Advance Praise for

OUT OF THE CUCKOO'S NEST

"*Out of the Cuckoo's Nest is a deeply moving memoir that transcends personal storytelling and becomes a quiet act of healing—not only for the author but for anyone who has ever carried invisible wounds.*

With unwavering honesty and profound emotional clarity, Shalom Saada Saar shares a life marked by displacement, misdiagnosis, and abuse, but also by extraordinary resilience, dignity, and compassion. What is most striking is not just the pain he endured, but the grace with which he reflects on it. There is no bitterness here, no accusation—only a patient, respectful search for meaning in the aftermath of suffering.

Saar's openness about the long shadow of childhood trauma—and how it shaped his relationships, self-perception, and life path—is courageous and disarming. He does not shield the reader from the rawness of memory. Yet, in every sentence, there is quiet wisdom that speaks not of blame but of reconciliation: with the past, with the people who failed him, and ultimately with himself.

Amid the darkness, what remains constant is the author's deep reverence for his parents. His gratitude for their strength, humility, and unconditional love grounds the narrative in warmth and humanity. It is this spiritual and emotional inheritance—more than any institutional redemption—that becomes the true source of his transformation.

Rather than presenting his story as one of triumph over adversity in a conventional sense, Saar offers a gentler truth: that healing is a long, imperfect, and deeply personal journey. And that empathy, presence, and service to others are the most powerful ways to give meaning to one's own pain.

Out of the Cuckoo's Nest is not a loud book. It is quiet reckoning. A generous offering. A testament to what becomes possible when we stop hiding our wounds and instead learn to carry them with integrity and light."

—**DR. URSULA SCHÜTZE-KREILKAMP, MD,** Former Head of Group HR Executive, Deutsche Bahn Germany

"*What a marvelous book! I was totally engrossed in reading it. This is a true page turner. Shalom Saada Saar is an amazing storyteller who combines fine literary prose with beautiful imagery to bring the story to life and make it so vivid. The courageous account of his own life's traumatic experiences and his ability to overcome despair is inspiring. The book is an account of how one can triumph over adversities to live a life of meaning, purpose, empathy, and significance. It is a story of pain and suffering, but more importantly, resilience and transformation that has led to a life of purpose.*"

—**HENRI R. FORD, MD, MHA,** Dean and Chief Academic Officer, Miller School of Medicine, University of Miami

"*For over ten years, Shalom Saada Saar has served as a leadership coach for Heineken's Americas Executive Team. I am familiar with the struggles of his upbringing and how he transformed those difficulties* into opportunities. I am grateful for the immense contribution he made to the organization as a whole and to me personally. This book is an emotional rollercoaster, filled with resilience and wisdom, and subtly highlights the power of love and generosity in the face of adversity. It is a must-read, as it serves as a powerful reminder that life, despite its ups and downs, is ultimately a story of success."

—MARC BUSAIN, President, Heineken Americas

"Out of the Cuckoo's Nest by Dr. Shalom Saada Saar is a rare and searing memoir that transcends the boundaries of personal history to become a profound meditation on resilience, dignity, and the human spirit. In deep lyrical prose, Dr. Saar recounts an extraordinary life journey. From the sunlit shores of Benghazi to the darkest corners of institutional neglect, and ultimately to the lecture halls of Harvard University and global boardrooms, the pages come to life with vivid imagery.

What distinguishes this book is not only the brutality of its realities but the grace with which they are told. Chapter after chapter, from the "Shadows of the Past" to "Flying Away from the Cuckoo's Nest," reveals a life forged in pain, redeemed through love, and given purpose through service to others. His reflections on trauma, identity, and leadership offer a rare insight into what it means to survive not merely as a victim, but as a visionary.

This is not just a memoir. It is a masterclass in empathy and courage. Anyone seeking inspiration in the face of adversity or looking to understand the power of compassionate and effective leadership must read this book. Dr. Saar's voice is unforgettable. Equally so is his message: out of destruction, we can construct meaning, purpose, and hope for individuals and society."

—DR. OMAIDA C. VELAZQUEZ, MD, Professor and Chair, Miller School of Medicine, University of Miami

"An inspiring and poignant self-reflection upon a life upended at a young age by a mental health misdiagnosis. Professor Saar shares his vulnerabilities and his ongoing struggle to cope as days half-full are inevitably followed by days half-empty. While the boy is so often the father of the man, openness to new experiences and to coaching by others can enable us to overcome childhood trauma and eventually contribute to the greater good. Any man can learn more about himself by reading this unique book."

—DR. JOHN A. QUELCH, Executive Vice Chancellor, Duke Kunshan University, China

"Out of the Cuckoo's Nest is both intimate and universal—a vivid reminder that the most extraordinary leaders are shaped not by ease, but by the courage to face what breaks them and still choose to build. Through unthinkable heartbreak and trauma, Shalom's story becomes a testament to resilience, reflection, and an unwavering hope that lingers long after the last page. It is a generous gift of humanity that calls us to lead - with empathy, with purpose, and with an open heart."

—JACKIE INSINGER, CEO and Leadership Consultant at Spark Brilliance; bestselling author of *Spark Brilliance*

"The shocking and chilling book "Out of the Cuckoo's Nest" is the fruit of several writers who make one author. Shalom Saada -- the joyful little boy riding on the strong shoulders of his father, the Rabbi of Benghazi, make his way to the sands of Ashkelon. Landed in the promised land he had to part from his father's broad shoulders, from his mother's warm and comforting embrace, and to confront, as a lost and humiliated child, a cruel world inside a demonic boarding school for children diagnosed —rightfully or mistakenly—as mentally disabled.

Yet the book is also written by Shalom Saar, the man who chose to charge life and manage to escape the inferno. He joined the Israel Defense Forces, and with the help of his commander -- a former partisan who fought the Nazis in his previous life -- Shalom changed the trajectory of his destiny. At the same time, the writer is Shalom Saar the winner, the mentor. The one who completed his studies at Harvard, who raised generations of students to face impossible challenges. To lead! The one whose counsel was sought by CEOs and Governments around the globe.

Anyone familiar with the experience of moving from one country to another understands the deep trauma involved with emigration. The journey of Rabbi Chai Saada and his family to the Land of Israel was the fruit of a dream and of compulsion. Shalom Saada Saar's story is particularly difficult because of the horrors he endured personally – experiences, that fortunately, many others did not face.

His life journey is turbulent and chilling, yet it instills hope and proves once again that at the end of the tunnel, there is light, there is life. The light at the end of his tunnel of struggle and perseverance transforms his book into a must-read for anyone seeking to confront impossible challenges and to be inspired by a story of rising from the depths of despair to the heights of success."

—**AVINOAM BAR-YOSEF, President Emeritus of the Jewish People Policy Institute (JPPI)**

"*Out of the Cuckoo's Nest* is a passionate, engrossing book. It will have you experience deep emotions as you travel with Shalom Saar along his life. An out-of-the-ordinary life to be sure!

This book speaks of deep wisdom and empathy, of resilience, emotional intelligence and courage – the courage to share, to explore, to revisit trauma and drama, to take our own responsibilities, to accept humanity and, therefore, flaws.

Saar's beautiful language and metaphors enfold the reader with love, (self)-compassion and hope."

—**LISA WENGER, Director of the Estate of Meret Oppenheim, Switzerland**

"Dr. Shalom Saar's life is not only a testament to the power of perseverance, but also a profound journey through some of the most turbulent chapters of the 20th century. His early years were marked by displacement, discrimination, and deep personal adversity. Through extraordinary resilience, Shalom emerged as one of the world's most respected scholars and teachers in the field of Leadership.

This book is more than a memoir —it is a wellspring of inspiration. Dr. Saar's life challenges us to re-examine our assumptions, lead with *empathy, and never underestimate the potential of the human spirit. His story is both a mirror of history and a beacon of hope for future generations.*

At the heart of this story is also a remarkable love—Ping, whose unwavering support, courage, and love gave Shalom the strength to confront the past and share his journey with the world. Her presence not only shaped his life but helped make this book possible.

Highly recommended for anyone seeking courage, clarity, and the true meaning of leadership."

—MING YUE, Managing Director, Union Science & Technology Co., Ltd., China

OUT OF THE CUCKOO'S NEST

A MEMOIR

SHALOM SAADA SAAR

WINDERMERE PRESS

COPYRIGHT © 2025 SHALOM SAADA SAAR
All rights reserved.

OUT OF THE CUCKOO'S NEST
ISBN 978-1-962341-80-6 *Hardcover*
      978-1-962341-81-3 *Paperback*
      978-1-962341-82-0 *Ebook*

In memory of my father, Rabbi Chai Saada, and my mother, Aliza Naiem Saada.

CONTENTS

Foreword		1
1	THE SHADOWS OF THE PAST	5
2	THE MESSIAH HAS ARRIVED	11
3	JERUSALEM, OH MY JERUSALEM	19
4	THE DARK SIDE OF SPAIN	27
5	TOUCHING THE ANCIENT SOIL	37
6	A DEEPLY ROOTED TRADITION	45
7	MY FATHER'S BURNING PLATFORM	57
8	CRYING OUT FROM THE BELLY OF THE WHALE	65
9	DAYS OF TRANSITION AND RECKONING	71
10	THE CITY OF SAMSON AND DELILAH	79
11	MEMORIES THAT REFUSE TO FADE AWAY	87
12	GUIDED BY THE SCRIPTURES	95
13	OF ANGER AND DISCONTENT	101
14	THE DEAFENING SILENCE OF HOSTILITY	113
15	MIRACLES DESCEND UPON US	125
16	ROAMING THE WILD DESERT	131

17	RISING FROM THE ASHES	143
18	THE JOURNEY TO CONFIDENCE	153
19	THE SEA WITHOUT HORIZONS	159
20	STIRRING THE MELTING POT	175
21	FORCING THE WINDS ON THE SAIL	183
22	RECOVERING IN DENMARK	191
23	EVENTS BEYOND OUR CONTROL	199
24	THE POWER OF EDUCATION	205
25	THE THICK WALLS OF ACADEMIA	215
26	REVISITING THE PAINFUL PAST	225
27	SPREADING MY WINGS AND FLYING HIGH	237
28	FALLING IN LOVE WITH THE DRAGON	245
29	FLYING AWAY FROM THE CUCKOO NEST	251
Acknowledgments		257
About the Author		259

Foreword

Life is a complicated experience, and all of us periodically experience adversity, disappointment, stress, pain and despair. Despite the fact that many times our problems are actually much less serious than they seem to be, perception trumps reality, and life can be and always is exceedingly difficult for all of us at some point in our journey.

Out of the Cuckoo's Nest provides many important life lessons and a unique and therapeutic perspective on adversity. Dr. Saar's life journey has been full of truly daunting and at times horrendous challenges, with pain, persecution, despair, hopelessness, and numerous experiences that most of us could never tolerate. Yet in every chapter, he provides us with important ways to transform despair into happiness, cruelty into kindness, hopelessness into optimism, and paralysis into action, leading to triumph and many times, salvation.

There are an infinite number of life lessons in these chapters, and each is important because it provides us with novel insights, new perspectives, and powerful tools that we can use in our own lives to overcome adversity and achieve fulfillment and joy from every life experience. In many ways, the experiences and their resolution are examples of the aphorism "What Doesn't Kill You Makes You Stronger."

Even more important than the stories with their challenges and the ways to overcome them is how such experiences can produce maturity and resiliency. I have known Dr. Saar for over 50 years, and his life experiences have produced a man who has true empathy and compassion, and incredible skills to help people navigate from seemingly impossible situations into profound and rewarding success stories. By focusing on solutions rather than problems, and by reaching down into one's soul and believing there is no impossible situation, we can achieve incredibly remarkable things in our lives. It is hard to focus on that in times of pain and sorrow, and Dr. Saar's chapters serve as an inspiration to all of us, demonstrating in each episode that we can make so much more of our lives and achieve our dreams and goals if we never give up.

Finally, and perhaps most importantly, these life experiences can provide us with perspectives that can enable us to help many others. The Oxford English dictionary defines empathy as the ability to understand and share the feelings of another person. It involves imagining oneself in another person's situation and experiencing their emotions or perspective. This capacity allows for a deeper connection and understanding between individuals

I can personally testify to the fact that Dr. Saar has done this with some of the world's most prominent individuals and organizations, when so many others have failed. The most important takeaways from this book are the lessons from each chapter, which provide an inspiration to all of us to take our life experiences and convert them into guideposts to help ourselves and others achieve greater meaning in our lives. Every religion and great spiritual leader believes that the key to fulfillment in life is in successful unselfish service to the betterments of others. This book and its lessons provide us with an illuminated path through the inevitable darkness we all encounter in life to do just that.

In the tapestry of human experience, it is often during our darkest moments that the seeds of transformation are planted. The stories we tell ourselves—and the stories we encounter in the lives of others—shape our understanding of resilience, hope, and the capacity to rise above even the most harrowing circumstances. When we look beyond the surface of suffering, we find that adversity can function as a crucible, forging within us qualities of strength, wisdom, and compassion that endure far beyond the initial

FOREWORD

challenges we face. Dr. Saar's life is a testament to this, and reading this book will be transformative for all. I am proud of him and his accomplishments and feel extraordinarily privileged to call myself his friend.

—David S. Baskin, M.D., FACS, FAANS
Professor of Neurosurgery, Weill Cornell Medical College and
Texas A & M Medical School

Chapter One

THE SHADOWS OF THE PAST

The deepest recesses of our mind hold our memories, enveloped in which are the sights, sounds, colors, and experiences that shaped us in many ways to be the person we are today. Everything is still vivid and alive, never fading with time.

It seems like only yesterday that I walked with my father along the beach in Benghazi as a child. The azure waters of the Mediterranean Sea offered a stark offset to the powdery white sand, which caressed my little toes as we walked. The translucent waters of the ocean shimmered in the morning sun, exuding a radiance that captured the state of my mind. It's a feeling that's hard to describe. I was loved. I was protected. I was home.

Fishing boats bobbed up and down in the distance as fishermen busily got their catch for the day. As the waves gently crashed into the sand, the beautiful backdrop framed my father's silhouette: his long salt-and-pepper beard, a defining feature of his face, and his long flowing black garb of the Rabbinical court waving in the gentle breeze. We walked together in this tranquil place, just the two of us and the sea. His firm, protective grip engulfed my hand as he gently squeezed my fingers.

These moments were precious. They were separate from the rhythm of our daily lives; they belonged to just the two of us. My father's intense but loving face reflected wisdom: the wisdom of life, the knowledge of experience, the wisdom that comes with having stoically weathered unspeakable tragedy.

As we walked, I assumed that he was thinking of far more essential things than the meanderings of a four-year-old's mind. But then he looked at me and smiled. He lifted me up and seated me on his broad shoulders.

"Look at the world from above," he said gently. "You'll see things that you can't see from below."

I took his advice and looked down at the sand. Then I squinted and stared at the boats on the horizon. I wondered what was so special about the view. I was too young to comprehend the wisdom in his words—it was only much later that I understood what he meant.

A wise man once said: "Life can only be understood backwards; but it must be lived forwards." I marvel at the wisdom of these words as I look back at my life, all 80 years of it.

The Talmud states, "A small ray of light can extinguish any darkness." My story is one of the searches for that light, of burning to ash and rising from the abyss, of a struggle for identity, for voice, and for a childhood that was snatched away, a journey of obstacles, of a ruthless environment, permanent wounds and lasting scars. Most of us, in one way or another, are locked in a virtual cuckoo nest, not fitting in where they are. The challenge is to break away from the shackles that others impose on us—and sometimes our own.

Ultimately, my story is one about hope, conviction, resilience and redemption. It is a journey of transformation, from the dark walls of the school for the developmentally disabled to the bright walls of academia at Swarthmore College and Harvard University. From a cry for help that fell on deaf ears, to becoming a coach to senior executives and state ministers. From drowning in a sea of misery without a compass, to consulting organizations across the globe on navigating their enterprises. From being out of control in the face of unbelievable odds to taking charge of my destiny.

CHAPTER ONE

My story has created in me resistance to the wrong and unjust, and rebellion to defy the odds.

We are all gifted with the ability to love, teach, coach, encourage and support one another to bring more meaning to our existence and fulfill our calling by serving others. It is in many ways, the Buddhist belief that holds that we arrive here for a reason. We all have a critical role to play. In fulfilling our part with a purpose, we will face numerous obstacles. We will be tested, knocked down, battered from left to right, but never defeated if we stay on the path. We must stay focused by knowing who we are, and by reaching out and enabling others.

Rabbi Hillel once said, "If I am not for myself, who is there for me? But if I am not for others, who am I?" This profound and common-sense concept propelled me to teach and coach others. After all, to bring meaning to our journey, we must reach out by making others better than us. This is true for the parent, teacher or manager. Connecting with others is not about imposing our will but about putting ourselves in other people's shoes. When we empathize, when we listen, when we probe, and when we give, we create an authentic and meaningful value that serves others. We can take others to a place they can't get by themselves alone. In doing so, we actualize ourselves. This is the fundamental purpose of our journey.

As the decades rolled by afterward, the childhood moments with my father on the Benghazi seashore stayed with me. And like the tide in the sea, those moments come back to me from time to time, sometimes gently as a mere whiff of a memory brightening my day, other times more strongly, blowing away my self-doubt. That memory has offered me the fortitude I often need during life's twists and turns. My father, with his broad shoulders, a face exuding strength with his piercing dark brown eyes, is the image of someone who could withstand any storm and overpower any obstacle.

Life is not shaped by a progression of experiences, but rather by singular events that mold and shape us into who we are. It is less about heredity and more about specific moments, hours, or days where we become their consequences for unknown reasons.

Good or bad, specific events tend to stay with us for a long while and often determine our destiny and purpose in life.

In so many ways, my life is like the history of my people. I was uprooted at an early age from the security of my home. At a young age, I confronted soldiers with machine guns; I had an unsettled exit into the unknown, sailing away on a refugee ship away from the comfort of my warm and comfortable nest. I constantly struggled with identity and recognition. Memories of being rejected, labeled as mentally underdeveloped, and an object to be mocked or abused are never easy to erase. We all carry those moments of our lives when we felt unloved, misunderstood and rejected. Yet, these experiences shape us and build a platform from which we can explore new heights, possibilities and better days.

I felt and still feel an inner force that pushes me forward to demonstrate that I am a man with an identity, with a curiosity to learn, and, most of all, someone to be accepted. Yet the journey has been painful and arduous; despite all my achievements, I still suffer from waves of desolation and loneliness. In many ways, the wounds of childhood never heal completely. They linger endlessly and erupt from time to time, leaving a trail of broken relationships and invisible scars.

My case is far from unique. I have witnessed it in every place I visited. We tend to look down on people who look or act differently than the rest of us. What fascinates me the most is that despite a landscape filled with human tragedies, there seems to be no progress in understanding or even a better sense of awareness.

The world-class schools I was eventually privileged to attend gave me stellar education credentials—and yet, to this day, I remain ignorant of the root cause of my frequent self-doubt—days of despair spent questioning my existence, my being, and my sense of purpose. And yet as I reflect back

CHAPTER ONE

on my parents' struggle in a newly founded land and their deep suffering in adapting to a new place, I find that it is a perpetual source of power and hope.

The experience of my people arriving from Libya, in general, and my parents, in particular, is a story of struggle blended with inner strength and fortitude; the struggle of my people in the new land after centuries of living among the Arabs continues to amaze me. An inner strength propelled them to withstand formidable challenges. Their narratives are carved in my mind and have served as a moral compass guiding me north. They were able to transform the tremendous disruption in our lives into days of love and passion, a source of resilience, redemption and calm for us.

Despite all the hardship, they never complained or raised their voices. They never gave up hope in their ability to protect us from neglect and disrespect.

My mother, Aliza, was a giant. With limited formal education, she single-handedly managed to be there for us even though she was the main bread winner. Working as a janitor never diminished her beauty and courage to face any challenge that came her way. My mother was always available to listen, to advise and offer encouragement and support; her love for us was the fuel that kept us moving forward. She saw life as a precious gift from heaven—for her, life had to be treated as sacred.

I never saw her depressed. Despite the hardship that was inflicted upon her, she never gave up hope and never stopped seeing the beauty in others. She cared deeply for my father, my siblings, our neighbors and anyone who needed some warm words or a hug to lift spirits. She once told me that when thousands of starfish are washed out from the sea onto the shores, there is a sense of hopelessness about how to save them; , she reminded me, we can each pick up one star at a time and bring it back to life by putting it back into the water.

My people, the Libyan Jews, managed to lift us up one at a time with their endless love and put us back in the water. They sacrificed themselves to show us the light, and in doing so, they raised an extraordinary generation. The essence of their journey to a new land was to inject life into our veins and air into our lungs. I have learned that despite all losses and pain, we must pick ourselves up; we must go on to complete the journey not by submission, but by the force of confidence.

Failure, according to ancient Chinese philosophers, is not falling, but the refusal to get up. I learned that whatever comes our way, whatever the challenge is, we must take it, even if it requires swimming against the tide. The secret to success is to forge ahead, running into the fire with courage, and adapting an unwavering conviction in your own strength.

This is the story of my life.

Chapter Two

THE MESSIAH HAS ARRIVED

I still have vivid memories of our lovely neighborhood in Benghazi where I spent my early childhood.

Each home had a single door, typically painted blue or green, with a small peephole for the owners to see who was knocking, and a spacious yard that allowed residents to plant vegetables. In the spring, the blossoming trees filled the air with their fragrant buds, while palm trees dropped fresh dates that we would pick up from the ground and eat without washing. Chickens roamed freely, accompanied by a noisy rooster that woke us up every morning. Fresh eggs would be waiting in a basket by our door. My mother would delicately crack an egg, sprinkle some salt and black pepper on it, and I would gulp it down raw. I can still remember the yolk being warm, coming straight from the hens that roamed freely in the yard without cages or supervision.

A man named Abu Sadie came daily with his donkey to deliver groceries and take away anything we wanted to dispose of or give away. During that time, there was hardly any trash. Groceries were packed in old newspapers. Abu Sadie would sing in Arabic, and women would appear at their doors, listening to his hoarse voice while laughing at his songs of lost love and beautiful women yearning for their men to return. My mother always greeted him with a wide smile as he brought the groceries up the steps of our home.

Among these treasured memories, of a place and people that defined my early life, are starker images—those of the day we left Libya, never to return. It was a concept that, at the time, my young brain couldn't quite comprehend.

My mother, Aliza, who I always called Ya-Emi (my mother), was determined not to shed any tears that day. The beauty of her hazelnut eyes matched her braided hair tucked under a colorful scarf as she carefully packed her jewelry. Her own mother had given it to her, and it was her most treasured possession.

My father packed his holy books, prayer texts, his tallit and tefillin. I vividly remember him climbing up the ladder to retrieve his handwritten interpretations of scripture from the top shelf of his library. He filled several suitcases with sacred texts such as the Mishnah, the Talmud, the Kabbalah and writings from Libyan sages. The idea that these sacred books were more important to him than clothing or blankets always left me in awe. He firmly believed that his God would never abandon him. In his mind, and in the minds of many of his followers, my father communicated directly with his Maker.

Mother was practical and managed to gather every item she deemed essential for our long journey and beyond. She packed the suitcases with underwear, jackets, blankets, pots, plates, tea kettles and her favorite item, a tablecloth designed especially for her wedding, which she hoped to use for Shabbat dinner. Deciding what to take and what to leave behind under such stringent time pressure was a challenge. I remember her selecting certain items and then dropping them onto the floor in frustration.

Reflecting on those moments later, I wondered what thoughts crossed her mind. When we leave places, we also leave behind our memories; how difficult must it have been to carry only a fraction of what she wished to bring along to preserve those memories?

Whenever I read about people who are forced from their homes and

CHAPTER TWO

become refugees overnight, my mind returns to those painful hours when I witnessed my family begin the long journey to a new home, neighborhood, friends, and country. Unlike many refugees who have nowhere to go, my parents and 30,000 other Libyan Jews chose to leave a land where they had lived for over 3,000 years. They saw themselves as the descendants of the Israelites escaping Egypt thousands of years ago, making their arduous journey to the land promised by their God.

With the establishment of Israel in 1948, several waves of immigration followed: the Jews who survived the Holocaust, then Jews who embraced secular Zionism, believing that the suffering of the Jews would end once they had their own land. Conversely, Jews arriving from Arab countries viewed the establishment of the state of Israel as a sign from heaven that the Messiah had arrived. For the Jews of North Africa and the Middle East, this was a messianic movement.

Additionally, there is a sect of ultra-Orthodox Jews who oppose the creation of the state of Israel. Their belief stems from the idea that the rebirth of Israel will only occur when God decides to send the Messiah. They argue that the coming of the Messiah is in God's hands alone, not in the control of mortals. Nonetheless, according to the sages, the Messiah would arrive riding on a donkey, symbolizing simplicity and humility.

In contrast, the Jews from Arab countries held a more pragmatic view of the Messiah; to them, there were no more excuses. The time was ripe for hundreds of thousands of Jews from Arab countries to realize a dream that had persisted for 2,000 years.

The old Jewish vision of the Messiah arriving on a donkey to gather them from the diaspora was transformed into reality. Most of the Libyan Jewish community was convinced that their destiny was in their hands. They believed they were the donkey, while the Messiah was merely a compass provided by God, guiding them toward the Promised Land. They felt that this time—after a long wait—God was finally fulfilling His promise. After thousands of years, the prophecies of Isaiah, Jeremiah and others from the Old Testament were being realized: "The day will come when I gather you from the four corners of the earth," and "I will bring you back on the wings of eagles."

Most families embraced the idea of leaving their homes. They saw themselves as the descendants of the Israelites in Egypt, led by Moses thousands of years ago. While European Jews were fleeing the brutal regime of the Nazis and facing betrayal from their neighbors, Jews from Arab countries were heading toward the Promised Land. They were willing to leave everything behind—homes, shops, synagogues, cemeteries, the places where they had celebrated their marriages, and the beautiful beaches along the Libyan coastline. Songs were written and sung by men and women to commemorate this incredible moment. There was no fear in abandoning their past; their conviction was so strong that it left a lasting impression on me about the nature of change and transitions.

My father's decision to leave was rooted in a fundamental belief that, with the establishment of the new state of Israel, the vision of "next year in Jerusalem" had finally become a reality. He was convinced that Israel's founding sent a clear signal that it was time for Jews to return to their homeland. He saw no reason for Jews to remain in the Diaspora. His faith in God was unwavering, and his conviction that we were the first generation in generations to cross the sea and reach the Holy Land was stronger than rock. "In every destruction, there is a construction," my father would say. He believed our journey was a divine sign; after years of exile, the moment had arrived to leave everything behind and step onto the soil of our ancestors. He envisioned a land where the ancient Hebrew language would once again be spoken. This was a gathering of exiles from more than 70 countries. He imagined a revitalized land free from exile and eviction—a place where Jews could walk the streets with their heads held high, unafraid of pogroms, defended by Jewish soldiers just like the ancient tribes of Israel.

CHAPTER TWO

Together, my parents managed to fit everything of value into just five suitcases. We had to leave everything else behind: furniture, clothing, artwork, even the large pots my mother used to preserve food for the winter. One large clay pot held the tomato paste she made from crushing ripe tomatoes and letting them dry in the hot sun. She would cover the tomato paste with olive oil to prevent flies from feasting on the freshly made condiment. Another pot was filled with pickled lemons that she would pick from our lemon trees, and more contained salty dried fish and large black olives brought to us straight from the countryside. The scent and aroma from the fermentation process were intense and my mouth still waters at the thought of them.

As we walked out our front door for the last time, I took a final look at the fruit trees that consistently yielded copious quantities of black figs, juicy oranges, and the ever-present pomegranates from which my mother would squeeze a glass of fresh juice to my father's delight.

In the courtyard a rope hung from one of the trees that my father had set up for me. He would swing me while my mother warned him not to push too hard. I played there endlessly, always under my mother's watchful eye. And now, I was leaving it all behind, taking only cherished memories that would never fade away.

Our Arab neighbors stared from their open doors in dismay. They held great respect for my father, who always greeted them with a smile and a blessing. He welcomed their children, often giving them coins from his pocket or candies from the pastry shop. My father, with his white beard cascading down to his upper chest and his piercing charcoal eyes, had a demeanor that captivated anyone who dared to look at him. Some neighbors even trusted my father to hold their gold in his office instead of keeping it in their own homes, convinced that no one would dare to break into the Rabbi's residence.

Years later, my mother shared with me an interesting story about my father coming home late one night after delivering a eulogy. He was stopped in the alley leading to our home by robbers. It was our Arab neighbors who bravely came out of their homes to yell and scare the robbers away. As the would-be robbers fled, they invited my father to rest and recover before escorting him safely home. These stories, along with many others of Arabs and Jews working together in Libya for centuries, provide a sharp contrast to the situation today. It is hard to accept, let alone witness, the constant wars and the ongoing conflict between Jews and Arabs.

I will never forget my father's face as we left—anxious, yet calm. My mother was tense but determined. She lifted her eyes to the sky and prayed, her lips moving silently. The hot, humid air was suffocating, and my mother wiped my father's forehead with her scarf—a surprising gesture in such a religious environment, where women typically do not touch men.

As we exited our home, my father, honoring his ancestors in Spain, removed the mezuzah from the door and held it close to his heart in his pocket. Outside, he lifted me into one arm and carried me, while holding whatever he could in his other hand. My mother brought my two sisters out of our beloved home, a beautiful place with wonderful Arab neighbors in one of the finest sections of Benghazi. From my father's shoulders, I watched till our house slowly disappeared.

We passed by my grandfather's spice and herb shop, a place my mother used to visit every Thursday as she strolled through the market, purchasing meat and vegetables for the Shabbat celebration. I can still recall the aromatic scent of his shop. He would sit on stools with his Arab partner, drinking mint tea with a few roasted peanuts. The shop was closed that day as he and his new wife were also making their way to the ship that would take him to his ancestral homeland. Years after we arrived in Israel, and before he passed away, he told me how much he missed his Arab partner. "We were like brothers. Finally, I am going to see him soon."

We also passed by the Great Synagogue of Benghazi. Its gates were

CHAPTER TWO

closed, and the five scrolls of the Torah held in the Holy Ark were being divided among the leaders to be brought to Israel and placed in the new synagogues. My father wore his Tarbush, a Turkish red hat, atop his head, and a regal Burnitz, a long blue robe that flowed down almost to the floor, balancing on his broad shoulders. This attire made him look more like a warrior or a king than a holy rabbi.

I couldn't help but wonder who would take care of our house and belongings once we left. Thoughts of the swings, the trees, and the beautiful arches leading to our rooms filled my mind, and sadness washed over me. Would I ever see them again?

Chapter Three

JERUSALEM, OH MY JERUSALEM

I had never seen something as huge as the ship before. It dwarfed everything in front of it.

Its rustic color gave way to faded old red paint above the waterline. A worn-out flag fluttered above a white-colored bridge, its steep gangway leading up to its deck. The old Greek sailors with their black caps and blue shirts were busy loading suitcases and fresh produce brought by the Arab merchants. The smell of produce and human sweat overwhelmed me, surrounded by the sea of people at the busy port of Tripoli waiting to board this old Greek ship.

The gangway connecting the ship to the port was the last connection between the ship and this land we had called home for several centuries now. Family after family ambled into the ship as the waves crashed below, sending up little splashes of water.

The atmosphere was thick with anticipation as hundreds of Libyan Jewish families entered the ship, determined to leave everything behind and venture into the ancient yet newfound land of Israel. The mood was a blend of excitement and anxiety, along with a strong sense of joy as these people returned to their homeland, a place where their ancestors had roamed thousands of years ago.

There was hope in the air. Promise. Happiness. And also, like a heavy blanket we would never quite be free of, the deep sadness at leaving our old home behind.

The women wore colorful scarves over their heads, men donned white Kabbalistic head coverings, and the children behaved more obediently in the face of the vast blue ocean. Adding to the melee was the noise of the old, cranky ship as it prepared for the long journey ahead, and the clamor of voices from all around. The men carried on their backs elderly grandmothers and grandfathers who couldn't walk, and they made their way up the gangway.

The sight was overwhelming for both the Arabs and the Jews. Arabs watched from a distance as their old friends and business partners left for good. People they had known forever, who had been an integral part of their lives, were departing the country, leaving everything behind – their homes, belongings, memories, friendships. They had lived among the Jews for centuries, and now, to their surprise, without any warning, their neighbors were embarking on a journey of no return. These emotions were hard to process.

Later, on the eve of the Passover celebration, I would, as tradition required, remind my parents that we left Libya just as the Jewish slaves had exited Egypt under the guidance of the prophet Moses. My father emphasized on every Passover that the primary purpose of the holiday was to ensure each new generation internalized the idea of liberty. That we must never forget that we were slaves in Egypt and that it was the invisible hand of God that delivered us from years of bondage to freedom. Tradition teaches us that freedom is much harder to sustain, and we must guard it with our lives. In many ways, the exit of my people from Libya was just like the exodus of the ancient Israelites who left Egypt after years of slavery more than 3,000 years ago.

Throughout Jewish history, fleeing from home has been a common occurrence, almost resembling a rite of passage. Many Jews have been forc-

CHAPTER THREE

ibly removed from their homes, particularly those living in Europe, where they were hunted down across various countries. Hardly anyone stood by to protect them; they were often at the mercy of kings and queens, swayed by anti-Semitic advisors who promoted increasing taxes on Jews or conscripting them into the army.

The deep-seated hatred of Jews never ceases to astonish me. Antisemitism, an incurable ailment, has existed for thousands of years; sometimes it lies dormant, while at other times it erupts like a volcano, leaving behind ravaged homes, violated women, slaughtered men and children, shattered hearts, and ruined lives.

Despite the tragic events that have plagued Jewish history, the Hebrew phrase "Ham Israel Chai"—The People of Israel are Alive—continues to hold true.

In the first half of the 20th century, while Europe was saturated with anti-Semitism, the experience of the Jews living among the Arabs was dramatically different. The incidents between Jews and Arabs in North Africa and the Middle East were far less bloody than the brutal pogroms in places like Poland and Russia. Jews of North Africa lived with less violence and a less hostile environment. There were times when Muslims considered the Jews brothers. While maintaining their distinct identity, Jews in Muslim countries were less likely to seclude themselves from the cultures they lived in. Each man carried two names, the Hebraic name and the Arab name. Abraham was synonymous with Ibrahim, Moses with Musa, Yaakov with Yakub, and Shalom with Salim. They dressed in the same clothes; they spoke the same language both at home and in the streets. Hebrew was the language of prayer and an expression of longing, they ran businesses together and most of all, they trusted each other more than the Christians and the Jews of Europe ever did – they were integrated but never assimilated. Violence between Arab and Jews broke from time to time, but never reached the scope and depth of the mass killings that the Jews of Europe experienced for hundreds of years.

Despite temptations and adversities, Arab Jews have rarely succumbed to or betrayed their faith and convictions. Their resilience is rooted in their deep faith and beliefs. They believe that their God delivered them from bondage to freedom and brought them to the Promised Land, where thousands of years ago King David established Jerusalem as its spiritual center. In their view, God chose them to be His representatives.

Over the years, Libya attracted Jews from various countries. When rulers implemented policies unfavorable to Jewish life in Libya, Jewish leaders often negotiated with or sought to influence those in power. If these attempts failed, they did not hesitate to adopt a tougher approach. When their lives were at stake, they fought back. Some Libyan Jewish communities even armed themselves during World War II. While hundreds of Libyan Jews were transported in trucks to the only concentration camp located several hours from Tripoli, many managed to survive this ordeal. It is important to note that the camp was not constructed by the Arabs, but rather by Mussolini's Black Shirts, who were following the orders of Hitler and his gang of killers.

The most significant influx of Jews into Libya occurred during the Spanish Inquisition when many, including my father's ancestors, escaped from Spain. Some fled to the remote caves of Carian in Libya, which were beyond the reach of the Inquisition. They transformed these caves into homes, establishing a synagogue, a *mikveh* (ritual bath) and a rabbinical court. After more than 500 years of living in these caves, these Jews gathered their belongings and made their way to the port of Tripoli, heading for Israel. Their physical strength and mental resilience laid the foundation for their future success in Israel.

Throughout history, Jerusalem has served as the spiritual core of Jewish existence. Just as Muslims turn towards Mecca during their prayers, Jews face Jerusalem. Given its importance to Christians and Muslims as well,

CHAPTER THREE

Jerusalem holds a special place in the hearts of all three religions. However, for Jews, it represents the very essence of their identity. And among the Jews, the love for Jerusalem has never faded. Almost every Jewish home in Libya displayed a photo of the Western Wall, also known as the Wailing Wall. My mother used to kiss that photo just as she kissed the mezuzah on our door. The image of the Wailing Wall was the only framed picture my mother brought with her—a reminder of the remaining wall from its second destruction.

Jews of Libya expressed their lamentation for Jerusalem by leaving a section of the house unpainted, as a reminder of the destruction of their land. When women prepared homemade bread, they left a portion of the unbaked dough as a reminder of Jerusalem. Wherever Jews lived and gathered around the world, at the conclusion of every prayer, they would shake hands and greet each other by saying, "Next year in Jerusalem". The desire to return to their homeland never ceased. On every anniversary of the destruction of Jerusalem's Holy Temple, known as Tishah B'Av, Jews fast from sunset to sunset and pray. Libyan Jews would walk barefoot to the synagogue, rubbing ash on their foreheads in remembrance of their lost temple. The pain of losing their land never faded. Each year, the solemn ceremony of fasting, praying and chanting hymns of remembrance instilled a lasting hope that one day the Jews would return to their homeland. "On the rivers of Babylon, we sat and wept."

Unlike many other Jewish communities, where the groom is expected to smash a glass covered with a cloth during the wedding ceremony, the Libyan Jewish wedding has a different variation. In this tradition, the glass is shattered without any cloth covering it. The sight and sound of the breaking glass serve as a powerful reminder that, amidst the wedding joy, Jerusalem is never forgotten. "If I forget you, O Jerusalem, may my right hand cease to function" – Psalm 137:5.

While the Libyan Jews were an integral part of the history, culture and the economy of the land, their love for Jerusalem was a burning flame and a dream passed from generation to generation. This explains the decision of many of the Arab Jews to leave everything behind and make their departure from the comfort of their homes into the unknown. None of the Arab kings and dictators attempted to stop the departure of Jews returning to their homeland. In fact, many Arabs were puzzled, and some were shocked to see their Jewish neighbors streaming to the land of their ancestors.

Holding my father's hand, I wandered throughout the ship, greeting people, praying, and expressing gratitude to the Almighty for delivering us from exile to the Promised Land. I remember my father wearing his beautiful prayer shawl, the Tallit, which he placed over the heads of others as he blessed them for a safe journey. We were making our way to join our ancestors, making history. In times when the world closed its gates, God reopened the path to rekindle souls and fulfill an historical hope that runs deep in every Jewish community anywhere in the world.

The old steamship we boarded was full of families from both Benghazi and Tripoli, clustered everywhere, occupying all the decks. We felt as if Israel were waiting for us with open arms, like a mother who had not seen her children in a long time. The men would occasionally burst into song and dance, much to the amazement of the ship's Greek crew.

I was with my beloved father, holding his warm and trusting hand as we sailed onto the horizon. We were heading toward the old new country. We would never again see the beautiful shores of Libya. My father would never again place me on his shoulders and walk along the sandy beaches of beautiful Benghazi. We would no longer feel its sea breeze on our face and draw circles in the sand with our toes. We would never breathe the scents of its intoxicating markets. This was the end of a chapter, a final goodbye.

Conditions on the ship were rough. My father spent most of his time with the families on board, offering blessings and words of comfort as babies cried. It was not equipped to handle such a big crowd. The men searched

CHAPTER THREE

for water and cleaned the overwhelming toilets—all this without access to showers. Despite the challenges, the women continued to sing about the new land. "Jerusalem, oh our beloved city, we are coming to kiss your soil and bring life back, just like in the days of Kings David and Solomon!"

The image of my father walking the decks of the ship, his beard billowing in the wind as he listened to and inspired gatherings of exiles, is etched in my memory. Years later, I would emulate his passion and encouragement as I listened to people from around the world. I inherited my father's courage and confidence to help others overcome their fears and insecurities.

I didn't realize then that I would never see my father's eyes sparkle with fire and joy again as he held me high to feel the ocean breeze. This would be the last time I would witness the land where my ancestors had lived for thousands of years, the place my mother never stopped loving, the land that gave birth to my father, the son of a blind baker who became a guiding light for his tribe.

Chapter Four

THE DARK SIDE OF SPAIN

To understand oneself, one needs to also comprehend one's background. In his diary, William A. Mann III wrote, "Just as the mightiest oak topples without its roots, so will a man without knowledge of his people come crashing to earth, dreamless and unfulfilled. We cannot hope to understand ourselves until we know something about those who have come before us." This understanding encompasses geography, history, upbringing, traditions and customs that have been held for hundreds of years. Our differences extend beyond mere fingerprints and transcend official documents; we are shaped by events and incidents that impact us in diverse ways, much like the combination of various musical notes results in a unique composition.

To understand my background, my behavior and my inner struggles—I must return to the land where my ancestors lived for centuries. I need to explore the experiences of my forefathers and comprehend their narratives, struggles and aspirations. It is essential for me to make sense of the shadows of the past, which leads me back to my birthplace: Libya.

Libya's coast had been home to my people for hundreds of years. Even before the Jewish exile by the Romans, which left the Jews without a state of their own, Jews from the land of Canaan sailed to the fertile shores of Libya. The first synagogue in Libya was established in the coastal town of Sirte in the tenth century B.C. King Solomon established trade routes with countries like Egypt, Greece and as far away as modern-day Tunisia. With promising commercial opportunities, the ancient Israelites arrived in North Africa and settled along the coastal cities of Cyrenaica, initially controlled by the Greeks and later by the Romans.

These early settlers established communities along the once lush and green Libyan coastal line and traded marble, swan meat, olive oil and livestock. Thriving, they upheld many original biblical Jewish customs throughout the centuries. They kept their values, norms, customs and practices. The Libyan Jews are different from their neighbors in Tunisia, Egypt and Sudan. Their Arabic is less classic and more robust; it is known as barbaric Arabic. They are known to be loud, stubborn, argumentative and impulsive, and they never shy away from a good fight.

One historical event that particularly impresses me is the bravery of Libyan Jews in their fight for freedom. During the Roman Empire, when Jewish slaves were brought to Rome for sale, the Jews of Rome and Libya collaborated to liberate these slaves by purchasing them from the Romans. Much like the zealots who rebelled against the Roman Empire at Masada, the Libyan Jews revolted against the Romans in the first century, forming a strong army to drive them away from the shores of Libya. In response to this rebellion, the Romans were determined to suppress the uprising, just as they did at Masada. They sent ships carrying thousands of soldiers to confront the Libyan Jews. Outnumbered and poorly equipped, many Jews faced severe consequences, as hundreds were hanged along the main roads of Tripoli, while their children were shackled and taken as slaves to be sold in Rome.

The massacre of hundreds of Jewish men during the first century left a deep and lasting wound in the community. On Tishah Be' Av, the anniversary of the Roman destruction of the Temple and a remembrance of the Libyan Jewish rebels, worshippers arrive at the synagogue with ashes marked on their foreheads, wearing slippers instead of shoes, fasting for twenty-four hours, and chanting hymns of pain, sorrow, and hope. When my family had

CHAPTER FOUR

our home painted, my father made sure the painter left a portion of the wall unpainted as a remembrance of the Temple's destruction and the lives of Libyan Jews lost during the Roman Empire.

Unlike many other countries where Jews often faced uncertainty under the rule of kings and queens, Libyan Jews generally maintained positive relationships with the local Arab population throughout the centuries. They played significant roles in government, with notable figures such as Pinna, a Jewish queen of Libya during the seventh century, who was well-loved by Muslims. They believed she was a descendant of Abraham, a key figure in both Jewish and Muslim traditions.

The history of Libyan Jews relied heavily on oral traditions, with stories passed down from generation to generation, often embellished over time. Through my research and by listening to a variety of accounts, I wrote an essay about my father's ancestry during my senior year at Naval School. In the process, I accessed documents concerning the Libyan Jewish community and its demographics, which were informed by those conversations. Ultimately, I compiled a narrative that echoes the experiences of many Spanish Jewish families who, refusing to convert to Christianity, chose to leave Spain. I envisioned the perilous escape of those who summoned the courage to take their families on a dangerous journey, fleeing the influence of the Church for safer havens among the Muslims.

The story, passed down through generations, begins on a dark night in the Jewish quarter of Córdoba, where bitter winter winds howled through the narrow alleys. Although it was late on Shabbat, the entire family was awake, anxious and prepared to leave their beloved home and community. The family patriarch was terrified but understood that leaving Spain was essential for his family's survival as Jews.

Converting to Christianity would have been the easier path to safety. However, such a conversion would have felt like a betrayal of the God of his ancestors and would not have brought peace to his tormented soul. His faith prevented him from embracing the cross and becoming like the Gentiles. To convert to Christianity meant turning away from his eternal God—the one who liberated his ancestors from slavery in Egypt and led them to the Promised Land. This was the God who parted the Red Sea, the one who promised to deliver His people.

While converting to Christianity might have seemed like the most logical choice for his family's safety, religious beliefs are rarely driven by logic or rationality. True belief compels individuals to act in accordance with the deeply held values of their convictions. As my father once said, when values are compromised, everything else becomes easy. This was not the case for many of my ancestors from Spain. For those who were true believers, embracing any other faith was seen as heresy. For my ancestors, God was powerful and invisible, and they believed that their fate and future rested in the hands of the Almighty.

He felt like Abraham, the patriarch whom God asked to sacrifice his son. He recalled the lessons from his rabbi, who taught that Abraham didn't challenge God, but rather obeyed His command with conviction. Abraham took his son Isaac to the field, tied his hands and legs, and placed him on the altar, preparing to sacrifice him.

It's likely that my ancestor felt a similar weight on his shoulders. He must have debated with himself about the merits and drawbacks of either converting or escaping Spain, leaving behind his vibrant community in Córdoba. He felt the burden of this test. Like Abraham, he was uncertain whether to accept his fate or feel anger toward God.

He lifted his head, hoping for a sign from heaven that it would be acceptable to convert for the sake of his family. He even considered the option of a temporary conversion, believing it would be better than fleeing suddenly like a criminal. He thought that if Queen Isabel were to die, there might be a chance that her successor would be more tolerant toward the Jews.

But no sign came from Heaven. He knew that unless he left Spain, he

CHAPTER FOUR

would be forced to make a choice.

He, his wife, and their five children would be tortured for refusing to convert to Christianity. Like many of his friends, he heard of the torture of Jews in the dark cellars of the Inquisition. Stories of severed limbs of those who refused to convert sent chills down his spine. He wondered why he and his family were being tested again and again. How long would his God test his believers? How long must he and others demonstrate their eternal loyalty? At what point would his Maker be satisfied with his anger at the Jews for selling Joseph to the Egyptian merchants for a pair of shoes? Couldn't his Maker strike a hand on those cardinals and those who hate the Jews and say, 'Enough is enough'? Why couldn't his Maker become angry with the Spaniards as he did with the Egyptians long ago when he delivered the Jews from Egypt? Didn't he strike water out of a rock? Didn't he split the Red Sea for his ancestors to cross the waters into the Promised Land? Didn't he shower manna from the sky to feed his believers? Why couldn't his God do it right now?

Time was not on his side. He couldn't afford to wait for a response or question his God. The strong winds and biting cold weighed heavily on his decision. In front of his family, he remained stoic, aware that the days ahead would be fraught with risks and dangers. Heresy was a tempting thought, and he wished he could discuss the matter directly with God, but there was no time. He had to prepare for the long and treacherous journey ahead.

He and his wife packed clothes and holy books, carefully wrapping them in blankets. To mislead the informants who reported fleeing Jews to the Inquisition, he left the fire burning in the fireplace. He added several logs to the flames and prayed to God for forgiveness for lighting a fire on the eve of Shabbat. He remembered his rabbi saying that when life is at stake, the rules of Shabbat could be bent. His heart trembled as he looked at his confused children and his unsettled wife.

Hearing a soft knock at the door, he opened it cautiously. It was the signal from the agent hired to take them away. Together with his wife and children, he stepped out of their home. Outside, two horses and a long wagon were waiting to take them to the port, where they would board a boat. He kissed the Mezuzah affixed to his doorframe, quietly removed it, and placed it in a pocket over his heart. Silently, he helped his children onto the wagon, and like many others, they managed to board a boat making its way to Tripoli, Libya.

The stories of my ancestors arriving from Spain to build new lives among Muslims have deepened my understanding and respect for the Muslim countries that welcomed them and thousands of other Spanish Jews. Many of these immigrants prospered in Morocco, Tunisia, Libya, and other Muslim nations. They adapted to their surroundings and coexisted peacefully with their Muslim neighbors, working closely with Arabs. As they had in Spain, they contributed to the fields of science and medicine and started businesses that led to economic growth in the countries that embraced them. Some were employed by various governments as financial advisors and held high positions in commerce and public service.

A notable historical example is when Hitler requested the identities of Moroccan Jews from King Hassan of Morocco. His response was, "We don't have Jews; we are all Moroccans."

There are also lesser-known accounts of Muslims who heroically saved Jews during this time. One such example is Abdol-Hossein Sardari, a young Iranian diplomat who protected Iranian interests in Nazi-occupied France during World War II. He negotiated with the Nazis in Paris and successfully saved hundreds of Jews from being sent to the gas chambers.

Another remarkable act of bravery was demonstrated by Nejat Kent, the Turkish consul general in Marseille from 1941 to 1944. Upon learning that hundreds of Jews were being rounded up and forced into cattle cars bound for concentration camps, he quickly went to the train station. There, he confronted the Gestapo commander and insisted that the individuals on the

CHAPTER FOUR

train were Turkish citizens. Despite attempts to prevent him from boarding, he managed to get on the train and refused to leave. He issued Turkish passports for all those detained and helped them board a ship bound for Istanbul.

These courageous acts from individuals in Muslim countries are often overlooked by historians documenting the horrors of the war. Even the Mufti of Jerusalem, who was pro-Nazi and met with Hitler, could not achieve what other European countries did in collaborating with the Final Solution, which was executed with chilling precision by the Nazis.

There are times when I wonder if there is a chance for a bridge that could foster a deeper understanding between Arabs and Jews. After all, the commonalities between Arabs and Jews are much more than those between Christians and Jews. In fact, some believe that Muhammad felt a closer connection to the Jews of Medina than to the Christians of Jerusalem. His attitude toward the Jews translated into many shared practices. For instance, both religions forbid pork; Friday evening is the start of the Shabbat for Jews as it is a sacred day for the Muslims. While Muslims pray five times a day, compared to the three daily prayers observed by Jews. Circumcision is also a common practice in both faiths. Unfortunately, these commonalities have not been as influential as they should be. For the past eighty years, relations have deteriorated, and the blood shed continues to take its toll.

My parents believed that the two religions, both tracing their origins to Abraham, could coexist peacefully, as they did for hundreds of years. Unfortunately, history has been revised by those who wrote it, often neglecting to credit Muslims for opening their doors to Jews fleeing the horrors of the Spanish Inquisition and the brutality of the Nazi regime.

The story of the Libyan Jews is not unique. Jews throughout the North African coast lived a life marked by pride and tradition. Libyan Jews possessed a remarkable talent for storytelling, which I believe plays a crucial role in preserving ancient customs across generations. The Jews of Libya lived their traditions with deep faith and passion. Many were engaged in trade and retail, with some founding companies that conducted business with other countries. They communicated in several languages, including Arabic, Italian, English, Spanish and Hebrew. Throughout history, they expressed gratitude toward the Muslims who welcomed and embraced them. Although they remained cautious with their Arab neighbors, they were always willing to negotiate, compromise, and assert themselves when necessary.

Morocco served as the intellectual and spiritual hub for many famous writers and merchants. This was also true for Jews in Yemen, Iran, Iraq and other Arab countries. Many were well-educated, and some families accumulated wealth and fame, extending their influence as far as Asia. For instance, the Kadoori brothers and the Sassoon family, the Jewish entrepreneurs from Baghdad, played an instrumental role in igniting an economic renaissance in Asia and opened China and Hong Kong to the world. It was the Kadoori and Sasson families who in 1928 built the famous and renowned Peninsula Hotel in Hong Kong and the Peace Hotel in Shanghai.

Libyan Jews became skilled craftsmen, known for their expertise in carving, jewelry-making, carpentry and fishing. They bravely ventured into stormy seas to bring the best catch to market and sailed to places like Italy to trade fabric and machinery. They also crossed the Sahara Desert to connect with traders from Sudan, Egypt and Tunisia. They built courtyards in their homes where they could grow fruit trees and vegetable gardens, successfully balancing traditional Jewish life with business partnerships among Arabs.

Despite the pressure from those who conquered the land, the local inhabitants learned to coexist with nearly everyone, including the Phoenicians, Greeks, Spaniards, Turks, Romans, British and other foreigners. They celebrated their holidays freely, maintained their customs, paid their taxes, and became an integral part of Libyan society. My grandfather ran a spice shop with his Arab best friend. Although his Hebrew name was Abraham, people preferred to call him Ibrahim. Together, they traveled to purchase herbs and

CHAPTER FOUR

spices from Tunisia and Sudan. They were like brothers and trusted each other completely until my grandfather decided to leave for Israel, entrusting the store to his Arab partner.

Unfortunately, the remarkable achievements of Sephardic Jews and their contribution in countries like Morocco, Iraq, Egypt, and Libya are not widely known among both Jews and Gentiles. Like the case of many immigrants arriving in Israel, Sephardic Jews had to abandon many of their old customs and grapple with a new set of norms and values in sharp contrast with their previous way of life among Arab communities. This was my heritage—strong yet tender, rigid but flexible, resilient yet sensitive, and swift to forgive.

As a boy, I listened to the stories of my neighbors, absorbed the details of their narratives, and immersed myself in this unique segment of the Jewish diaspora. Their fervor for their faith, tradition and family helped them survive and maintain their identity. Many of these stories, along with others, provided me with strong roots and guided me as I navigated my youth in Israel.

Chapter Five

TOUCHING THE ANCIENT SOIL

It was early morning when the old Greek ship approached the port of Haifa.

Our Coptic Orthodox Christian captain had been sailing boats for over thirty years; he studied the map intently, discussing the route with his first mate. Looking down from the bridge at the decks, they might have noticed men in their prayer shawls wrapping the tefillin around their hands and over their heads. The tefillin is also known as phylacteries of two small leather boxes worn during weekday morning prayers. Inside these boxes are scrolls written on parchment using specific ink and script according to strict Jewish law signifying the binding of the heart and the mind to God.

Unlike other morning services, this one was exceptional. It was a Thanksgiving celebration expressing gratitude to the Lord for bringing them back to their homeland. This was a historical moment they had dreamed of for so long—a miracle reminiscent of their ancestors' exodus from Egypt and God's invisible hand parting the Red Sea.

The decks trembled with songs and dances. The sight was so moving that the captain and his officers, watching from above, were in awe of what they witnessed. Everyone could see the shores of Haifa approaching, with the Carmel Mountains in the background—the very mountains where the prophet Elijah brought the dead back to life and where the Maccabees fought against the invading Greeks.

The excitement and anticipation were palpable; children ran along the decks while women brought hot coffee and pastries they had hastily baked before boarding the ship. Those pastries reminded many of the unleavened bread that their ancestors had taken with them when they left their bondage in Egypt eighty generations ago.

My father led the prayer, and as everyone listened, tears welled up in their eyes. He chanted words of gratitude, thanking the Maker for the gathering of the diaspora. Soon, each person knew they would kneel on the ground and kiss the soil where their ancestors had walked—the very soil of their forebears. The women wept as they heard the shofar, a traditional musical horn, that my father had brought with him. Even the children fell silent, captivated by the thunderous sound emanating from the shofar, while tears of happiness rolled down my father's cheeks.

On the bridge, the captain rolled down the glass to listen to the hymns of the service. The melodies may have reminded him of the beautiful music from his church in Alexandria, which he attended as a young boy. That church was filled with incense and chanting. Just like the Jews he was ferrying from Libya to Israel, the Copts—his people—also endured suffering. His religion originated in the Middle East, and its ancient practices held a history as rich as that of the Jewish faith. As a minority in Egypt, Copts have faced persecution throughout history. The captain told the officer standing beside him that they should pray for the day when the Copts of Egypt could make their exodus to the Holy Land. He quietly urged his mates to pray for a future where they could worship their Lord without fear.

His prayer was abruptly interrupted when a sailor informed him that a pilot boat flying an Israeli flag was approaching the ship. Slowing down the engines, military officers from the Israeli boat climbed up to the bridge to help disembark the excited passengers, who were praying and dancing.

The sight of Israeli soldiers carrying rifles sparked a wave of joy and pride

CHAPTER FIVE

among the newcomers. Everyone stood up on the deck and began singing the new anthem. Some saluted the soldiers, while the women, with their scarves covering their heads, threw candies at the Israeli guards. They welcomed the soldiers with smiles and songs in Arabic, praising Ben Gurion, the new Prime Minister, the newly named King David and the newly founded land.

But as we disembarked the ship in Haifa, there was no band playing the national anthem, no children with flowers or waving small flags to greet us, and no official representatives in formal suits to welcome us. It was a hot day. The images of our arrival remain vivid in my mind—shining faces, trembling hearts, and the anxiety of facing the unknown. After all, this was the land of milk and honey, the Promised Land that Jews had yearned for thousands of years. I was too young to fully appreciate the historical significance of the moment, clinging to my mother and making sure that none of our belongings were lost on our way off the ship. I remember the blue sky, the mountains surrounding Haifa, the flag adorned with the Jewish star and the oppressive heat.

To our shock, we were asked to line up under the scorching sun while two men dressed in white gowns and masks sprayed us with a cloud of disinfectant chemicals. My sister coughed, and other children cried as men grumbled about the treatment. My people dislike standing in line, following any structure, or having the patience to listen to instructions. Some complained while others tried to calm the crowd. My mother was searching for water to quench my sister's thirst, but there was no one to ask. It was a chaotic morning, a far cry from the songs and dances that had taken place on the ship's decks. In many ways, it felt like a letdown; no one was prepared for such treatment. The joyful songs sung on the ship turned into anguished cries from infants and anxious women trying to protect their children from the fumes being sprayed by workers from the newly established Health Department. One man shouted: "This is how you treat animals before slaughter!"

It was an early sign that the promised land of milk and honey was different from what everyone had imagined all these years.

Children coughed incessantly as their mothers became angry and the men stood silent, at a loss for words. In Libya, they would have stopped the misery and subdued those with the spraying machines, but on the shores of Haifa, in their new homeland, they submitted to their hosts, a process of submission that would define many of the immigrants arriving from Arab lands. As we would soon learn, the underlying attitude of the residents here was that Jews from North Africa and Middle Eastern countries were primitive, uneducated, and dirty. While the founders' intention was to avoid any diseases or viruses picked up along the journey, the process was humiliating.

Immigrants from European countries were treated differently. They were not disinfected by spraying fumes on their faces. They did not have to live in tents and transition camps. They were housed in major urban centers, spoken to in Yiddish or Russian, and assigned decent jobs. They were treated with generous benefits and compensated for all the suffering that most of them had experienced at the brutal hands of the Nazis.

A loud voice boomed from a megaphone held by the announcer, instructing us to climb onto the trucks that would take us to our new homes. We were transported to a transition camp known as Beer Yaakov, which resembled a large tent city. Some women from the Jewish Agency served water and biscuits, which the crowd consumed hungrily. Despite the discomfort we experienced, we viewed our situation as the necessary pain of being the first generation to connect with this ancient land and touch its soil. Amidst the confusion, chaos and unfriendly attitudes we encountered on our return, my people remained forgiving. They held no feelings of revenge; instead, they accepted their circumstances as an integral part of their journey.

As I later reflected on those challenging days, I was amazed by their strength, resilience and support for one another. Their invisible anger transformed into a boundless love to protect their children. Their confusion over the unfair treatment was softened by their willingness to lower their expec-

CHAPTER FIVE

tations. The hundreds of newly erected tents served as a reminder of their ancestors' escape from Egypt, evoking memories of roaming the Sinai Desert while sleeping in tents made from sheep skins. This was a generation of lions, embracing whatever came their way and facing each challenge with courage and an endless love for their newly founded land.

My mother, like many others, justified the special treatment given to Holocaust refugees. She often told her friends that, considering the brutal actions of the Nazis, these refugees deserved better treatment. The love my people have for others humbles me; they rarely expressed jealousy or envy over the privileges afforded to those arriving from Europe. The general sentiment was that these refugees deserved better lives than we did. For over three decades, my people accepted this reality, often walking away undeterred as they faced barriers to better job opportunities and admission to institutions of higher education.

Their ability to endure such a harsh reality continues to amaze me. This conviction came from a deep faith that greatness can emerge from pain and suffering. My father frequently reminded his congregation about the ancient Israelites, who wandered in the desert for forty years before reaching the Promised Land. "Think of the struggles our forefathers endured to transform a small tribe into a nation," he would say. He often referenced the extraordinary life of Job, who faced immense suffering and was tested repeatedly to recognize the power of his Maker. He would also speak of Moses crossing the Sinai Desert, where food and water were scarce as they journeyed toward the land promised to Abraham. He conveyed to his congregation that God fulfilled His promises.

"Our God," he would say, "is the one who gathered us from the four corners of the earth and brought us to this land. This is our only homeland, and there is no other place for us to go. We will stay, multiply and rebuild."

Our small tent had two regular beds and two bunk beds, along with a pinewood table and four chairs. We also had several pots, plates and a device known as a primus, which served as a cooking stove fueled by kerosene. Cooking on the tent floor compared to her beautiful kitchen in Benghazi was a significant challenge for my mother; the constant black smoke from the primus and the risk of flying embers landing on the mattresses stuffed with dry hay or cotton weighed heavily on her mind, causing her a great deal of stress.

With my youngest sister, Rachel, in her arms, cooking became an even heavier burden for my mother. As her anxiety grew, my father was too busy with his rabbinical duties to lend a hand. I remember watching her as she tirelessly tried to clean the tent, where dust and flies were ever-present. Her eyes often appeared tired and distant, and her memories of Libya seemed to be her way of coping with the harsh situation.

Her sadness reflected that of many other women in the tent city. In hindsight, caring for their children was often what kept them going in such a challenging environment. When the women gathered around the tents, they rarely spoke of their better days in Libya. Instead, they discussed how to prepare various dishes, ways to keep the tent free of dust, and how to care for sick children. Occasionally, they would break into Arabic songs, reminiscing about beautiful beaches, fresh grilled fish from the sea, and the delightful aroma of hot coffee made from dark roasted beans mixed with rosewater. However, when the men arrived, the singing would stop, and the women would lower their heads as they returned to their tents.

One day, I fell from my bunk bed and my thigh hit the frying pan on the lit primus. My mother had been frying potatoes for lunch. I don't remember crying, but the smell of the burned skin catching the hot oil made my mother run to me. She looked at my thigh, and the sight of the blackened, blistered skin panicked her. Thinking that the cold margarine in the ice box might ease my pain, she rubbed it against the skin. The melting stick on my burning skin increased my anguish, but I gritted my teeth and bit my tongue. I couldn't bear to increase my mother's anguish. To this day, the scar

CHAPTER FIVE

on my right thigh reminds me of those painful days in Beer Yaakov.

Seeing me lying in bed with a towel wrapped around my leg was the first time I had ever seen my mother angry. Her face was tense, her eyes filled with fury as she paced anxiously in the small tent, waiting for my father to return from the synagogue. When he finally arrived, she wasted no time in telling him what had happened to me, her voice trembling with emotion.

My father listened to her without interruption. He approached my bed, placed both hands on my head, and began to pray. Although I couldn't hear the words he spoke, the comfort of his hands on my head and face helped alleviate my pain. I then heard my mother mention how she missed the times in Benghazi when life was better and more beautiful. With a sad tone, she expressed her longing for those days in Libya.

For several minutes, my father remained silent. Then he walked over to my mother, took her by the arm, and led her out of the tent. In his calm yet intense voice, he addressed her, saying, "My dear, look at those hundreds of tents. Do you know any of the people living in them?" He didn't wait for her to respond. He gestured toward one of the nearby tents. "Do you see who lives there? The famous Teshuva family. Next to them is the Arbib family, and nearby is the Saadon family. They were all wealthy families in Libya, living in palaces with servants and cooks. But now, look at them. Their wives are cooking meals on the tent floor, and they sleep on iron beds."

He paused, turned to her, and in a stern yet loving voice, said, "You see, my beloved wife, they are just like us." His serious tone was softened by love and compassion.

My mother straightened up, lowered her eyes, and replied, "I see."

Tears welled up in my eyes as my heart broke for the pain and suffering my mother had to endure.

My father returned to my side of the tent and held my hand. This was the last time my mother spoke about our poor living conditions in the tent. She accepted his message: we were not going back; the bridge to Libya

OUT OF THE CUCKOO'S NEST

had been burned.

    We were there to stay.

Chapter Six

A DEEPLY ROOTED TRADITION

After we left Libya, I found myself clinging to the stories of our old life that my mother and father had told me. Together with my own recollections, they formed a tapestry richly woven with memory and tradition.

I recall this tapestry now with the intention to weave it again, so that it may continue to live on—but first, I would like to explain why I feel it is so important for me to do so.

I want to make sure our traditions are remembered not just as a collection of stories, but as a direct counterpoint to the erasure we faced upon our arrival in Israel. We came from Libya with a rich culture and a proud history. We were not fleeing tragedy the way many European Jews were; no one forced us to leave Libya. In fact, some of us stayed behind, prosperous and rooted in centuries of life in North Africa. Others, like my own family, came to Israel carrying generations of songs, customs, and scholarship. But when we arrived, that richness was dismissed.

In Libya, we were never ashamed of who we were. We carried our heritage with pride. And yet, in Israel, we were made to feel embarrassed by our traditions, our impulsive spirit, our language, even our music. When I weave the tapestry of our traditions, is it not from a place of nostalgia. It is from a place of resistance. The Libyan Jews came to the Promised Land with a rich and vibrant history, but as I sat in school in Israel, the curriculum acted as if we had no history at all.

We were not seen as we saw ourselves: as a people of culture, of art, of commerce, and of scholarship. In Libya, many left for countries like Italy, England, and Canada had been university professors and successful business leaders, but in Israel, our contributions were invisible.

Only recently have those narratives begun to be restored. I insist on telling them because remembering is a moral obligation and an act of survival. Our history deserves to stand in its full truth, with all its complexity and pride intact.

My mother always painted a picture of Benghazi as beautiful and charming, with old buildings, courtyards and colorful markets bursting with spices, alive with people from various religions and backgrounds. Fig and pomegranate trees dotted the expansive yard at our home, providing tantalizing scents, shade on hot days and delicious fruit in the summer.

Whenever my mother spoke of her old kitchen, her thoughts would linger on the fruit baskets atop spacious countertops, the cupboards filled with fine glassware, and the pantry large enough for homemade jams, carafes of olive oil, fresh wine straight from the vineyard outside the city, and bread that had just come out of wood-fired ovens. Even years later, I can still smell the deep, aromatic scents of cumin, curry, cardamom, and cinnamon from her cooking.

The Jews in Benghazi, Tripoli, and other cities in Libya lived separately from their Muslim and Christian neighbors, divided—but not at odds or in any serious conflict—by religion. And yet, while our traditions of worship were different, when it came to our geographical history and many of our shared cultural values, we learned how to live with each other.

My mother was equally comfortable with her Arab neighbors as she was with her Jewish neighbors. She spent time playing with the Muslim children who lived next door, enjoying their pastries, listening to their stories,

CHAPTER SIX

and singing along to Arabic songs about love and desire. These memories stayed with her for many years. Her passion for the Arabic language later hindered her ability to learn Hebrew. Arabic was her expressive language; her songs were in Arabic, her metaphors were drawn from Libyan culture, and her affinity for people from all walks of lives in Libya was profound. I experienced something similar during my time teaching at Harvard and the University of Hartford, where I had students from Libya under the Gaddafi regime. They were more comfortable with me than with their other professors. We used to meet on weekends to cook, converse in Arabic and sing Libyan songs together. They offered me any assistance I needed, and when Gaddafi fell from grace with the United States, my students had to return to Libya. They communicated with me freely from there, without fear. They never asked for anything from me, nor did we discuss politics. One of them was the daughter of the Libyan Chief of Staff, while others held positions in the Libyan government.

My mother respected the Arab way of treating their elderly, their warm hospitality and their humility. She often reminded me that throughout the ages, rabbis have warned their communities, both in writing and orally, that neglecting the elderly in their old age is a sin. For the Arabs in Libya, this respect is ingrained in their culture, and no admonition from their spiritual leaders is necessary.

I rarely heard my mother speak negatively about the Arabs in Libya. In Israel, when she experienced racism and discrimination, she longed for the friendship and respect she had with her neighbors in Benghazi. As the conflict with the Arab states along the Israeli border intensified, she was puzzled by the sudden animosity that arose between Arabs and Jews. She always believed that peace between these two civilizations would lead to a better world.

My mother attended an Italian Catholic school for five years, which she regarded as the best place to learn good manners and receive a meaningful education. She adored the nuns and their disciplined approach. For her, the years at the Catholic school in Benghazi were a refuge, allowing her to regain her confidence after losing her mother at the age of 13. Following her mother's death, she was the only single girl in the household and assumed responsibility for all the housework. Her father was strict, and her childhood was marked by pain and a longing for love. The Catholic school became her sanctuary, filled with serenity and care.

The love and support from the nuns nurtured her soul and exposed her to customs and habits unfamiliar to her in the Jewish quarter. An open-minded woman, my mother embraced all religions and felt comfortable among both Christians and Muslims. Throughout her life, she saw beauty in people and focused on their positive qualities, making their weaknesses seem insignificant. My mother's influence on me was far more subtle than my father's. Her positive mindset, her sense of humor despite the economic struggle, her compassion, her generosity, and her rich reservoir of love were the very forces that kept us going. In many ways, my mother was one of the strongest and most resilient people I have ever encountered. While life treated her harshly, she held no contempt.

Among my most precious memories as a child are the ones of breakfast with my mother. Since she had to leave for work early, we would all gather around the table with a cup of coffee loaded with sugar and fried dough. During breakfast, Mother would ask us if we had any dreams the night before. For each dream we shared, she had an interpretation. Water symbolized blessings, fish represented good fortune, lions stood for strength, snakes indicated lurking enemies, and falling into dark wells was a sign of impending trouble—though by dreaming of it, we could avoid its occurrence. Sharing our dreams with the family and waiting for Mother to explain became a kind of therapy in those trying times. After we described our dreams, she would always smile and comfort us, assuring us that the dream was a blessing in disguise. She consistently emphasized that we would have a wonderful

CHAPTER SIX

day and that we should have no fears since God was watching over us.

Despite her busy schedule, Mother encouraged us to talk and express our emotions. Withholding feelings was discouraged; her belief was that once we expressed our emotions, the fear would dissipate. This became a guiding principle in my work with others.

The most memorable times with my mother were Thursday mornings when we walked together to the crowded market. Donkeys brayed and wagons stood by the wayside. The vendors were primarily farmers from neighboring villages. They displayed a wide variety of fresh produce – fruit, vegetables and herbs – all integral to our cuisine. It was a heady mix of intoxicating scents: the aroma bursting from mint leaves, the fresh smell of cilantro, and the pungent whiff of fresh onions. The vendors and their children loudly lured shoppers to their stands, resulting in a deafening but engaging cacophony. The produce itself was a feast for the eyes.

This was my personal time with my mother. Undisturbed by my siblings, she was there with me and no one else could have shared her beauty and determination as I did. Looking at my mother's tense face convinced me that she was more focused on the mission of buying the best products for the lowest price than enjoying the scene as I did. Mother would hand pick each tomato or onion and bring the item close to her nose and inhale its scent, then she would squeeze it delicately to determine its quality. I loved those long moments watching her concentration and intensity. Later I would follow in her footsteps, selecting vegetables and fruits using her subjective methods of quality control. She had specific vendors whom she believed were honest and reasonable. Following the two-hour long shopping tour, we would haul the harvest home.

The most memorable dish we prepared was a traditional Libyan Jewish dish made especially to honor the Shabbat. It is known as *mafrum*. This tasty dish consists of layers of potatoes, meat and vegetables, all seasoned with a unique blend of spices and then baked to perfection.

Mother would start first by peeling six to eight large potatoes. We then cut each potato into thick wedges. Mother taught me how to slice each wedge creating space for the stuffing. In a large mixing bowl, mother would place the chopped meat with two eggs, salt, black paper and spices that included cumin, caraway, curry, cilantro, parsley and hot grounded pepper. I liked helping mother create balls out of the mix and placing each ball into the potato wedge. As I was inserting the spicy meatballs into the potato and covering each *mafrum* with a dusting of flour, mother heated a big frying pan of oil. When the oil was hot, we carefully dropped each stuffed potato into the pan. Listening to the sounds of the sizzling oil and inhaling the scent of heaven coming from the blend of spices and potatoes uplifted my soul. Once the *mafrum* browned, she would pull them out one by one and place them in a large pot filled with onion and tomato. The pot and its wonders would be simmered for hours before it was served on a bed of couscous and garnished with fresh cilantro and parsley. As my father recited the blessings, we impatiently waited to devour the *mafrum*. Mother was always excited to serve my father first with a plate of *mafrum*s and couscous and like a little kid, she waited for him to display his amazement at her creation. Only after my father expressed his delight, she would then proceed to serve us. Those moments of my parents connecting with each other remain unforgettable and are carved in my memory for eternity.

I also have fond memories of my father during our time in Libya. The synagogue was a focal point where those with means supported the less fortunate. Like other places, synagogues reflected the wealth of their members. I have an old picture of my father as a young rabbi placing the cornerstone for the great synagogue, known as *tslah*. Each *tslah* united Jews in a single, unbroken link.

My people were never known for being shy or reluctant to express their feelings. It was common for them to raise their voice, curse and quarrel with one another. Nevertheless, it was my father's role as a rabbi to mend

CHAPTER SIX

fences when things got out of control and repair broken relationships. Like other rabbis, my father would call the disputants to his rabbinical court. He encouraged them to speak about their emotions. With his calm, soothing voice, he persuaded them to eliminate the anger that poisoned their relationship. I was always amazed to see how two men, who entered his office ready to fight, would leave smiling and reconcile.

Being quick to temper and fast to reconcile placed a strain on my community, but it ultimately kept them mentally healthy. Consequently, rabbis had to be soft-spoken, great listeners, and possess a delicate sense of humor, much like my father. Humor often served to break the ice and create a rapport among those who had issues with one another. The *tslah* was more than a place of worship; it was a venue for discussing current matters and determining a course of action. It also served as a place for young men to gaze at the young women watching from the balcony where women were separated from men during the services. However, eyes had no boundaries; they were free to roam and scan the entire hall. The balcony offered young women a better vantage point to observe the men below, enabling them to distinguish true worshippers from those there for other reasons. Matchmakers were always present, scanning the crowd, recruiting and taking mental notes to predict the best matches, thereby building their reputation as the best matchmaker. Their success was measured by the happiness of the couples they brought together.

Compared to many other Jewish communities, Libyan Jews were less strict, although rabbinical authorities maintained some notable exceptions. Even among the rabbis, though, there was a degree of flexibility and compassion. Jewish laws were often interpreted and reinterpreted to provide a more liberal understanding.

Cultural traditions encompass not just Jewish law, such as circumcision and the use of the *mikveh*, the ritual purification bath, but also the cuisine, which is just as bold and spicy as the Libyan people themselves. Libyan Jews learned fishing techniques from their northern neighbors in Sardinia and Sicily. They would venture out to sea at night to ensure a fresh catch for the morning market. One of the most common dishes is *charaimi*, a spicy sauce made from hot peppers, garlic, cumin and tomato paste. Fresh fillets of fish, such as grouper and snapper, would be immersed in this sauce and cooked over a low flame for several hours. This dish was typically served as an appetizer on Friday nights. Several years later, I was thrilled when my *charaimi* recipe was published in *The New York Times*.

It seems that almost every Libyan is an excellent cook, having learned from their mothers and grandmothers, just as I learned from mine. We discovered the secrets to making delicious dishes that uplift the spirit and inspire joyful conversations around the table. The special recipes, stories from our days in Libya, rich traditions and warm hospitality kept our community connected. I can still recall the enticing aromas of cooking filling the air before sunset on Friday evenings as my mother prepared us for Shabbat.

Libyan Jews excelled not only in commerce, but also in literature. Jewish scholars and rabbis in major cities like Tripoli and Benghazi authored numerous works, including historical accounts highlighting the vital roles Libyan Jews played in trade, as well as literature and poetry. Some focused on the mysteries of the Kabbalah, while others interpreted scriptural texts and their significance for Jews living in exile. Influential writers such as Rabbi Mordechai Hacohen, Rabbi Nathan Haddad and Rabbi Yaakov Rokach explored the complexities of the Kabbalah and the Mishnah. Many of the hymns sung in Libyan synagogues in Israel and Italy today were composed by these Libyan rabbis and scholars.

The most famous rabbinical scholar and poet was Rabbi Shimon Lavie, who left Spain during the Spanish Inquisition and made his way to Jerusalem. During his journey, he stopped in Tripoli, where he was pleasantly surprised to find the Libyan Jewish community living much like they had centuries ago. Jews in towns like Derna and Benghazi practiced their religion

CHAPTER SIX

with complete freedom. Legend has it that Rabbi Lavie was so impressed by the way Libyan Jews lived in contrast to the Jews of Spain, that he decided to stay there. His work in enhancing Jewish life in Libya is celebrated every Friday evening by chanting a poem – in both Hebrew and Arabic – after Shabbat dinner.

As a rabbi, my father held a special place in our community's traditions. When someone in town fell ill, a family member would visit him with a cloth-like scarf or a shirt belonging to the sick person. My father would take the scarf in both hands, placing his fingers on the still-warm fabric and immerse himself in prayer. He would close his eyes and whisper the names of angels. He concluded his ritual by declaring that the "evil eye" placed on the suffering person had been lifted. The visiting family members would then hurry home, asking the sick person to wear the scarf. To everyone's surprise, the sick individual would often rise from their bed, reporting that they felt better.

I used to think of my father as a medicine man, but he was more than that. He was a Kabbalist who employed a combination of angelic names and specific verses from various Jewish texts. In his mind—and in the minds of others—my father possessed the power to heal through his holiness, prayers and a mysterious connection with the Creator. I firmly believe that part of healing was a result of mind over body; the conviction people had in the power of Kabbalah and their trust in my father as a healer led to positive outcomes.

My father believed his role as a rabbi was to serve God by helping others in their times of need and despair. I learned that there are often unseen lights around us. My father was like a lighthouse, guiding people toward purpose and conviction. Simply being in his presence helped people see the positive side of life, put smiles on tired faces and eased the anger stemming from being misled and mistreated by those in power.

In almost every Jewish home, it is common to find the amulet called *chamsah*, which features the symbol of an eye within the palm of an open hand with five fingers. This symbol is believed to protect against the evil eye and is typically hung prominently in the foyer, ensuring that visitors see it and are distracted from wishing ill upon the household. My mother hung our *chamsah* on the wall separating our small living area from the kitchen, facing the front door, thus providing protection from any ill-wishers upon entering our home.

If a child fell ill, the mother would burn resin from the tree known as Washka, allowing the sick child to inhale the scent, which were thought to drive evil spirits from the body and promote quick recovery. Over the years, the soothing scent of Washka helped me, and my siblings recover from fevers and the flu, especially since money was scarce and doctors were often unavailable. I still burn Washka in my home when I feel down. In cases of more serious illness, however, medicinal experts in the community would use various plants and fervent prayers to counteract the destructive power of the evil eye. If a child's life appeared to be at risk, the rabbi would perform a ceremony to change the child's name, believing that such a change would lead to a more favorable outcome and recovery.

At nine years old, I developed a stone in my bladder, making urination an excruciating experience. The situation worsened until my pain became unbearable, prompting my mother to take me to the hospital. Doctors determined that I needed an emergency operation to remove the stone that was blocking my urinary passage. Although my father had named me after his eldest son from a previous marriage—who had been killed in the war—he conducted a special ceremony, calling upon God to change my name to Shu-Shan. I eventually recovered, but the surgery left me hunched and unable to walk straight for several years, which further isolated me from the other kids. My new name didn't last long. My parents loved my original name and continued using it until their last breaths.

My parents were different from most of the families in our neighborhood.

CHAPTER SIX

They never raised their voices or used physical punishment. My mother felt sorry for the boys and girls whose parents were strict and used severe methods. She often told me that hitting children indicated that parents had lost control over them. Instead, my parents chose to appeal to the softer side of discipline, which, in most cases, proved to be more effective.

When my father's eyesight was good, he would give us a piercing stare to get our attention. Once he had that, he would quote verses from the Bible or Halacha to teach us right from wrong. Those verses still resonate in my mind.

My mother would often refuse to look at us when we strayed from the right path. Her silence was so disturbing and painful that none of my siblings or I could bear it. Within several minutes, we would approach her with simple, leading questions like, "Ya-Emi, are you upset with me?" or "Ima, did I do something wrong?" These questions felt like trying to break down a dam, releasing a torrent of guilt and shame. But then came the forgiveness, manifesting through her unconditional love. In those moments, with her braided hair escaping from her scarf and her beautiful, shining eyes, she would appear both stiff and loving. She would offer us a Libyan biscuit known as *kaak*, which was as sweet as her eyes. Her love captivated us. We were like butterflies hovering over the sweet nectar of a flower in Paradise.

I still take pleasure in preparing Libyan Jewish dishes for my friends. The hours I spend cooking, inhaling the spicy aroma of roasted garlic, feeling the smoke rising from *mafrum*s sizzling in hot oil, watching the steam rise from fresh couscous, and savoring the spicy fish simmering in *charaimi* sauce evoke sweet memories and transport me back to my mother's tiny kitchen in Israel filled with her radiating warmth and inspiring smile.

The customs, ceremonies, traditions, delicious meals, blessings, singing, tough discipline and the overall ambiance of our beautiful culture—all of this I carry with me to this day, even if only in memory.

Chapter Seven

MY FATHER'S BURNING PLATFORM

During those early years in Israel, my father's old age started affecting his movements, and his energy dwindled. Watching my sixty-year-old father running around looking after the community's needs brought my mother to frequent tears, which she hid from us. My mother could not linger on that long because we were all young and needed her care. It was perhaps a blessing to her, as young children help a mother escape the anxiety of the unknown.

There were rare moments when my father asked me to walk him to the synagogue. Those moments of him holding my hand were the best. His warm, strong palm covering my entire hand always brought infinite security and comfort. From time to time, my father squeezed my tiny hand as if he were telling me, "All will be fine, my son." I always wondered how he felt during those days. His ancestors from Spain left one foreign land for another, and now he was finally home. I wondered what went through his mind and heart as he looked at his flock settled in different parts of the country. Did he feel like a lost child returning to his original homeland? Or like a man from another land and a generation becoming irrelevant in the new land?

Libya and Tunisia had been all he and his ancestors had known for several generations. It was where his grandparents and great-grandparents had sustained the Jewish flame.

My father was the youngest and only son in a family of six daughters. In my culture, not having a son was a heavy burden. His mother, a strong-willed woman and master of the house, never gave up on having a son. In her misery, she would sneak into the synagogue and pray to God with trembling hands holding the holy scrolls, begging for a son to please her humble husband, to gift him with a boy. She felt like Hannah, in the Bible, who couldn't bear a child, walking into the Holy Temple begging God for a child. Hannah's cry was so loud that Eli, the high priest, thinking that she was drunk, advised her to stop drinking and go home. I always admired Hannah's courage in responding to authority by letting him know she was not drunk but filled with sorrow and a broken heart for not bearing a child. Eli sent her home and promised that God had heard her prayer. Sure enough, she later gave birth to the prophet Samuel.

My grandmother's life echoed Hannah's. She never let go of the power of prayer, and her love for my grandfather ran deep. Though he wasn't a scholar or a learned man, he loved her fiercely in return and never once raised his voice at her. His devotion never wavered, even when friends mocked him for having six daughters and no son. Even when the town rabbi reminded him that Jewish law allowed him to divorce and remarry in hopes of producing a male heir. In those days, a son meant continuity, a way to carry the family name forward—a name, Saada, that had endured for centuries. But my grandfather never faltered. He remained loyal to her. When she died a month after giving birth to my father, his spirit broke. His world fell apart. Nine years later, he, too, was gone, leaving my father an orphan at ten.

Throughout the ages, in cities like Tripoli and Benghazi, unity existed as one of the most emblematic elements of the Libyan Jewish community. Taught the values of generosity and harmony, children were the shining lights of the community, which shared the responsibility of raising them. I

CHAPTER SEVEN

am told that at least five nursing mothers shared their milk with my father when he lost his mother.

When my father lost his father, the community came together again to find him a home with a loving family. A wonderful family adopted him. They identified his unique talents: quick mind, love of reading the scriptures, unforgettable memory for Jewish law, deep knowledge of the Talmud, and mesmerizing voice. From a young age, my father would rise early to head to the synagogue for the morning service and then stay for hours to read. Eventually, his sisters married, and some ventured to Tunisia to follow their husbands. My father was left behind. He attended a reputable Yeshiva in Libya, where he was ordained at age seventeen as a rabbi and a spiritual leader of the Jewish community in Benghazi and Tripoli. His sharp mind in dealing with day-to-day issues among members of the Jewish community and his ability to negotiate with the Muslims and the Christians in addressing religious and secular matters amazed those who knew him.

He became a Talmudic scholar, an expert of the Kabbalah, an extraordinary orator, and a man of gravitas. In Benghazi, my father earned the love and respect of Muslims, Christians and Jews alike. At first sight, people trusted him. His burning eyes and generous heart created an aura around him, enabling him to settle conflicts peacefully, find the right man for an orphaned girl, counsel broken hearts and encourage those who lost their business or needed good advice. In the new land, what was he? I could sense his emotions and the general feeling of age coming upon him.

My father rarely revealed his thoughts, let alone his feelings. I watched him from the corner of my eye as we made it to the synagogue. I admired him for his unshakeable belief in God and his endless love for his family. His beard had grown white and rolled down to his chest. But his eyes were still young, still full of intelligence and life, and they communicated far more than his lips. Despite his age and declining sight, he walked with energy, propelled by purpose. Even when he stopped, it felt as though he was still moving. Perhaps it was this energy that drew people to him.

As a rabbi, he was known as intense and reserved in his demeanor but liberal in his interpretations of Jewish law. Some years later, when we were settled in Israel, and he led a congregation again, I saw him forgiving congregants for breaking religious customs. Unlike his peers, he felt religion had to adapt. He was always against the extreme and conservative interpretations of Jewish law. Once, I observed him looking outside our window at a man returning from his shop after the sun had set and Shabbat had begun. He didn't reprimand him publicly but pulled him aside later in the synagogue. He never placed anyone on the spot, only trying to determine if things were right. In doing so, people felt comfortable sharing anything with him. When people confronted him about his silence in moments when a person circumvented a religious law, he would respond by making those who complained feel uncomfortable for throwing stones at their neighbors. He would advise them that compassion is more powerful than blaming and loving their neighbors, which is the essence of Judaism and the reason underlying the survival of our people. He was a true spiritual leader. His sermons often brought people to tears. His metaphors and quotes from the Bible inspired people to stay the course despite all obstacles. Father demonstrated everything he believed in through his conduct. From his point of view, people were not bad; they were lost or imprisoned in their own cells. He strongly felt they needed guidance the most. Reaching out to others by extending a hand was his purpose in life. Yet, in instances of serious violations, such as a man hitting his children or wife, he wasted no time in demanding an immediate meeting with the abuser. He probed, and listened to find the reasons behind such conduct. His body was tense, and his voice was low but clear; he radiated a stern demeanor without space for negotiation or excuses. Eventually, he would bring the man to tears due to shame and warn him that hitting someone, especially his wife, constituted one of the greatest sins, with no room for God's forgiveness.

CHAPTER SEVEN

He mastered the art of getting people to do the right thing without imposing his will or rabbinical authority. I have tried to adopt some of his extraordinary skills in getting people to do the right thing. When my mother would praise him for his gift, he would dismiss the compliment and let her know that he was only a messenger of God. The Bible was his compass; the Psalms were his medicine; the tallit on his shoulders and over his head signified a moment of intimacy with his God; the blessing before he consumed anything was an expression of gratitude; and washing his hands before meals was like entering heaven while on earth. God was part of his existence, almost like two lovers, as the Song of Songs by King Solomon depicted, and his covenant with the Maker was unshakeable regardless of any difficulty he faced.

He had an aura that the townspeople were convinced that he was a messenger of the Almighty. Thus, he was endowed with the aura of the Schinas, the spirit sent from heaven. They looked up to him as their shepherd and a spiritual healer. People lined up to see him for multiple reasons. One might be worried parents who had not yet received a proposition for their daughter well into marriageable age; another, a patient with insomnia who had found no relief from Western medication. A couple might be unhappy because the wife couldn't get along with her in-laws. Others just wanted to be in his presence, bowing and kissing his hands and asking for his blessings.

At times, I grew up in the shadow of a spiritual messenger whose love for his flock carried him through age and exhaustion. Those seeking healing came to our home, waiting for my father to return from his morning prayer. My mother greeted them with sweetened coffee laced with rose water, offering comfort for their anxious hearts. When my father arrived, she guided them to his small study, a space he carved out by partitioning part of our bedroom. Inside stood a simple desk, crowded with holy books and his own worn notebook filled with the names of angels known for their healing power. One by one, the visitors entered. I would slip behind the wall or hide beneath the bed, listening closely to their stories and, above all, to my father's replies—his voice steady against their sobs and pleas.

Most of the time, my father said little. His style was to ask simple but direct and straightforward questions. The answers by the grievers were always long, and the emotions deep. Through this process of probing and quiet inquiry, asking relevant and piercing questions, he brought them to understand their situations. Unlike other rabbis who were quick to advise and tell people what to do, my father encouraged them to make their own choices. "Tell me how you are feeling," "Share with me something good you did for others," and "Explain to me more why you have to hit your wife when you are upset."

As they finished telling their stories and responding to his questions, he would quote a statement from the sages to make a point—never to embarrass or place the person in a corner—only to get them to see that the choice was theirs and God's role was to support them once the decision was made.

Depending on the circumstance, he might then hand them a Kamiah, a charm, his handwritten note carved by a fountain pen made from bamboo. This charm was precious for many of its holders. They would place it in a case hanging from their neck. My father's writing on a small piece of paper covered the names of angels like Gabriel and Malkiel and secret words and graphs drawn from Kabbalah to get the demons out of their existence and transform their fears into a sense of hope. He created a safe environment for them to pour their emotions, pain and suffering into the open. As a result, they left feeling more liberated, more relieved and more confident of themselves.

Father gave so much to others, but he never seemed to need intervention for his own concerns. He was much older than my mother. He knew his wife would survive him with seven children when he was called to see his Maker. Yet he never discussed his worries about the future with us; neither did he discuss the pain of the past. He never mentioned his days as an orphan. He

CHAPTER SEVEN

never talked about the days of horror when he lost most of his first family to the fascists during the war. All I know is that after the loss of his family, the sight of his children and wife lying dead in front of him forced him to stop conducting any circumcisions or slaughtering animals. He dumped the knives and never looked back. His ability to hold things deep and not burden others with the weight of experience deepened my admiration for him.

Father never talked about the death of his first wife and their four children and grandchildren; altogether, thirteen family members died in the bombing of Benghazi and Tripoli. In an article written in the local paper in 1942, the reporter described my father's moments of seeing his loved ones being pulled out from the rubble of his home where they all sought shelter from the long arm of the Nazis and the constant bombing by the Allied Forces. Despite General Mussolini's promise to protect the Jews of Libya, the Nazis ignored his commitment. They planned on continuing their Final Solution in North Africa. They sought to extinguish the Jewish existence in every land on earth.

Like many survivors, my father preferred to remain silent about his traumatic early life. But my mother knew his story and would tell it. On the anniversary of the killing of my father's first wife and children, my father fasted and said the Kaddish in his synagogue. Still, my mother stayed with us to recount the pieces and fragments she could recall. I regret not having the courage to get closer to him and beg him to share more of his life, its many twists and turns, and his struggles with me.

I can still smell the powdered tobacco he used to sniff, known as *nafa*. I loved the yellow streak the tobacco left on his white mustache. He kept the powdered tobacco in a small silver container. He used to tell me that it helped him stay awake at night to dwell on Jewish mysticism. I would come close to him to enjoy the wonderful scent of tobacco that wafted from his whiskers. I loved the moments when he touched my head to bless me. For me, it was less about the blessing and more about his warm scent and touch, and the feeling of his caring presence.

While he slept, I would quietly sneak to his desk and open the silver container to take a tiny amount of the powdered tobacco and inhale it. The first time I did it, I sneezed so hard that the powder spread like dust all over his desk. That night, I couldn't sleep out of fear of his inevitable discovery of the empty silver case and the powder covering his piles of books. The following day, he must have seen the empty container and powder all over his desk, yet he never said a word. My father and mother must have wiped away the powder from his books.

He never criticized any of us. His eyes said it all. We knew when he was joyful, sad, preoccupied, or going deep into his reading of the Kabbalah. He was always with and apart from us, yet we always felt safe around him. Like everyone else in the community, we believed he was endowed with the power of the angels. After all, we knew that his life was frequently on the line, but he always managed to get through whatever came his way. My father never held any negative emotions toward others, even those who tried to kill him or hurt him. He always believed that nothing was coincidental, but only messages from above. He was a true blend of a warrior and a monk at the same time.

My father believed in the power of love to transcend all barriers and to overcome old assumptions and groundless prejudices. He always thought that anything that had to do with human life must start with the heart. From the heart, everything else can be connected and integrated. Living in Israel with conflicting values and clashing cultures, my beloved father always believed that love was more powerful than hatred. In his view, hatred was a force of destruction, and love was a force of healing, building, and reconstruction. He was indeed a man for all seasons.

Chapter Eight

CRYING OUT FROM THE BELLY OF THE WHALE

One year after losing thirteen members of his family, my father had to make a choice. The custom among Libyan Jews held that the spiritual leader would mourn for a year if he lost his wife. At that point, he needed to decide either to remarry to stay at the pulpit or to remain single and in mourning and renounce his rabbinic position.

The custom always seemed a beautiful interpretation of a rabbi's role. It did not condemn the rabbi who chose to mourn; it simply dictated that a spiritual leader who wanted to serve as an advisor for married congregants with the authority to decide on marrying or divorcing them must be married himself to have such a capacity. My father decided he would not renounce the rabbinical pulpit and the passion to lead his people in trying times.

Back then, the concept of dating didn't exist. Marriages were arranged through a delicate negotiation process, beginning with designated matchmakers, who approached the fathers of single daughters in the town. In my father's case, one of these matchmakers came from a spice shop owner. He was a widower, earning just enough to get by, with a seventeen-year-old daughter, his youngest, still at home. Marrying her off seemed the most prudent step. And so, my mother became one of three potential brides.

The next phase occurred in a courtyard, where the prospective brides strolled as if they knew nothing of the matter, modestly glancing at the interested suitor. My father, in turn, observed them subtly from afar. My mother told me later that she fell in love at first sight when she glanced at his way. On that day in the courtyard, he chose her over the rest. The couple had a more formal introduction to the following Shabbat. My father, accompanied by a few friends, presented himself at the shop owner's home, bringing platters of food and fruits for the occasion. The young bride-to-be served food, fruits and tea, limiting herself to only eye contact. At the afternoon's close, her father and the aspiring groom shook hands in agreement.

But my grandfather struggled with the decision. He got cold feet. People in town mocked him for agreeing to marry his young daughter to a much older man—my father, after all, was fifty-six. Yet, in those days, one did not renege on a handshake. Bound to the decision, he determined to make things difficult for his future son-in-law, refusing, for example, the tradition of paying for the wedding as the bride's parent. But my father accommodated his wishes, and the attempts to anger my father failed. My poor grandfather also faced my mother's rebellion. In defiance of the protocol against challenging one's parents, she repeatedly asserted that she would not agree to marry any man other than my father. Succumbing to the circumstances, my grandfather complied. They got married.

Despite the wide gap in age, my mother loved my father with her whole being. He was her North Star—a man of wisdom who guided her with unwavering love. After his greatest loss, he believed God had blessed him with the perfect partner. She was loyal and steady, a woman who met whatever came her way with conviction and grace. My mother carried a strength rooted in quiet confidence, certain that God had sent her to care for him. His life had been filled with sorrow, and she wanted to give back what had been taken. She poured her love into small, steadfast gestures—never through words, rarely through touch, but in her constant attentiveness to

CHAPTER EIGHT

him. Each morning, after his first service at the synagogue, she greeted him with a cup of coffee and freshly baked salty cookies, carefully hidden from us children who would have devoured them at once. Later in the day, as he sat reading Psalms, she would slip into his study with a tray of mint tea and two raw eggs. She believed the yolks strengthened his voice for sermons. Standing at his side, she watched as he made his blessings, swallowed the eggs, and finished with a sip of mint tea.

My father wanted a child after the loss of his four children. My mother had grown up without her mother and wanted her child to have a purpose and please my father. After me, my mother would give birth to six more children, pleasing my father to no end and endlessly worrying him at the same time. My father knew that, given his age, he wouldn't see us get married or witness the joy of having a new generation of grandchildren around. He told my mother half-jokingly and half-seriously that he had met her young and would leave her young, to which my mother used to say: "It is in God's hands."

When my father passed away in 1966, at age seventy-eight, the town of Ashkelon shut down. Hundreds of people from all over the country attended his funeral. He left his mark on everyone who came to know him.

My mother was only thirty-seven. She never remarried. Years after his death, I made several attempts to match my mother with a decent man. I knew a few men who had lost their wives and would have loved to marry my mother. I hated seeing her alone. But she refused any of the men I proposed. One such suitor came knocking at her door one day, holding a large bouquet of flowers. She threw the flowers away and closed the door in his face. Another man approached her in the evening as she walked home carrying a basket of vegetables. As they walked, the man attempted to ingratiate himself by placing his hand squarely on her back. My mother swung the basket across his head, and he fell to the ground. After that, any possible suitor knew she was off-limits.

Mother had always been gracious and willful. She had beautiful hazelnut eyes, a quick and sharp mind and soft, strong hands. She could influence her children without raising her voice. She would walk in the marketplace without lifting her eyes, still seeing everything. I never knew someone with such relentless energy and a delicate touch. I always felt that my mother was my goddess. Her ability to size up my moods, anger, and discontent in later years and soothe my pain created the support I needed. She managed to provide the entire family with very little money.

Her steady optimism and the blessings she poured over everything—and everyone—around her left a lasting imprint on me. She blessed the meals on our table, the farmers who brought their produce to the market each Thursday, and the neighbors to whom she wished good health. She blessed God for the little we had. She blessed my brothers and sisters, morning and night. She even blessed those who wronged us, asking that wisdom soften their hearts. She blessed the garbage collectors, the street cleaners, the burial society, and every day she blessed my father's memory, praying that his soul rest in peace and vowing she would one day join him. Those prayers, rising from the deepest part of her being, became a guide for me. In time, I learned to use prayer as she did—to cry out to God against injustice and the wounds inflicted without cause. What set her apart was her unwavering ability to see goodness in others, even in the midst of poverty, prejudice, and pain. Her love for a man four decades her senior, her devotion to her seven children, her dignity in the work of a janitor, and her unceasing prayers carried her through.

Those images of my parents struggling but loving, suffering but never complaining, left a deep mark on who I am today. I internalized their experience. Some of it empowered me later to withstand harsh and painful events.

While I forgave those who inflicted pain on them in many ways, I have, on many occasions, imagined how their lives could have been had they experienced a more comfortable existence. There was little I could do to help

CHAPTER EIGHT

them. At a young age, I worked various menial jobs to make some cash, which I brought home with me and tacked into the box where my parents kept their meager savings. While I felt good about it, it never eased the pain of seeing my parents' poverty. Yet the real beauty of the experience is that we never felt poor; my mother made sure that the kitchen had plenty of bread, olive oil and fresh tomatoes, which we converted into delicious sandwiches. The beds were always cleaned, even though we shared the same mattresses and covers; the place, despite its age and the infestation of rodents and spiders, was always washed, and the scents of her cooking enriched our hearts and appetites. The endless love poured from all corners of the house made us feel rich with the abundance of love.

Chapter Nine

DAYS OF TRANSITION AND RECKONING

During the early stages of getting used to the new landscape of a tent city in Beer Yaakov, my people found comfort and purpose in a new synagogue my father and community leaders arranged in one of the tents. They assembled some chairs from the local branch of the government, and a carpenter named Zebulon constructed a podium and a closet known as the Holy Ark to house three Torah scrolls brought from Libya. Despite the heat and the dust, our new neighbors came to pray and socialize. Father would walk from tent to tent, blessing each family and ensuring that people were okay. I remember women smiling, children surrounding him for a blessing, and men bowing respectfully.

The congregation members viewed my father as another Moses who led his people to freedom. My father endeavored to do the same. He often delivered sermons, reminding them they were making history despite their pain and difficulties. He explained that any form of construction was the outcome of trying times. He elaborated that struggle is a precondition for redemption and that suffering was trivial compared to being part of the messianic movement moving to Israel. In his words, this was the glory of God and the fulfillment of God's promise to Abraham, Isaac and Jacob that one day, his people would return and rejoice in the Holy Land. He told them to be proud of being the first generation to fulfill the promise made to our ancestors.

We were to go from being stateless to having our land, country, national anthem and flag. People trembled when they saw the flag with its blue stripes and the Jewish star. For two thousand years, we had no flag and no anthem. The flag, with its humble look, united people despite all differences.

My father believed that without the blood and smoke and the killing fields of Nazi Europe, Israel wouldn't have come into existence. To him, the valley of the bones coming back to life in the book of Ezekiel was a prophecy realized before everyone's presence. He read the Bible both literally and metaphorically. He was never convinced that, as the tradition stated, the Messiah would arrive on a white donkey; and yet he was convinced that we must be aware of signals sent from God, and that our ability to interpret those signals was the power that made God's wishes come true.

My father's metaphors, analogies, stories, ability to connect with people at their level and humility became my foundation for understanding how leaders must lead and conduct themselves under the most challenging circumstances. His losses, tragedies and sufferings never surfaced to his followers, but they all knew. He was less focused on himself and more on others and saw no reason to dwell on the difficulties or negativity. Looking forward and believing in oneself was his constant message.

One day, as I walked with my father on Shabbat morning from the Mishkan to our tent, we encountered my mother with my sister Rachel—named after my grandmother who died young and left my mother at a very young age. Rachel was very sick, suffering from fever and having difficulty breathing. My mother had left us alone to look after Rachel. She had my infant sister in her arms, holding her tight as she ran toward the large building left by the British, which served as a hospital. The nurse examined my sister while my mother waited anxiously. After a while, the nurse approached

CHAPTER NINE

my mother in the waiting room and told her not to worry. She advised her to go home and return the following day to pick up my sister.

However, my intuitive mother had heard of many babies left in the emergency rooms for treatments, only to never see them again—and to be told that their child had died in the night. "I am no fool," she told us, after grabbing my feverish sister from the nurse and leaving the clinic. Upon my mother's arrival at the tent, my father called upon the angels to descend and heal my sister while my mother prepared a concoction of herbs boiled in water. She helped my sister slowly sip the homemade medicine. To my surprise, my sister recovered, and there was a smile on her face.

My mother had good reason for her suspicions. Many Sephardic Jews, and the Yemeni Jews in particular, fell victim to a governmental policy aimed at snatching babies from their mothers only to hand them to the Holocaust survivors, now known as the Yemenite Children Affair. Many survivors suffered the pain and consequences of the Nazis' biological experimentation, unable to reproduce or having lost children in the concentration camps. Many survivors were eager to adopt a child. The government perceived the Sephardic Jews as an abundant source of supply of babies for these desperate parents coming back from the worst disaster in our history. Governmental officials had no qualms in making such decisions. Only later did the newer generation demand an investigation. The government dragged its feet, and the true story was revealed to the public only years later.

The wife of a good childhood friend, Hertzel Atia, tells a similar story. Her family arrived in Israel with her six-month-old brother. The boy developed a fever, so his parents took him to the nearby hospital emergency room. After the child was admitted, his anxious and trusting parents were told to leave the child overnight in the hospital and return later. Upon their arrival the morning following, the parents were told that their child died during the night for unknown reasons. The shocked parents asked for the body to be buried as the tradition required. The cold and distant nurse told them that the hospital had already buried the baby, and they should go back home and try to bring a new baby into the world.

The naive parents believed the nurse and went home to mourn their child for the seven-day shiva, as the religion requires its followers to do. Seventeen years later, the parents received a letter from the Department of Defense informing them that their child had to report to the draft office to be ready to serve in the military. It was clear that the baby had never died, since there was no death certificate. All attempts to find their stolen child were in vain. They faced a thick wall of bureaucracy and heavily protected state secrets. Like many hundreds of other Sephardic babies, they were given up for adoption to European families. The government's official policy was that their actions were justified to compensate those who suffered from the Nazi horror. Still, it was done at the tragic and unforgivable expense of the hundreds of Sephardic families who trusted their new government.

To the best of my knowledge, such a policy has no parallel with other civilized nations, and my people took it with complete innocence and trust in their government. Years later, when the whole story broke, many of the young Sephardic Jews walked away from the Labor Party founded by David Ben Gurion and shifted to Menachem Begin, the formidable leader of the Likud Party. I have met some of those families. I have listened to their nightmares, to the stories of loved ones taken away from them, never to be found. Things like that had never occurred in places like Morocco, Tunisia or Libya. . We were not prepared for such an experience. We swallowed it. But we never forgave those officials who caused so much pain to the newcomers in the new land.

Most immigrants from Arab countries were placed in strategic locations close to the borders to avoid wide geographical gaps and desolated areas where an enemy could cross the border to spread terror and fear. These towns—called Development Towns—had no infrastructure, factories, or opportunities. Towns like Sderot, Netivot, Ofakim, Kiryat Shmona

CHAPTER NINE

and others primarily harbored immigrants from North Africa and Middle Eastern countries. They were the laborers who worked for the neighboring *kibbutzim*. It was cheap labor in the fields, picking oranges, tomatoes, cucumbers and cotton. These towns, since their inception, have been in dire condition. The cries of their citizens remained silent for more than five decades. Many of these towns were the first to suffer from rocket shots from Gaza and Lebanon.

For the European founders, the Jews coming from Arab countries were an enigma. We looked different than them. We spoke the language of our neighboring enemies. We wore the traditional gowns of the Arabs; those long white garbs made from Egyptian cotton were suitable in the scorching sun and easy on the body. But to the European Jews, the customary dresses and clothing reminded them of the enemy at the border. Thus, the traditional clothes from Libya slowly gave way to a more Western look. There were, nonetheless, some Libyan Jews who refused to adjust and wore their white garb to the end. We didn't speak Yiddish, and were made to feel ashamed of speaking Arabic. We spoke Arabic only at home. They listened to classical music while we were ashamed of listening to Arabic songs. They ate with forks and knives, and some of our Libyan dishes, like Basin and Assita, were eaten with our fingers. In many ways, to them, we appeared to be from another planet.

Some Jewish sociologists from North Africa teaching in leading institutions like the Sorbonne University and other leading academic institutions perceived the Israeli government to be indifferent to the plight of Sephardic Jews from Arab countries. Our history was ignored, and we plunged into despair and shame. Our narratives were never part of the school curriculum. All courses at all schools focused on the history of the Western world. To be enrolled in high school, we needed to learn about European Jewish poets and writers like Ahad Haam, Theodore Herzl, Ben Yehuda, Brenner, Bialik, and Agnon. There was nothing about our writers and poets. There was a general recognition that the melting pot of Israeli society was never stirred, but frozen.

In a way, I lived in two worlds—at home with the customs that didn't die but prevailed and the second which was European, studying about Russia and the Holocaust and Herzl. None of what they covered in my curriculum had anything to do with my history. The pressure to adapt was huge, and our teachers wanted to mold the students into the European way of thinking and behaving. While the policy intended to transform the new society into a modern state, the strong European influence had a bitter and lasting taste.

We had no choice but to adapt. Most of my generation felt less proud of who we were and worked hard to shed away our old customs and habits. To pass the national exams, we had to shed our narrative. We had no identity. Leaders like Ben Gurion and Golda Meir looked down on us; in private conversations, they mocked us. They saw us as the laborers who would carry out the manual work. We became welders, builders, carpenters, plumbers, janitors and trash collectors. What amazes me about the entire experience is that my people, like many other Sephardic Jews, never complained or compared what it used to be to what it was. Without exception, they did it with dedication to their new homeland.

Over time, Israeli society consisted of three strata: those coming from Europe, the Ashkenazim; those arriving from North Africa and the Middle East, the Sephardim or the Mizrahim; and the Arabs who opted to stay after the War of Independence. By all measures, the Sephardim held manual jobs, dropped out of high school, and were at the bottom of the nation's socioeconomic structure. For instance, while 80 percent of the incoming first-graders were Sephardic children, only 10 percent graduated from high school with a matriculation card. As a result, 90 percent of those who entered universities in Israel were of Ashkenazi parents.

In many ways, we became the Black Jews, or as they used to call us in Yiddish, the *Shwartzes*. We were compared to the Black community in America—our

CHAPTER NINE

culture disregarded and our social mobility hampered by obstacle after obstacle. Later, during the mid-sixties, a new movement led by Moroccan activists called the Black Panthers was formed, and thousands of Jews from countries like Morocco and Algeria demonstrated in the streets, expressing their anger and despair at ongoing discrimination and persistent poverty. Unfortunately, far from the land of milk and honey many of the immigrants from Arab countries arriving to Israel during those years began to recognize that the Promised Land had become the land of broken promises and shattered dreams.

Chapter Ten

THE CITY OF SAMSON AND DELILAH

Ashkelon, known as Migdal to the Arabs, would be our first home as newcomers to the new state of Israel. We had lived in a tent for nearly a year at this point. It was a typical quaint Arab town. At the town center was the mosque with its high tower from which the muezzin announced the call for prayer. The town had one main street lined with retail stores. The many small alleys along the main street housed Muslim families from all levels of society. We were among the first sixty families transferred from the tent camp in Beer Yaakov to this old southern town known for the ancient Philistines and Samson's encounter with Delilah.

Though I was just a young boy, I still remember donkeys and mules pulling wagons filled with the local Arab inhabitants' furniture and mattresses as they fled town out of fear of the Israeli army. When we entered the Arab house assigned to us by the new local government, the Arab owner was still packing his furniture. A mule was outside with a cart filled with the family belongings, and the Arab man lifted his three children on the wagon. He looked at my father not with anger, but with sadness as he gave the key to the main door to Father. His words have stayed with me for decades.

"I wish you happiness in this house."

As I reflect on that moment, his wife and children were confused about the departure from their home. I am still amazed by his submission without any anger in his eyes. Watching a man give up his family's home to strangers was surreal. We were in the same position when we left Libya; the only difference was that we left to return to our promised land, and he left for an uncertain future.

This historic incident accelerated the widening gap between the Israelis and its Arab neighbors. The reality of displacement worked slowly on me as a young boy. The Arab family joined many other residents and left for Gaza. This refugee camp would later become one of the arsenal incubators of the most profound hatred against the Israelis. It would serve as a center of violence, launching raids and rockets on Israeli towns and settlements. In many ways their escape was motivated by the neighboring Arab leaders promising them that one day they would return to their homes; this was the origin of a guided vision of what became known as the aspiration of Arab leaders 'to throw the Jews to the sea.'

From the several thousand Arabs who once lived in Migdal, only three families remained, placing their trust in the newcomers. Among them was the family of the town's sole pharmacist—Dr. Zachariah, his wife, and their two children. He was kind, confident, and gentle, with a smile that never seemed to fade. I often wondered what he thought as he watched the town's Arab population replaced by Jews arriving from every corner of the world. His family lived above the pharmacy, on the second floor. A Christian, he spoke Arabic, French, and English with ease, making him the most educated man in that ancient biblical town.

Whenever I stepped into his pharmacy, he welcomed me as though I were family. On the glass counter sat a ceramic dish filled with sugar-coated almonds, fanned, and he always encouraged me to take as many as I wanted. To my mother, he was a reminder of her Arab neighbors back in Benghazi. Each time she came to his pharmacy, she blessed him in Arabic, and he

CHAPTER TEN

returned her blessing in kind. I never once saw anger in his eyes. His circle of relatives, friends, and Arab clients had vanished, leaving him alone among strangers, and I often wondered why he chose not to follow them. Still, his warmth and respect for every person embodied the very spirit of coexistence. Sadly, those days of such tolerance and mutual respect now belong to the past.

Those days, it was common to go to the pharmacy and describe your pain and symptoms to the pharmacist. Once Dr. Zachariah understood, he approached his desk, which was crowded with chemicals and minerals. He then mixed various liquids and minerals pulled from his shelves and ground the mixture into fine powder. He would add liquid to it, making it drinkable, and place the concoction in a small bottle. He presented the medicine to the anxious mother with a feverish son or the mother worrying about her aging father with difficulty walking. His patience was remarkable. He ensured his patients understood the steps to be followed in consuming his medications. His consideration made him more respected and trusted than other local physicians or retailers. Dr. Zachariah was a man whose compassion for anyone walking into his pharmacy melted away boundaries. After several years, he worried about his two children growing up in a lonely place without friends. He eventually left town and immigrated to Canada. He was missed. Once, I heard my mother telling her neighbor that the town had lost a good man.

Mother got to know him well, because those were hard days. Shortly after we arrived, my mother was pregnant again. Without telling anyone, including my father, she decided to terminate the pregnancy. This was not an easy decision for the wife of a rabbi.

She went to Dr. Zachariah's pharmacy, and without a word, he prepared the chemicals for her to drink. I was there when we stood in our small kitchen, where she mixed the chemicals in a glass of warm water as instructed. With her face twitching and hands shaking, she drank it before me. I was too young to comprehend but old enough to understand her decision. I remember the shadow of my father sitting at his desk, totally immersed in his daily prayers and unaware of what my mother was doing. This woman, my mother, was made from a rare material of inner strength blended with care and compassion.

It took several hours for the poison to reach my mother's womb. First, she sat at the kitchen table, scared and praying for the fetus to be washed away, never thinking of the danger and risk she was taking. Then, as murky blood marked her flowery dress, she lay on a towel placed on the cold floor as she convulsed. I pulled the blanket from her bed and covered her sweaty and shaking body as blood soaked into the towel. She didn't resist; she was shivering and helpless, as was I. All my siblings were at school.

She whispered to me to call the midwife named Zulla. She lived several blocks away, and I ran barefoot, like a scared animal, praying that Zulla would be home. When she saw me, she moved quickly, complaining that Mother should have called her before taking the medicine.

When we arrived, Zulla ordered me to heat water on the stove while she placed old towels and sheets under my mother. I remember shaking with nerves. Looking at my mother lying on the floor, shivering and sweating without a sound of pain, shocked me. I brought her the hot water, and she asked me to leave the room as she pulled my mother's dress upward. She kept coming in and out of my mother's room with bloody towels, washing them in the kitchen sink. She came out two hours later, asking me to keep my brothers and sisters away when they returned from school. She instructed me to have my mother rest and serve her hot tea. I walked into the room to see my mother lying on the cold floor, covered with an old blanket, silent and tearing. I wanted to hold her but was afraid to touch her. I instructed my sister to look after our mother and make her tea with mint leaves, her favorite drink. I then walked to my father's room, escorting him to the synagogue for the evening service.

CHAPTER TEN

On all our walks, my father would always chat with me about a verse from the Talmud. Not this time. This time, he was silent as I guided him to his chair in the synagogue. I left him there and walked back home quickly, making sure that Mother was recovering from her abortion and the pain of loss. Later, when I asked her to tell me more about the incident, she said that the tears rolling down her eyes were more from the sadness of losing a child than the physical pain she encountered in carrying out a dangerous home abortion.

That was our connection to Zachariah—his kindness and genuine respect left a deep and lasting impact on me. Deep in my soul, I have always believed that coexistence is possible. The long and untaught history of Arabs and Jews living next to each other with mutual respect can be revived. Israel, with its neighbors can transform that small and pain-filled region into the Switzerland of the Middle East.

I am still driven with the hope that one day, Jews and Arabs can live in coexistence and harmony. I remember when, right after the Six Day War in 1967, the Palestinians in Jerusalem looked forward to the Israeli soldiers marching over the land. After years of suffering under the Turks, the British, and the Jordanians, they had hoped that the brilliant minds of the Israelis and their progress would impact their quality of life. I remember going shopping in Gaza with my mother. We, and thousands of Israelis, were welcomed. They opened their homes and offered coffee and pastries. Their eyes were filled with hope that the Jews would bring peace and prosperity.

Their hopes were shattered. Later, with no sign of any redemption, some resorted to violence. Their leaders misled them and refused to accept Israel as a legitimate state. Driven by a dream of throwing the Jews into the sea, acts of violence and terror were on the rise. Since then, the gap has widened to a point where building any bridge is almost unreal. On the day of October 7th, 2023, with the brutal slaughter of more than 1500 children, women, and men by the Hamas, the hope was shattered among many of the Israelis who believed that such coexistence could become a reality. I mourn those losses and am saddened by the missed opportunities for both people to live side by side as my parents did with their Arab neighbors back in Libya. In many ways, the entire region became a landscape of casualties; the land of milk and honey was soaked with blood and bullets. It became an eternal cuckoo nest.

Besides Zachariah and his family, there was another Arab family who decided to stay—the Mahmud family. The family owned a sizable citrus orchard and a car dealership. Unlike Dr. Zachariah and his introverted family, the Mahmud family was more outgoing with the newcomers. I thought of them as descendants of the people who made peace with the outsiders who conquered this old land: from the Babylonians to the Crusaders, from the Turks to the English, and now the Jews. They seemed to be accustomed to invaders and made the necessary mental adjustments to adapt and accommodate the influx of new and different residents. Their home was close to where we lived and was always crowded with visitors and potential customers. They always welcomed me to their house and had a basket of oranges to deliver to my mother. They stayed long enough, and only later, like Dr. Zachariah, did they sell their properties and leave the country.

The last Arab to remain was a man from Sudan who had first come to work in the orchards and later became the town's only shoe polisher. An older man, known simply as "the Sudanese," he had arrived at the turn of the twentieth century and was hired by a wealthy Arab family to tend their gardens. To supplement his income, he polished shoes. When the Arabs left, he chose to stay, earning his living by shining the shoes of the new residents. His cheerful face and sparkling eyes posed no threat to anyone. From his low stool, beside a beautifully carved shoe box edged with brass, he watched the Israeli army march into town, polishing shoes for a nickel just steps from the ice-making factory.

He shined shoes through three different eras: under the Turks, the Brit-

CHAPTER TEN

ish, and now the Jews. Each time I passed him, he lifted his face and greeted me with a toothless smile. He asked about my family, blessed me with prayers for Allah's protection, and always blessed my father, who often stopped to check on his health. To this day, his smile remains one of the most beautiful I have ever seen—innocent, unguarded, and flowing straight from his heart. He loved to tease me, asking if I wanted him to polish my sandals.

When I was thirteen, not long before his death, I asked why he had stayed. In a gentle voice, half Arabic and half broken Hebrew, he replied, "Shoes are shoes, and it matters not who wears them; they need to be polished." His simple words carried a depth I never forgot. The day he died, he was laid to rest in the Arab cemetery with no ceremony, just a nameless stone marking his grave. He passed away alone, the last Arab in Ashkelon.

The mosque was at the center of town and several yards from our place. It was a large building with several domes on its roof, culminating in the large tower from which the muezzin called upon believers to kneel and pray. This was the only building that was not disturbed by the newcomers. It stayed there for many years unattended, unmaintained and slowly deteriorating. As a child, I would sneak into the mosque and climb the steep stones leading to the top. From there, I could see the entire town's houses, markets and orchards encircling this beautiful place where Samson met Delilah. The silence of the tower always served me as an escape from the noisy streets of Ashkelon. Looking at the entire town from the tallest structure in town reminded me of my father in Benghazi by the sea holding me on his shoulders, letting me see that things always look different from distance.

The Arab cemetery was about half a mile from the center of the town. It was enclosed by a beautiful stone wall and covered with trees. The two tall columns at the entrance were simple but beautiful. There, among the hundreds of simple gravestones, I used to walk around, reflecting on those who left, unable to visit the graves of their loved ones. The entire history of the town was right there. All you had to do was read the carved Arabic letters.

Over the years since, the beautiful stones have gone. The wall has crumbled, and one of the two tall columns has disappeared. Now all that remains is a large field covered with a rough carpet of wild grass and shrubs, leaving only traces of what used to be.

I was aware that the Arabs of Libya and other Middle-Eastern countries demolished Jewish cemeteries and converted synagogues into retail stores. Yet Jewish cemeteries in Morocco, Tunisia, Egypt, and Algeria remained intact, a testimony of the Arab respect for the Jewish tradition. I am a great believer that as Jews, people of peace, we have the moral obligation to honor all holy and sacred places. After all, we pray three times a day, and the last phrase of each service ends with the words begging God to bring peace upon us. My father named me Shalom, meaning "peace," lasting peace after the horrors of the Holocaust. I still believe that as Jews who have suffered so much, we have an obligation to be different and to serve as role models seeking justice and peace. Upon my last visit to Israel, I witnessed the great economic conditions of the Israeli Arabs. They have become an integral part of Israeli society. They attend universities to become managers, physicians, and lawyers. Their women don't have to wear the *hijab* if they refuse to do so. In talking to them, I was impressed with their good fortune and the freedom they experience in Israel.

Any person visiting Israel will be impressed with its beautiful landscape—a desert turned into a green land and amazing advances that are exported to other countries. Thirteen Israelis have won the Nobel Prize since 1966, and the winners have contributed much progress in medicine, science, agriculture and technology. But despite all these incredible achievements, there is the invisible pain and the continuation of an unresolved conflict. The horrible images of innocent lives from both sides of the border continue to bleed, and antisemitism is once again on the rise.

Chapter Eleven

MEMORIES THAT REFUSE TO FADE AWAY

In the Ashkelon of my youth, the orange orchards surrounding the town were the most captivating feature of the landscape. The intoxicating scent of their blossoming flowers infused freshness into the crisp air of the spring season. Sand dunes filled with fig trees and wild vineyards left from centuries ago stretching all the way to the beautiful beach reminded me of old Benghazi.

Today Ashkelon is a changed place. Those orchards are gone, replaced by condominiums that now serve as homes for new immigrants coming from all over the world. The only historical landmark remaining from the thousands of acres of orchards is an old structure that housed the diesel pumps used for irrigating those beautiful trees.

Hundreds of empty homes, vacated by Arabs, became available to the new immigrants, including my family and others from Arab countries. We were not the only newcomers; Jews were also arriving from Yemen, Iraq, Egypt and Iran.

Vittorio Teshuva from Benghazi opened a grocery store near the mosque. My uncle Sfani established a barber shop. Joseph Britto, from Darna in Libya who lived next door, opened a shoe repair shop, while Abraham Buchnick opened a furniture store. Sassy Jehan from Amrus started an herbal and spice shop, and Joseph Berda converted an old store into a restaurant serving dishes from Tripoli. Our neighbor Alfonso Zentara opened a cinema, and Kafela, a famous pastry maker from Benghazi, opened a humble bakery that offered a variety of Libyan cakes, sweet pastries, and Rossata, a drink made from fresh almonds.

Yosef Mesika, a wealthy man from Benghazi converted an old warehouse into a glass factory, replacing old windows with new ones. Several yards away, Chawato Tanaka ran a shop that made and repaired pots and frying pans. After Chawato passed away, new owners took over the store and became rich overnight when, during renovations, they discovered a bucket filled with hundreds of gold coins buried just a meter beneath the floor. The original Arab owner, unaware of how destiny would play out, had believed he would one day return to reclaim his fortune.

Our neighbor Chalafo, affectionately known as Laffa, opened a butcher shop. Bechor Makhlouf started a construction company that has become one of the largest enterprises in Israel today. Ben Zion Charia, along with his brother Rachamim, took over a large, old restaurant and transformed it into a large grocery store.—a place where I used to work for several hours a week assembling old bottles. My nephew, Baruch Guetta, ventured into running one of the largest electrical companies in town, executing significant electric projects and completing all the infrastructure needed for new housing and shopping centers. Most notably, the Chalfon family opened a soft drink company that produced a delicious sparkling orange drink. They named it Sapir, after Pinches Sapir, the newly appointed Ashkenazi Minister of Finance.

One of those old homes became my father's synagogue. It was a house with a large yard and a beautiful fig tree at its center. On one side, a spacious room was used for prayers during the weekdays. The small Holy Ark held the scrolls that my father spent hundreds of hours writing. The room featured

CHAPTER ELEVEN

dozens of benches painted gray, and, according to Jewish law, there were no pictures on the walls as it forbids any images or artwork. The Holy Ark was adorned with beautiful needlework, known as Parochet, featuring gold letters that commemorated a woman who had passed away. Hanging from the ceiling on both sides of the ark were glass containers shaped like bells, known as Kendil. Each Kendil was filled with water and topped with olive oil, from which a cotton wick emerged. This wick was lit every day. I still remember the intoxicating aroma of the slowly burning oil, cooled by the water beneath.

On the wall, a small poster displayed my father's beautiful handwriting, naming the deceased person and the date of their passing, accompanied by prayers for the soul to find peace. The hope was that the departed soul would be included in the Day of Revelation and brought back to life. The sight of the humble ark, the flickering candlelight, the musty smell of the prayer books piled on the table, and the simple pulpit from which my father led the prayers all elevated me from my gray reality into God's presence.

In another small room, a three-meter-long bench was placed against the wall, used only the day before Yom Kippur, known as Nar El Araba. My father would angle the bench against the wall and administer an ancient ritual. Each man removed his shirt and leaned his bare chest against the bench. My father would then symbolically flog each person with a leather belt ten times, as a gesture of God's forgiveness and an expression of humility and guilt. This was the last and most significant act before the men would return home to shower and dress in white robes and sandals, preparing for the holiest day in the Jewish tradition, collectively praying for good health, prosperity and longevity. The symbolic ceremony left a strong impression on me, reminiscent of the Catholic tradition of confession.

The left side of the building was reserved for services on Shabbat and special holidays. The Holy Ark contained five Torah scrolls, each housed in a beautiful wooden case adorned with two silver bells, known as *paamonim*.

The *paamonim* chimed delicately as the scrolls were removed from the Holy Ark and placed on the podium. Strong men would lift the Torah for the congregation to see while they sang, "This is our Torah that Moses placed in front of us, and we are grateful to the Almighty for choosing us." These special moments always uplifted the congregation and helped them face the challenges of people struggling under the sun for a new home in ancient land.

The old Arab home we moved into had two bedrooms with a large yard, leading to a small kitchen and a restroom. The restroom had no shower; it only featured a cold-water faucet sticking out from the wall and a hole in the ground, with two stones placed for your feet while relieving yourself. As kids, we were always scared of that hole since it often housed rats and other creatures. Walking to the toilet at night required courage, as we never knew what might leap out at us. The open sewage ran into the alleyway, leaving a stench that would make you gag. One bedroom was occupied by my parents, while the other bedroom, which had two beds, was shared by my siblings and me. With only lamps filled with kerosene by my mother, we grew up in darkness. Those dark nights when we were all huddled in two small bedrooms would leave a deep mark on me: of being edgy in dark valleys and always searching for light and spacious places to avoid the suffocating feelings of nine people jammed in a place crowded with rodents and hissing snakes.

Watching snakes come out of the stones was scary at first, but quickly turned amusing. We got used to them. They crawled out at night, searching for mice and rats, and ventured out during spring days, searching for warmth. It was common to see some of them coming out from their tunnels during the hot summer days, searching for cool spots.

I remember one day when my younger brother, then aged five, was playing with something odd in the yard. I saw my mother with a panicked face, recognizing that he was playing with a long, yellow snake that had gotten into the house through tunnels in the old walls. She froze with such fright

CHAPTER ELEVEN

that no sound escaped her lips. My father, who was close by, noticed her silence and saw the snake wrapping around my brother's body playfully. In her wisdom, my mother went to the icebox and filled a bowl of milk, which she placed not far from my brother, who was still patting the snake with innocence and delight. The snake slowly unwrapped itself from his body and made its way to the bowl of milk. My father, out of character, persuaded the playful creature into the alley, where he smashed its head. I felt bad for the snake—executed for no other reason than having fun with my brother.

The rodent problem in our home was quite serious. Rats sneaking into the house at night were a nightmare for my mother, who worried they might bite us while we slept. At that time, there were no pest control companies to call for help. One day, after returning from the academy, I decided to act. I brought home several glass bottles and shattered them into large and small pieces. With my brother's assistance, we inserted the broken glass into the tunnels inside the walls that the rats used to enter our house. Once we filled the tunnels with the smashed glass, I sealed them with cement. To my mother's relief, the rats stopped visiting us. I remember her lifting her arms to the sky and thanking God for blessing her with such an intelligent son. Watching her praise her Maker brought tears to my eyes. Although my mother was not much of a hugger, her love for us was always evident in her eyes.

Next door lived a single woman named Fannie, the only resident on the second floor in our neighborhood. She was a Holocaust survivor from Romania. Unlike most of her surviving friends who settled in major cities like Tel Aviv and Jerusalem, Fannie preferred to live among us, where she felt safer. Her striking blue eyes contrasted with those of her North African neighbors. Despite the suffering she endured in the concentration camps and the loss of her entire family, she carried herself with an air of elegance and always wore a smile. She lived in a lovely two-bedroom apartment and had access to the entire roof through her living room, which she transformed into a beautiful flower garden. Fannie had no relatives and lived alone. Well into her sixties, she was tall and slim, and her soft white hair framed her gentle face. Her eyes reflected the scars of the hell she had faced under the Nazis. I distinctly recall the blue digits on her left arm, which she typically kept covered.

One day, my mother noticed Fannie struggling to carry her shopping bags from the market and asked me to help her. Together, we went upstairs, and I placed her bags on the kitchen table. As I was exiting, I caught a glimpse of her beautiful garden and was mesmerized. She came out of her kitchen with a glass of lemonade and asked if I wanted to take a stroll through the garden with her.

As we walked together, she explained the names of the flowers, speaking in a mix of half-broken Hebrew and half-Romanian. She had grown them in pots all over the roof.

I quickly fell in love with the tranquility of her upstairs space. Her flowerpots brought me comfort and a sense of peace. Everything felt safe up there.

Noticing my fondness for her garden, she invited me to help water the flowers and look after her place when she was away. I started going upstairs several days a week, and she was always ready with a glass of lemonade and a plate of chocolate cookies. Occasionally, she would hand me a few coins and cajole me to use them to buy ice cream.

There were many times when I returned from school and, instead of going home, I climbed up to her garden while she made me a sandwich or served me vegetable soup. The scent of her flowers, the lovely tablecloth, the warm bread and the soup created a striking contrast to the constant noise of my siblings and the crowded two-bedroom flat that my large family shared. This continued for almost a year.

Then, during one of my visits, I saw she had hired a young woman to look after her since her health was failing. The caretaker told me to go home, and there was no need to worry about the flowers. One day, when I arrived

CHAPTER ELEVEN

home from school, I noticed an ambulance next to her door and two men carrying her with a white sheet covering her entire body. I felt numb at the sudden and abrupt end of a beautiful relationship. I would no longer climb up the stairs leading to her beautiful garden, watch the town from the roof, and enjoy a cup of tea with a delicious pastry. I remember her fondly to this day.

There was a Turkish coffee house across the street from where we lived. People stopped by, sitting on the small stools, drinking coffee and playing backgammon. One day, around five in the afternoon, I heard several gunshots. I ran to the street where the guests in the coffee house stood over a woman who had been shot several times. I approached the scene to see her chest was wide open and her breast half hanging from her body, soaked in a large puddle of blood. Within minutes, the ambulance arrived, and the torn upper part of her body was placed in a black blanket. At the same time, the police arrested her husband, who stood by in a total haze.

While the husband was guarding the orchards at night, he discovered that his wife had been sleeping with the neighbor who often visited the Turkish coffee house. Suspecting her infidelity and having received a message from friends about the rendezvous location with her lover, he called in sick and made his way to the coffee house where they met. In a fit of rage, he used his rifle and fired more than three shots at point-blank range. As a result, he was placed in jail, and social services took away their five children. The image of the dead woman was so intense, traumatic and disturbing that I often woke up screaming, frightening my siblings.

Like many North African Jews, we believed in ghosts and demons. There was a common belief that when people were killed before their time and under tragic circumstances, their spirits would linger at the scene. Several months after the murder, I experienced this firsthand. I woke up at 3:30 in the morning to walk my father to his synagogue, and as we walked, I saw a ghost—a giant wolf with long hair staring at us. I knew it wasn't my imagination; the sight was vivid, and the shiver it sent through me is still alive in my memory. I held my father's hand tighter than usual. He sensed my fear; I think he saw it too but said nothing. He began to walk much faster than usual. I managed to whisper to him that there was a ghost by the Turkish coffee house. My father got me closer and whispered, "My son, please don't look there; just look forward."

I couldn't help it and took another glance as the wolf stood there silently, big and threatening. I felt like Lot's wife, desiring to look back as my father squeezed my arm warning me not to do that.

The poverty and the difficulties in adjusting to the new society made a strong impact on me and in many ways shaped the kind of person I am today. Many of us felt like second class citizens—and we had no choice but to endure it. The entire generation strongly believed that this was the last foothold for the Jews to live without the fear of being exiled. We endured it because of our fathomless love for Israel. Despite the blend of beauty and ugliness, the old with the new, the joy and the sorrow, one thing was clear to all of us: we were in our land, the land that the Almighty promised. We would stay, putting down deep roots, sticking to the vision, and not being distracted by poverty and unjustified treatment.

These reflections empowered me during periods of hardships. As my father once told my fuming mother outside the tent, in a clear and passionate voice, "We are staying. We are not going back. We will make it."

Chapter Twelve

GUIDED BY THE SCRIPTURES

I grew up amidst colliding cultures, and felt the impact of that clash.

During my first year at school in Ashkelon, my classmates perceived me as quiet and timid. I rarely played or laughed with them, and I seldom spent time with my peers during breaks or after classes. Instead, I often found myself daydreaming. In class, I learned to disconnect from my surroundings, immersing myself in an array of stories from the Bible. These stories fascinated me and provided an imaginative escape. I would embellish them and personalize the narratives, particularly the story of Cain and Abel, which offered a rich exploration of the darker aspects of humanity.

Abel came across as kind and gentle, while Cain was rough and aggressive. I spent time pondering over their dynamics and how they treated one another, imagining them in conflict: Cain as the provocateur, and Abel as the timid one. The scripture empathizes with Abel and vilifies Cain, making the jealousy and bloodshed between brothers difficult to comprehend, especially for a typical eight-year-old.

In my imagination, my peers became Cain, and I was Abel. Like Abel, I was not afraid of them, but I was too naïve to anticipate their capacity to bully me simply for the pleasure of seeing someone else hurt. Unlike other creatures, humans have the capacity to kill for sport and to abuse one another for pleasure, intimidation and control. The kids in my class bullied and mocked me. I felt like Abel, as I let them hit me, allowed them to throw olive pits at me, and endured splashes of paint from the janitor's closet on my head. While everyone else laughed or remained silent, I felt scared. Yet, I continued to show up at school, taking different routes every time to avoid my abusers. Despite the pain, I attended school every day, driven by the strong influence of my father's emphasis on education and the importance of learning.

Knowing what awaited me never dissuaded my thirst for learning. This desire later sustained me as I dedicated myself to the world of lifelong education. Today, in my work with global organizations and public agencies, I consistently advocate for the idea that organizations should be unconventional and hire agile learners who can ask the right questions, think critically, and have the courage to speak truth to power. Learning is the key to change, and this thirst for knowledge continues to fuel me.

I often think of my father's ability to withstand the storms he faced. His faith, in general, and his deep love for learning, in particular, were both his shield and his purpose.

When we studied the story of Jacob and Esau, I was struck by the timeless jealousy that exists between siblings. It troubled me that their mother favored Jacob. I felt that Jacob never truly forgave himself for being his mother's favorite, while Esau, the hardworking son who tilled the soil and hunted, was overlooked by her.

Throughout my experiences with my own siblings, I became aware of the toxic feelings that can develop among brothers and sisters. How often do siblings treat each other as enemies, refusing to yield or forgive?

Later, my siblings became angry with me for reasons I could not comprehend. Was their anger rooted in their observation of the special relationship I had with our mother? She often viewed me as a caretaker and an understanding companion, expecting me to be a disciplinarian and a commanding voice amidst confusion. She anticipated that my siblings should honor me

CHAPTER TWELVE

and follow my lead.

Or was their anger stemming from their jealousy of my education while they remained at home? While I am proud of them for being wonderful individuals, I sometimes wonder if that pride is mutual. Did they resent me for trying to discipline them and for using my authority as the oldest brother, causing them to fear me? Perhaps they needed distance from me to discover their own identities and places in the world.

Like Abel, Cain and Esau, I often felt rejected. Rejection at any age tends to bring out the worst in us. The anger of a child abandoned by parents, dismissed by teachers and bullied by peers leaves a lasting mark—a mark that occasionally resurfaces, leaving behind a trail of insecurity masked by anger, outbursts, and discontent.

The struggles of the characters in the Bible provided me with solace during my isolation. I no longer felt alone; there were others before me who had experienced similar narratives. Reflecting on these figures offered me temporary refuge. Being lonely and timid, I immersed myself in deepening my understanding of the scriptures. My father encouraged me from a young age to explore not only the Bible, but also the Mishnah and the Talmud. I found many of the figures relatable on a personal level. The suffering of the old rabbis, the pain endured by the famous sages, their sacrifices and their brutal deaths at the hands of the Greeks and Romans brought me an unexpected comfort—a comfort derived from recognizing that pain can be a part of life.

I came to believe that pain is a natural process that in many situations empowers us to become stronger and resilient. As strange as it may sound, humans have the capacity to adapt to almost any situation. Bad things happen to good people, like in the story of Job, and the Almighty is not always involved in every event that occurs under the sun. These images and painful memories inspired me to publish a book of poems titled *Poems of Love and Loss*. Recalling the story of my father being saved by our Arab neighbors, and the current conflict between Arab and Jews, I dedicated one of the poems to the tragedy described in the Old Testament of the forced separation between Isaac and his half-brother Ishmael.

My Brother Ishmael
As you grew older without me
Wandering with your mother Hagar
Watching the desert sunset
Did you miss me?

As you learned
Riding wild horses
Taming mountain goats
Did you think of me?

As you learned how to shear the
Wool of the sheep
Not cutting their skin
Did you laugh at me?

As you made your way to hunt
A fast gazelle with one arrow
Do you recall?
My lost arrows?
As you followed our
Father's request to
Pray to one God.
Did you pray for me?

As you raised your own children,

CHAPTER TWELVE

Taught them right from wrong.
Did you tell them about it?
Your lost brother?

As you approached heaven
Making peace with God
And our good father
Do you think of me my beloved brother?

Reading about the prophets of the Old Testament inspired me. I found a sense of virtual recovery in their stories and struggles. I imagined them walking through the alleyways of ancient Jerusalem as they preached their messages. I envisioned them being mocked, with eggs thrown at them for their frightening proclamations. Yet, their sermons, poems and profound warnings often fell on deaf ears and blind eyes. Only later did I realize the strength I gained from those prophets and their courage. They warned that cruelty and ignorance toward the poor would ultimately come back to haunt the perpetrators. The message that the real enemy is always within resonated deeply with me.

The bullying at my school rarely stopped, and I didn't know how to cope with those who took pleasure in hurting me. Once, I read about Steven Spielberg, who was also bullied as a child. He channeled his fear of bullies into filmmaking, transforming those same bullies into heroes in his stories. I felt less intelligent and creative than Spielberg. Instead of fighting back or developing a new way to cope, I allowed the abuse to continue. Rather than refusing to go to school, I returned to the battlefield every morning, facing a new day with no hope of victory or escape.

Solitude was comforting for me in Ashkelon. I learned more by observing others than by trying to make an impression on my peers or teachers. In many ways, I was influenced by my father's demeanor. I never heard him complain or express anger towards anyone. Lacking his inner strength, I often found myself yelling more at God than at anyone else around me. My father, on the other hand, accepted his fate with grace. Sometimes, I would see him outside, lifting his hands toward heaven and thanking the Almighty by saying, "Gam Zu Letova," which means, "I am okay with where I am."

At times, I wished my father would get angry, yell, renounce his Maker, raise his fist, and confront whatever life threw his way. But that was simply not who he was; it was not his approach. His ability to absorb shocks and difficulties only deepened his convictions while diminishing mine. I used to provoke him by questioning God's existence. He never reproached me or reacted the way I wanted him to. Instead, he looked at me with fiery yet sad eyes and said, "It is okay, my son. Go through your anger phase; I know that one day you will find peace with God, and ultimately, with yourself."

For my father, the Bible was a source of inspiration; for me, it was a shelter. However, doubt and anger often clouded my thoughts. How could there be a God when circumstances were so dire? I expressed my feelings to my father. He always listened, nodded his head, but never challenged me regarding God's existence. I have struggled with the concept of God throughout my life. At times, I feel His presence, yet there are moments when His absence bewilders me completely. I have struggled with my God my entire life. It has not been an easy journey. As a son of a Rabbi, I was taught that one must not question God's presence—one must embrace it without doubt. This has not been my experience. As I would soon discover, it would be my ultimate trial during the next difficult years of my adolescence.

Chapter Thirteen

DAYS OF ANGER AND DISCONTENT

To survive my gloomy environment, I developed a constant and uncontrollable desire to be outside in the fields. I felt at peace among the citrus and fig trees, away from the noisy school, the mice that ran throughout the house, the frustrated husbands yelling at their wives and the sounds of my young siblings quarreling.

On the outskirts of the city, there was a water tower. The spiral steps leading to the top of the tower were encircled with wire to prevent people from entering. One day, I managed to manipulate the wire, and, despite some bloodied scratches, I entered and climbed the concrete stairs to the top. I started doing this often, taking refuge in the isolation of the tower. There I would sit on the edge without any railing, watching the landscape and feeling the salty wind blowing from the sea. I felt free here. I knew that no one would dare to enter the tower. I spent hours watching the sunset over the Mediterranean Sea and dreaming of better days.

At a young age, I began to wonder if the entire country was like the city of Ashkelon. I had heard about *kibbutzim*, where children were raised far from their parents. One of my teachers was from a kibbutz, and he described it as a place where children worked on the farm, enjoyed their freedom, had a lot of fun and explored wild landscapes blanketed in golden yellow wheat and hills, riding horses and driving tractors.

I enjoyed those after-school walks. Discovering a wild plum tree or a fig tree thrilled me. I would climb the old trees and indulge in the large, juicy fruits. As I meandered along the paths, I found my secret route to the sea. I cherished those moments of escape, almost a quiet rebellion where I stood at the edge of the orchard, with the earth bearing fruit behind me and the vast, mighty sea before me. The elements came together in that place, filling me with a sense of belonging as I listened to the sound of breaking waves and felt the salty water on my feet. This was much more enjoyable than the chatter of townspeople or the silly games of children, things I could never identify with.

As a boy, I seemed physically weak. My movements were hesitant, and I often appeared frightened, even by my own shadow. Because of this, I became an easy target for bullies. In class, kids would place thumbtacks on my seat and laugh when I jumped up in shock and pain. I don't remember crying or complaining about being singled out; instead, I would stare into their eyes with silence and acceptance.

At times, I would find a dead mouse in my school bag. Other times, an olive pit would volley across the room and suddenly hit my surprised face. On some mornings, as I walked to school, classmates would hide behind a low hillock near the main building and throw stones at me, using me as a target to hone their aim.

One spring day, neither the crisp, blossoming mood of the season nor the few branchy bushes lining the hill could save me from the gravel stone that landed squarely on my left temple. I remember coming back to consciousness with blood trickling down my face. Next, I remember wiping it with my undershirt as I stumbled to my classroom late. When I walked in, the class grew silent. The teacher rushed towards me and escorted me to the nurse. The nurse attended to my wound, her hands gently wiping the blood

CHAPTER THIRTEEN

and wrapping a bandage around my head. I told my scared mother that I fell from a fig tree.

Hiding the truth from my mother became a habit. I never complained to my teachers or my parents; I wanted to protect them from the pain of feeling helpless and powerless. If the teachers knew about my situation, the other kids would likely increase their torment on my way to and from school. After class, I would hide in the restroom, waiting for the last child to leave the schoolyard. Only then did I feel somewhat safe enough to go home.

To my teachers, I was an enigma: unable to respond to their questions, daydreaming during class, and always the first to arrive and the last to leave when the bell rang. The government-appointed teachers at our school were often untrained and had little regard for their students' backgrounds or experiences. They were baffled and somewhat frightened by children who appeared confused and unsettled. For instance, a Yemenite Jew with black curls and dark skin or a Libyan Jew like me with dark eyes and hair bore little resemblance to the idealized image of the pioneers from the *kibbutzim*. We seemed more like savages than lost children caught between two clashing cultures.

It was common for many teachers to hit our palms with sticks or to slap and kick us frequently, sometimes for no clear reason. In those traumatic moments, some kids fought back, some ran away, and others, like me, just took the abuse without tears or cries, but with a smoldering anger and a deep desire buried within me to one day settle the score. The teachers did not view themselves as protectors of children; instead, they acted like disciplinary guards watching over those they did not understand.

I reacted with silence. When a teacher asked a question, I often didn't respond. I didn't complete my homework—a nearly impossible task in a noisy house with six younger siblings demanding my attention while my mother worked. I was quiet, unresponsive and distant, which made me seem different and strange in the eyes of both my classmates and teachers. Despite this, my advanced skills in reading and writing, which surpassed those of most other students in my classes, puzzled them. My teachers had no idea that my father had started my reading lessons before I even entered first grade. He would have me memorizing chapters from the Bible by heart. My situation was enigmatic to most of my teachers, and they were unaware that every morning, I woke up at four, dressed in the dark, and walked my father to his synagogue, where he led his congregation for the morning service.

When I was eleven, my situation caught the attention of one of my teachers, who decided to call the only psychologist in town to examine me and provide a diagnosis. This well-meaning teacher likely had no idea of the consequences that would arise from his goodwill. Sometimes, good intentions can lead us down a difficult path.

On the day the psychologist was ready to administer a series of psychometric tests to evaluate my problem-solving and social skills, I received a pass allowing me to leave the classroom and go to the designated office. There, I encountered a man with a thin, gray mustache that matched his hair. He instructed me to take a seat with a robotic voice, suggesting that he had performed this procedure at least a thousand times before. He appeared to be an educated man, likely from Poland. He proceeded to ask me questions such as, "What is the capital city of Germany?", "Convert thirty-five centimeters to inches," and "Convert twenty-two degrees Celsius to Fahrenheit."

The questions came one after another in an endless interrogation, and I couldn't understand why. I handled this uncomfortable and confusing situation as I did all the others; I responded with silence, which he met with a raised eyebrow. He showed me drawing after drawing and requested that I explain them in my own words. Everything seemed confusing, and I just wanted this ordeal to be over. He continued with a barrage of questions about my likes and dislikes, but I saw no point in responding. He grew restless and annoyed, releasing impatient sighs and raising the pitch of his voice. I could sense his displeasure from his facial expressions, which seemed to say,

CHAPTER THIRTEEN

Here is another dumb child from the caves of North Africa.

The session ended with a simple statement addressed to the school principal, declaring that my intelligence was below normal. He turned his attention to the paper before him, looking focused as he wrote, consigning me, at the age of eleven, to the label "mentally disabled." He formalized the document, signed it and sealed my fate with permanent black ink. Little did I realize what kind of life this blot of ink had condemned me to.

I remembered the prayer on Yom Kippur, in which we believe that God seals the fate of everyone—who lives or dies, who is imprisoned or liberated, who survives stormy waters or sinks into the depths of existence. On that fateful morning, I was condemned to touch the bottom of murky waters. To my misfortune, the concept of Special Education would not be introduced till much later. Back then, there was no distinction made between behavioral or social deficiencies and cognitive ones.

Years later, when I was sixteen, I was evaluated for mandatory military service. This new assessment revealed that my IQ was far above average. However, this correction came too late, and the stigma had already left its mark. The label became a source of enduring insecurity, a fear that would haunt me for many years. It fueled bottomless anger and a determination to prove to the world that I was neither inferior nor lacking in intelligence. By all cognitive measures, I was normal. Yet, the emotional toll lingered, leaving a path of depression and trauma. Despite the pain, this trauma also served as a catalyst, propelling me to achieve the impossible and pursue the unimaginable.

After the psychologist's formal diagnosis, the school authorities, alarmed at the prospect of having a mentally incapacitated child among them, decided—without consulting me or my parents—that I needed to be removed from regular school and transferred to a school for the mentally impaired. I will never forget my last morning at my old school.

Shortly after I arrived, a man with a stern face entered the classroom.

Upon a silent signal from the teacher who had requested my examination, the man beckoned me to follow him. As I approached, he took hold of my right arm and led me out of the classroom to a government vehicle. I can still recall the expressions of the children in the classroom—some were confused, others surprised, while some remained oblivious. I stared out of the window as the car moved through the neighborhood, sitting in silence and wondering why, yet not asking. Adults rarely offered guidance at school, and their responses were often dry and incomplete. To those few students who dared to ask questions, teachers would frequently respond with, "Just do as you're told," or "It's not time for questions."

Besides, I didn't want to disturb the man sitting next to me. I noticed how far on the outskirts of town we were heading and how much longer my walk home would be compared to my regular school. The car eventually turned onto a newly paved road. Ahead, I could see the school—a collection of wooden structures surrounded by barbed wire fences. Soon, I could read the large bold letters on the side of the gate that declared, "The Fountain: School for Mentally Impaired Children." Another line under it expressed gratitude to an American-Jewish donor for his contributions.

We arrived at the security shed before the gate. The stern man beside me exchanged a few words with a tough-looking guard with a long black beard at the security cabin. The guard opened the gate, and we drove through. We parked in front of one of the wooden buildings. The man called me out of the car and took hold of my right arm to prevent me from running away. Inside me, a voice screamed for me to escape his grip, jump the gate and dash to the beach and the blue waters of the sea. I felt empty and numb, like a chicken hanging by its feet, being dragged to the slaughterhouse. Those moments lingered within me, festering in my soul and stirring waves of anger at myself for lacking the courage to heed the urgent voice urging me to run until I collapsed.

All the structures looked the same: small, faceless one-story buildings,

CHAPTER THIRTEEN

each standing on cement posts. The building was new but dark, almost inhumane. I was sweating, and my legs were shaking. My mind raced, but my body was immobile. I prayed for God to get me out of there. I wondered why my parents weren't pulling me out of what would become my hell in the Promised Land. We walked to one of those monstrous buildings where I was ushered to the classroom. As always, out of fear, paralysis and shock, I obeyed. I was not prepared for what I would find.

Inside, I saw the contorted faces of children my age. Some were making loud, incoherent sounds; others stared out the window as if they weren't there. One child was laughing loudly for no reason while the one next to him was gyrating his body back and forth. The sight terrified me. A piercing stench of urine rose from the floor, and I was gripped by fear, despair and confusion, a mix of emotions of the kind I had never experienced before. Something bitter crept up my throat, and I thought I was going to vomit. I tried to lift my head, imagining that it was all a bad dream, but the stench, the twisted faces and the cold voice of someone asking for my name convinced me that I was indeed awake. He instructed me to take a seat, and I chose the desk closest to the door.

I looked closer at my classmates. I can still see the anguish in their eyes, the forced and twisted smiles, and the vacant stares with mouths open wide.

I felt pity for the kids who were caged like chickens, and pity for myself, who was to join them; my new reality was that I would be confined to my will. The scene still haunts me; I often wake up sweaty, plagued by nightmares of being snatched away and dragged down a dark tunnel.

The building stood in a peculiar state of premature decay – its walls still bore their original white paint, unmarred by the usual scuffs of age, and the metal desks their factory sheen – yet something more insidious than time has taken root here. Like a person aged not by years, but by grief. The structure felt abandoned, as though decades of despair had compressed themselves into mere months. I would soon discover that this accelerated deterioration mirrored our fate within these walls; that each of us, regardless of our own strength upon entering, would find ourselves worn down to the same smooth resignation, our spirit eroding as surely as we'd spent a century in this place rather than just a handful of seasons. As I would learn in a short time, only a brief period in this place could engender a long term of internal anguish and the surrender of one's will.

I sat there, my legs shaking and my fingers trembling. My silent voice cried out to God and His angels to descend upon me and take me out on those chariots of fire I used to read about, leaving a trail of flames as we ascended to heaven. Here is a poem I wrote years later, reflecting on those dark hours:

Chariot of Fire

Last night, I saw chariots of
Fire led by angels.
Their faces stern and
Wings wide and white.
Moving quietly and gracefully,
    Trailing fire in their wake and
Floating on pillars of orange smoke.

I watched them descend upon me.
Like God on Mount Sinai
I knew then that I must stop.
No longer hide or run.
My ancestors sent them.
Embraced by beauty and the
Warmth of godly fire.

CHAPTER THIRTEEN

They descended upon me.
Lifting me up with a force
That lacked gravity, and
There, for the first time,
My wings stretched.
And I was awake while.
I was asleep.

The entire experience haunted me for many years and had a lasting impact on my emotions. In times of joy, my mood would sharply swing back into darkness and loss. In moments of peace, I would feel relentless waves of anger. Many days passed when I questioned my existence. I often wondered how it was possible for the son of a holy rabbi—a scholar who devoted himself to serving his Maker—to feel so cursed. As I grew older, my father encouraged me to read the Book of Job. After reading it numerous times, I became increasingly frustrated by Job's patience and my father's acceptance of fate and destiny. Only later, after experiencing my own losses and betrayals, did I begin to understand the metaphorical lessons of Job.

After what felt like an eternity for a lost and scared boy—about an hour later, an older nurse with a boring look on his face, escorted me to another wooden building. Upon stepping inside, I realized from the equipment that this was the school clinic. The smells were nauseating. No one seemed to be treating injuries here. Instead, a couple of boys stood in separate corners, receiving instructions from other nurses. I was too focused on following my nurse to fully grasp their situation until he instructed me to remove my clothes at the third station in a chilling voice.

I couldn't understand, but I couldn't object and reluctantly obeyed. I stood there, naked and shaking despite the hot temperature outside, stripped of my dignity. The nurse held a hose with a showerhead at its end and sprayed me with a disinfectant powder. A fog engulfed me; the chemical smell choked me. I was burning both inside and out. I wanted to scream, run back to the fig trees, climb up like a monkey and never come back down. I imagined myself walking on my beautiful secret path leading to the sea. I remembered myself on my father's broad shoulders, walking down the beach in Benghazi. I thought of my father's burning eyes. How would he save me from the shock and humiliation if he were there with me? Would he use his soft voice to persuade them or lift his arms and knock them down to the ground?

Another nurse ordered me to his station. I was shaking as I headed toward my clothes on a chair. This second nurse shaved my head and smeared it with a yellow lotion, oozing a strong, medicinal smell. The yellow lotion was smeared over my head to kill any lice…but I had none. Confused, frightened and angry with my parents, particularly with my God, who was not there to protect me, I embarked on one of the most painful journeys of self-inflicted wounds. Those hours of humiliation sowed the seeds of wrath and sparked a fire deep in my soul that would continue to flame for years to come.

Later, I learned that the push to enroll so many children in the school was less about their cognitive deficiencies and more about satisfying the Jewish-American donor. As the saying goes, "If you build it, they will come." School leaders from nearby towns were encouraged to refer any child who behaved differently to this "special" school. Many of the misdiagnosed and wrongly selected children, stripped of their childhoods, grew up to become petty criminals filled with anger and resentment toward a society that punished them for no justifiable reason. I could have been one of them. However, being the son of a rabbi meant that obedience and adherence to the rules were absolute requirements. It also instilled in me an innate necessity to search for answers about the human condition.

I often woke up startled from nightmares, my body soaked in sweat—dreams of being hunted and tortured, filled with visions of fire and smoke,

CHAPTER THIRTEEN

and bottomless wells into which I was falling in the dark. I would shout so loudly that the noise deafened my own ears, yet no one else could hear or extend a hand to help. At times, I woke up screaming, terrified of those around me. I would get up shaky and trembling, wandering around while wishing for better days to return. Those moments when my past came crashing down on me felt like hot lava flowing over my soul. The eruptions affected my mood. My shame was buried under hundreds of masks; only my eyes were clouded, lacking their usual brightness, reflecting the darkness of a black hole.

Those days parents were powerless. Once government officials decided that a child was mentally unfit, there was very little that parents could have done. My father, almost blind, and mother working as a school janitor had no tools to fight the system. They just went along. Those days their love for the new land overpowered the strong will of my people to fight back. Only later, the Libyan Jews, like all Jews of Arab descent, would use their votes to demonstrate their disgust in a government that couldn't identify with the plight of living in poverty with a limited access to govern and the exercise of power. In retrospect, it was the disenchantment of the Sephardic Jews who were fed up with the Labor party that brought Menachem Begin and the Likud party to power.

Throughout my life, I have come to realize that my journey is not so different from the painful journeys of others. I have watched and studied people from all walks of life, discovering that tragic events and unintentional neglect often become defining moments in their lives. The struggle for belonging, a place under the sun, simple recognition and the desire to be loved and accepted lingers like an unquenched thirst.

At the Fountain, there was no one to help, no one to inject life, and no one to extend a helping hand. These are the wounds of youth that follow us for years to come. Some of us surrender, while others shake off the pain and get back on their horses, channeling that energy towards a more positive outlook and a clearer purpose. I had to decide which path I would take.

Chapter Fourteen

THE DEAFENING SILENCE OF HOSTILITY

In the quiet moments between dusk and darkness, when memories float like moths dying in sunlight, I often find myself thinking how anger threads through generations like a jagged vine, taking root in the most tender places of our hearts.

During my years as a counselor, I have sat with countless souls carrying the weight of old wounds. Their stories show themselves in furrowed brows and clenched fists. Patterns reveal themselves like constellations—anger handed down like an unwanted heirloom, each generation adding its own bitter ornament to the collection. I have heard every variation of rage and resentment: anger at parents who failed to notice them, anger at siblings who let them down, anger at abusive and toxic bosses, even anger at God for seeming absent during their darkest hours.

But I never saw anger in my parents. They accepted their fate as it came. I, on the other hand, carried the anger they never allowed themselves to feel—angry at their losses, angry at their surrender, angry at a childhood stolen from me.

While many took the trials of life and learned how to live with them, some became aggressive. I remember a Moroccan man with seven children who couldn't afford to support his family with his work in the orange field. He decided to take the law into his own hands. One day, he walked to the welfare agency office and turned all the desks upside down. He was subdued by the police and placed in jail for his violent behavior.

Others, like my parents, took the treatment without protest. My childhood friend, Lillo Guile, born in Benghazi, became a taxi driver. Mario, whose mother spoke Italian fluently and looked like a movie star, became a bus driver. Yehuda Salhub opened a place to train new drivers. Ephraim Makhlouf became a contractor and my nephew Baruch Guetta an electrician. They all served in the military, raised great families, sent their children to serve the nation, paid their taxes and rarely complained.

At times, I envy them for making peace with their circumstances. I came to believe that they were wiser than me. Those moments caused me to reflect and agonize over the opportunities my peers missed. I knew how smart they were. The streets and their conditions were their best schooling. They never lost hope and sincerely believed their children would one day stand up for their rights.

If the opportunities were the same as the European Jews, many of these young people could have become today's engineers, accountants, scientists and physicians. I have learned firsthand how it feels to have the poisonous sting of labels and their impact on those who suffered the most. It does not take a long time for those who are labeled to live up to the labels that are imposed upon them.

My narrative was different. Instead of submitting to what came my way, I fought back. I kept an account of every insult and injury, and under the surface my blood was boiling, and I was seething with anger. I still can't fathom why I resisted the status quo and where the power that inspired me to fight back came from. The stones thrown at me from the hill on the way to school never deterred me. The painful punches in my face, and the kicks all over me never discouraged me from showing up to school every morn-

CHAPTER FOURTEEN

ing. Even the mocking and the verbal insults did not stop me. I was like the North American buffaloes, who fight storms not by running away from them, but by charging ahead toward the coming winds. I developed strength I never thought I could have, a strength that enabled me to charge ahead, fail and rise again.

While the European Jews were rising from the smoke of the concentration camps and my father from the memories of heartbreak and sorrow, I was lost in ashes. Day by day at my new school, I drifted further and further from reality. My memories are scattered, and my recollections of those days are embedded in nightmares and an array of backflashes that surface unannounced. When I feel lost, I wander among the demons, engulfed in heavy clouds of darkness. Those moments of darkness occupied much time in my adolescence and early adulthood. I was thrust into desperation, wanting to hide but finding no safe place to shelter. Like a frightened scorpion, I crawled between the tight spaces of cold rocks, sitting there with my eyes darting, knowing I had no claws or poisonous sting to fend for myself. Out of touch with time and reality, I found solace in silence. Time was different at the Fountain. Minutes felt like hours, and I felt like Daniel, the prophet who was thrown into a den as a punishment for praying to God despite a royal decree on some occasions. I have imagined myself hauling the memories to the landfills of my mind. There are wounds we can rarely heal and ugly scars that can never fade. I thought of my father's scars that came from all that he went through, though he never said a word.

The therapy room at the Fountain was located between my classroom and the lunchroom. So rarely during my day did I find respite from the dreadful sounds and smells that came from it. These shrieks are, to this day, ingrained in my bones, and the dreadful sounds echo in my head. Though the abyss of sins separates hell from heaven, the two existed only a few miles apart in my town. My formal diagnosis prevented me from receiving this therapy myself. I don't know the details of what occurred in that room. I only saw the broken and angry faces of those that emerged.

I did, though, receive another kind of treatment. For a shy child to join, mentally impaired children proved no small matter. Since I acted differently from the other kids, their attention gravitated to me. Senseless hits and kicks for no reason became part of my daily routine once again. I was quiet, non-aggressive and didn't look physically healthy. The surgery on my bladder had gone wrong a couple of years earlier, leaving me unable to walk straight. My back curved in an arc and forced me to walk with my face down, like a hunchback. Though the effects eventually subsided, the "hunch boy" became my nickname for several years. My only comfort in such a name was that, at times, I could be alone when their exhaustion and other attractions swayed them away from me.

Teachers found me an easy scapegoat. One teacher perceived my silence as a sign of disrespect or resentment and used me to frighten others. The teacher would routinely ask me to walk to the blackboard. He would then pull out his belt and whip me several times in front of the laughing class. I had to protect my face from the lashes. Once, I escaped the classroom, only to be brought back quickly by the guard. The teacher slapped me in the face several times. He stopped only when he saw me urinating in my pants to the loud and euphoric laughter of most of the twenty kids sitting in the room. It became a ritual that once a week, as the kids became unmanageable, this teacher would call me to the front of the class to hit me with his belt. When he pointed at me to step forward, my pants were already wet, my legs shaking and my soul ready to depart from my aching body. In retrospect, I have limited recollection of the physical pain, only of being numb and nearly oblivious to my surroundings. I managed to detach myself from the physical abuse of teachers and students. The screams, the smells, the darkness and, most of all, the sense of abandonment were forces I had to learn to live with and absorb without letting them destroy me. Many times, I have wondered about our ability to disconnect from reality. How does the mind navigate

CHAPTER FOURTEEN

to other places when what we see radically differs from what we want? Yet, it still amazes me that I didn't run from there right away. What propelled me to stay there and take the abuse and the insults? Why didn't I leave and join a street gang or go somewhere else? I am still puzzled by my temporary surrender. At times, I feel like the many Jews who were reluctant from escaping their ghettos and the concentration camps. I guess like them I was mentally paralyzed

During breaks, I would crawl under the building that stood on cement posts. In the semi-darkness, I found a rescue, a temporary shelter. Weeds and wild shrubs filled the space. I could hear hissing snakes and occasionally a frightened rabbit. Yet, I had no fear of them. I remember watching a butterfly fluttering on a shrub. I felt a sharp pain, recognizing that no wings could get me out of this place. Here, I allowed myself to imagine better days. I would relive the scene of my father carrying me on his shoulders down the beach of Benghazi; I would remember walking into the grand Libyan synagogue holding my father's hand and seeing the congregation standing and bowing to him; the look on my father's face as he greeted my mother coming home from a long day of work; the loving tune that he would hum as she approached his desk and the smile that he would pull from her face as tired as she was; and most of all the loving gaze she returned to him, a gaze without touch. As a wife to an Orthodox Jew and a rabbi, she couldn't touch him in public. Yet despite the distance, her eyes were always filled with love. Her love sustained him despite all the poor conditions he had to endure. They could not physically demonstrate their love for each other as other couples did, yet it ran deep like a river flowing with passion and care.

Right there under the wooden building, standing on several posts, in the coolness of the place and among the shrubs, I found comfort in my visions of my loving parents and happier times, and then I mustered some courage to move on, to take the slaps, the insults and the mistreatment. And I could only hope that somehow, I could be back in the world that I belonged in.

OUT OF THE CUCKOO'S NEST

The Fountain was a frightening place, and I was a scared child tucked under the building, away from sight. No child should go through his childhood in a place like the Fountain. However, my misdiagnosis occurred due to neglect and profound indifference by "the educators" at the regular school. In previous years, before the Fountain, nobody knew how to inquire about the causes of children suffering from traumas or who are autistic. I was told later that, most likely, I was an autistic child. I certainly had all the symptoms, but teachers and school officials lacked the knowledge or skills needed to treat children of different cultures and backgrounds. My teachers were like everyone else—they, too, struggled for survival, moving in small and cautious steps to make a life for themselves in the new land.

During those years, how children were treated—with little or no empathy—was hard to swallow. Good teachers these days operate from a clear set of policies. Back then, teachers were oblivious to the needs of their students and not versed in child psychology. They believed that discipline and toughness were the only ways to assimilate children from different cultures into one mold. The nation needed one culture driven by its founders. Any tolerance or a policy toward diversity was smashed.

One sunny afternoon, however, my hideaway became a false sanctuary. It became more treacherous than the snakes that dwelled there. It morphed into a dungeon from which I'd take many years to escape. On this day, relaxed in the shade and comfortable in the tall weeds of my retreat, I dreamed. In my dream, I wandered into orange and pomegranate orchards and followed my secret trail to the ocean. I climbed a tree and tasted the juiciest fig I could recall. I smelled the fruits and the scent of the sea. The water spread far and wide across the horizon and glistened under a radiant sun. The waves rhythmically lapped at the shore. It was paradise.

And then, I heard voices. At first, the voices were distant, the kind you hear without knowing if they are from a dream or real life. Then, it was touch. That did the trick. I woke up startled. Three older kids, easily in their

CHAPTER FOURTEEN

mid-teens, had started fondling me. Startled and enraged, I tried kicking and punching my way out, but they were big and bulky compared to me. They quickly turned me around and pinned my arms and legs to the ground. They forced my face deep into the soil. They whispered words that I couldn't understand. I yelled many times, but my screams faded into the dirt.

Their nails dug deep into my flesh as I struggled to escape their hold. They held me tight, glued to the decaying leaves of the shrubs. I could smell the stench of their bodies, feel their heavy breathing on my neck, and their sweat dripping on my back. I froze and became stiff; my mind was racing, but my body shattered. I prayed for a snake to show up to scare them off, but like me, it was frozen from what it was witnessing.

I struggled to no avail, immobilized, while their hands and bodies were on me. When dark clouds overshadow my existence and my mood swings into the abyss, I agonize about the excruciating pain piercing through my body. I can still taste the stems of the wild grass my face was shoved into. The sickness in my stomach and the blood streaming in the bottom of my pants didn't bother me as much as the shame that engulfed me. Despite all these years and the fathomless trauma, my entire being is hijacked. My vivid memory of those moments is etched into my soul; a painful reminder of a time I wish I could forget.

During those moments that lasted forever, I imagined myself as David overpowering Goliath. With David's aim, I would emerge from under their grip and throw sharp stones directly at their foreheads. In my darkest hours, I remember yelling for God. I called Him, but there was no response. I still wonder why God did not enable me to do the impossible, like Samson destroying the six cement posts that held up the building and the six deceitful posts that created this cave, where my haven became my inferno. I would bring down the building upon my attackers, dying with them with dignity, buried under the debris. On that day, when everything was taken away from me, the God that I worshipped was as far away as the moon.

I don't know how long I was there. I only know that a voice suddenly rang loudly in the air. The janitor had been cleaning the classroom above and heard noises underneath. He had followed the sounds and investigated the crawlspace. I heard him yelling at them and felt their weight lift from my body as I raised my face from the soil and took a desperate, broken breath. The three assailants quickly crawled out. I barely saw their faces. They remain faceless to this day but never forgotten. The janitor locked eyes with me. I could see his thoughts, trying to make sense of what he had just witnessed, grappling with the sight of my muddied face and half-naked body.

In pain and with a shattered spirit, I fixed my clothes. He extended his hand. With whatever strength was left in me, I rolled towards him, and his hand grasped my arm. He pulled me out from under the building, dragging me into the open, leaving me in shock and confused. My memories of those hours are scattered. The janitor walked me to the restroom and helped me wash my face and arms. He then walked me home. He left me at my front door. I barely knew myself as I crossed the threshold into my house. My mother was at work, and my father was with his books in his study. I made my way to the washroom. I washed off the physical aspects of my tragedy. Inside, the wounds bled. I carried them with me as I slithered into a corner of the bed I shared with two brothers. There I stayed, alive but wanting to die.

The burden grew through the coming days, weeks, months and years. I became a stranger to myself. The trauma, to its core, never deserted me; it stuck me like an albatross. I would become angry and, for no apparent reason, would fall into the abyss. I would burst out in rage, always fearing that someone was going to push me down to the ground and diminish my existence to nothingness.

I lost the sacredness of my body, and fuming anger would burst from nowhere—a trauma response I would later learn. Even well into my adulthood, there were times when my depression couldn't be contained. Those

CHAPTER FOURTEEN

were hours of loneliness and melancholy. Sleeping during the afternoon hours and waking up irritably, depressed and frightened. I began to avoid sleeping during the day, knowing a mix of unsettling emotions would follow. There were times when I was rude to the people I loved. There were things I said in anger to my mother that I never meant. Until today, I cursed myself for being unkind to her during those dark moments.

Yet, my mother took it all. She would slowly approach me, rub my head, place a warm towel on my forehead, and tell my siblings that it was not me, but it was the demons who hijacked me, that it was the evil eye that brought me down. She would explain that I was a man with a good heart, with a soft and tender soul. She endlessly explained to others that I was no longer myself when darkness took over me. My mother noticed that out of the blue, I started banging my head against the pillow every night and wet my bed while I was asleep. Neither my mother nor any family members ever learned about the event and its traumatic impact or how much the experience made a profound mark on me. I needed a resolution, an absolution, but I couldn't find one. The despicable words I used in anger haunted me for years. I destroyed wonderful relationships and moved away from anyone who tried to get too close. Without warning, I became defensive, needing to control all aspects of a situation to avoid the potential pain of being deserted or reopening a wound that never entirely closed.

For a long time, the trauma took over my existence. Later, I was told that my behavior, never letting anyone get too close or intimate, stemmed from the fear of betrayal. It took many years of self-discovery to control the demons of rage. In the workplace, during these moments, I would go for a walk or a run to suffocate the pain. I learned how to suppress the moments when the past would start dripping in unannounced. I worked hard to sublimate the wilderness of the pain. Over time, I managed to detect the arrival of these emotional storms.

Only later in life, when I found my true soulmate, a woman of strength who understood my injuries, did I find the love that helped me to venture and trust again. I didn't express the darkness of my world to my parents. They knew little about the mistreatment that I experienced from week to week. I wanted to protect them more than I expected them to protect me. All they could offer was simple and pure love. My love for them moved me to shield them as deep as depth can be measured. I would not have tormented them by my struggles. They had enough of their own. They were unaware that the school was damaging my ability to be normal again. They only knew that the state had transferred me to another school. My ordeal occurred silently, away from their eyes.

To hide my torment from them, and as a registered student required by the state to be educated within the confines of the Fountain, I was back in my classroom the next day. Nothing was different. Not that day, nor any other after it. The mentally disabled kids continued to kick or hit when they could. The worst of my teachers continued to submit me to his public lashing. The screams from the therapy room continued to linger in the air in endless shrieks.

My mind wandered into illusions and daydreaming more often than before, and I created my alternate reality, a coping mechanism. I started fantasies of escape or being the strongest kid in the neighborhood. But my mechanism of survival didn't go unnoticed. One of my teachers, annoyed by my mental absence, made it a point to bring me back to his world by pulling my left ear and yelling that I was the dumbest child in class. His loud voice and the lashes with his belt were hellish. The impact was a disaster. My behavior started to change. I started behaving like all the other kids, talking to myself and shaking my head constantly.

Years later, while in the military of the Israeli Defense Forces, I considered looking for the psychologist who misdiagnosed me—my inquisitor who unleashed years of torture—and imagined myself harming him. My commander convinced me that such experiences, as painful as they might

CHAPTER FOURTEEN

be, could become our greatest source of inspiration. He knew what he was talking about. He escaped from the concentration camp and joined the Russian partisans. He fought hard and with endless anger. He was more than a commander to me; he was my mentor, guiding me through the years with tough love and with a lasting impact.

Years later, I wanted to find that psychologist for a different reason. This time, I wanted to forgive him for his error. I discovered that there are times when the pain inflicted on us becomes the catalytic force for a meaningful transformation. Surviving traumas transforms us in unpredictable ways. The anger that eats us from the inside can become a driving force in our lives. Such power enables us to forge ahead with courage and conviction. At the medical school of the University of Miami where I teach today, faculty and staff nicknamed me "the healer of healers."

I know pain, but none was as painful as what I experienced at the Fountain. Right there, under the cursed building where I felt deserted, I left my God behind, never again to trust anyone not even myself.

Chapter Fifteen

MIRACLES DESCEND UPON US

Despite all the cynicism and doubt, miracles do happen. I've experienced it.

Miracles may not necessarily bring happiness or wealth, but they have the ability of pulling you out of desolate circumstances – the Israelites' crossing the Red Sea, Moses striking water out of a rock, Elijah reviving a dead man, Jesus walking on water, Israel emerging from ruin. My miracle was more humble and less glorious, yet it saved me. I was eventually granted the opportunity to leave the Fountain without having to escape or venture into the unknown.

My miracle came from a clerk at the Department of Education in the city of Ashkelon. His name was Nissim G'ean. "Nissim" in Hebrew means "miracles," and he was the man who facilitated my miracle. A short, stocky man with a kind and warm face, Nissim – like me – came from Benghazi. He was well-educated in both secular and religious studies and spoke four languages fluently. He attended an Italian school in Benghazi and earned a diploma that brought immense pride to his family and secured him a decent job at the town hall. He always spoke highly of my father, considering him his true teacher. Nissim's father was a renowned rabbi and Talmudic scholar named Rabbi Sassy G'ean. My father had the privilege of sharing the rabbinical court with him back in Libya, but Rabbi G'ean passed away shortly after arriving in Israel.

My father knew that I was depressed, even though I had spared the details of my torment. He sensed my misery through my silence. He could feel the scars of the abuse I had endured. Like all sensitive parents, he recognized that I was not myself. I had stopped asking him questions, challenging him about God and inquiring if he needed anything. As a man who spent his life sorting out truth from lies as a judge of the rabbinical court in Libya, I believe he picked up on my distress during services, especially when he placed both hands on my head to bless me. He could detect that I was losing weight, that I wasn't as cheerful or interactive as I once was.

Nissim came to my father's synagogue only on special occasions, usually during the morning services on Shabbat. Despite Jewish tradition prohibiting discussions about business on the holy day, my father approached him after the service. He had asked me to wait outside the synagogue while he talked with Nissim. It was only later that I learned from Nissim that my father had shared details about my situation with him. Nissim understood and successfully convinced the Director of Education in the city hall and the Education Inspector from Jerusalem that I belonged in a different environment. Despite his efforts to have me sent back to the regular school in Ashkelon, he could not persuade the authorities to see either justice or the facts. The only option he presented to my father and mother was to transfer me to an agricultural boarding school in the famous Negev desert of Israel.

Israeli leaders had a grand vision of transforming the Negev into fertile land by channeling the waters of the Sea of Galilee into the arid dunes. The very waters that Jesus walked on were now flowing through wide pipes stretching from north to south, nourishing the soil that is the source of all life. To realize this vision, Israel needed to prepare farmers for the future.

I had no idea where I was going or what I was going to do in the desert; all I wanted was to escape at any cost. My desire to leave the situation I found myself in was so strong that I ignored everything important, includ-

CHAPTER FIFTEEN

ing the burden of leaving my family behind. It meant I would miss walking my father to the synagogue at dawn, I wouldn't have his determined hand holding mine, I wouldn't be able to inhale the sweet scent of his tobacco, share strong coffee in the morning with the other worshippers or serve as a role model for my siblings. Leaving would also mean abandoning my mother, who relied on me for so many tasks around the house. She never expressed the pain she felt watching her oldest son leave, aimlessly, leaving her to handle all the burdens on her own.

I was the one who painted the entire house before Passover. I was the one who poured cement and installed metal posts to protect our home from the trucks passing by.

I wouldn't cross the street to visit Abraham's grocery store anymore. Abraham, a warm Hungarian Holocaust survivor, had always let us take what we needed without immediate payment, writing it down in his accounting book. I would no longer stroll through the orchards or walk to the sea, breathing in the fresh air and watching the waves.

But the desire to leave the place I hated so much overpowered everything else. Several days after meeting Nissim, he returned to my school. Escorted by the headmaster, Nissim walked into my classroom. He looked at me warmly as the principal asked the teacher to excuse me from class. I stood up, trembling yet excited, leaving my personal belongings behind as I stepped out. We made our way to a minivan that would take me to the desert. Before we left, I approached my father. He stood up, placed both hands on my head, and blessed me. I felt a tear from his eye drop onto my head, its warmth piercing through my soul. I could still feel his trembling hands resting over me. There I was, the son of a rabbi, leaving everything behind to become a farmer. Yet, my father never objected, as other parents might have. He only blessed me. In that moment, I felt like Jacob receiving his stolen blessing from his father, Isaac.

Inside, I was brimming with shame. I felt ashamed for leaving home instead of following my father's footsteps and becoming a rabbi. Upon arriving in Israel, my father recognized the urgent need to cultivate the soil and defend the new and vulnerable country. He understood that the nation required fewer spiritual leaders and more productive citizens working in factories and on farms. After years of waiting, religion was less of a pressing concern than the need to build a new nation.

My father was a man for all seasons. His ability to see, feel, adapt and foresee was extraordinary. His wisdom in interpreting Jewish law to fit the moment served as a lifeline for others. It took me a long time to fully grasp his philosophy and way of thinking. Only later, as I reflected on his thoughts, vision, sermons and flexibility, did I come to understand his uniqueness and forward-thinking nature. As quiet as he was, and despite his blindness, he saw everything and understood the needs of the nation.

He focused less on combatting large societal issues like discrimination and concerned himself more with the day-to-day struggles of the many immigrants under his guidance. He had to help them make a life to build a stronger nation that would never again place Jews anywhere under threat of eviction or gas chambers.

After I received my father's blessing, my mother became emotional. Her tears weighed on me for days and months to come. She handed me one of her scarves, which she had sprayed with rose water, and asked me to keep it deep in my pocket and take it with me wherever I went.

As I left home, my mother sprinkled water behind me for good fortune. I departed from a place where I had experienced so much pain and from the home that had offered me unconditional love.

There are times when we must leave things behind; times when memories should be erased, deleted from our minds and blocked from recall. Otherwise, we risk becoming victims of our own recollections, pulled into the abyss. During those difficult moments, we must rise, lift ourselves up and unshackle ourselves—not just for survival, but for the sake of purpose,

CHAPTER FIFTEEN

hope, and a good fight like the buffalo running toward the wind.

Chapter Sixteen

ROAMING THE WILD DESERT

It was a spring day in the Negev in 1959. Vibrant red poppy flowers were in bloom. The wandering nomads known as the Bedouin, accompanied by their flocks of sheep, stood out in the pastures like pearls embedded in a crown. I took in the sight as the old minivan transported me to my new school. At thirteen, I no longer hunched over; the horizon signified a new beginning for me.

At the new agricultural school, I would be trained as a farmer to meet the demands of a budding nation. In exile, Jews in many countries were not allowed to own land, so they developed 'portable' professions. They could become jewelers who wrapped their jewels in boxes or physicians who carried their medical tools in bags. However, this new country needed farmers and ranchers. This vision had spread across the nation, and schools to teach agriculture and farming were established in every corner of the land. My school was nestled among the desert hills, not far from where Abraham, the father of Judaism, had dug seven wells more than 3,000 years ago. The seventh well became the origin of the city later known as Be'er Sheva.

Jewish immigrants from more than seventy countries arrived with little knowledge of plowing fields, milking cows, or herding sheep. Yet the school's head, Mordechai Ayalon, was tasked with shaping the youth into cattle raisers, shepherds, poultry experts, and wheat growers. At his side was agronomist Samuel Cooper, a fellow Holocaust survivor. Both men had left behind academic careers to settle in the desert and help bring to life the vision of Israel's founders.

The school's mission was clear: to turn the children of aspiring financiers, retailers, physicians, lawyers, and jewelers into farmers. Only farmers, it was believed, could transform the dry, barren soil into land overflowing with golden wheat and fruit trees. And so the school offered everything a future farmer could need—hundreds of hectares for growing wheat and corn, orchards heavy with peaches and plums, more than fifty cows for milk and meat, a large facility for hens producing eggs, and a tractor workshop where students learned to repair the machines essential to working the land. Established just ten years after the nation's founding, the school stood as a bold experiment in turning dreamers into cultivators of soil and life.

A newly built facility featured a pen for more than 200 sheep situated near the cattle housing. Several hundred meters away from the livestock facilities, wooden structures served as dormitories for the boys and girls. Each room contained four iron beds with hay-stuffed mattresses. The girls were housed in one structure, while the boys were in a separate one. These six dormitories shared one large toilet and shower facility, ensuring a clear separation between the boys and girls.

The six classrooms were built on a hill, where, on a clear day, one could see the expansive desert dotted with black tents used by the Bedouins, along with their sheep and camels. Located further away from the dorms and other school facilities were twelve to fifteen single-family homes that accommodated the faculty, instructors and administrators along with their families. In total, we had about 250 young boys and girls, mostly from families who had arrived from Arab countries.

The vast, open space, the distant horizon of desert hills, and the distinct smells of cow and sheep manure were invigorating. It felt like a warm welcome, the entire scene serving as a breath of fresh air to my suffocated

CHAPTER SIXTEEN

soul.

I walked around, waiting for someone to notice me and direct me to my new home. The head of the dormitories, an older woman named Lola with several numbers tattooed on the lower part of her left arm, welcomed me. She had a warm smile and radiant blue eyes. As she walked me to my dorm room, she showed me the large dining hall that served three meals daily. There, a Holocaust survivor from Romania, a tall woman named Dalia with a smile that could disarm any lost soul, offered me a cup of tea and toast generously spread with butter and jam. I gulped it down without hesitation.

Later, I learned that Dalia had escaped from a train leading to a concentration camp, joined the partisans hiding in the forests during the day, and bombed train stations at night. I could hardly imagine her as a fighter resisting the Nazis. She gave me a hug that I would never forget, and for the first time in a long time, I felt safe and comforted. From that day forward, she became my dearest protector and a surrogate mother. I later found out that she couldn't bear children.

She lived next to my dorm, and I frequently visited her humble home for a cup of hot tea and the pastries she baked herself. I would go to the orchard at dawn, pick beautiful peaches and bring them to her. Other kids were intimidated by her strong voice and demanding appearance, but for me, she always had a smile.

The sudden change in my life brought a sense of liberation, but also depression. I felt guilty that I was able to escape while my family continued to struggle in Ashkelon. My boarding school was intended for those deemed less academically sound, aimless or school dropouts from the nearby towns.

Each newcomer had several options to choose from, and there was no pressure regarding which area one could select to become an expert. This was the first time in my life that I was given the opportunity to make a choice. The school offered various tracks: working the soil, which involved driving tractors with plows; attending to cows by feeding and milking them twice a day; looking after hundreds of hens by collecting their eggs, feeding them constantly, removing their manure, and injecting them with antibiotics; or tending to sheep, which meant taking them into the surrounding pasture, milking them, shearing them, and assisting them during the birthing of their newborn lambs. Most boys wanted to work with tractors and horses in the fields as it was considered the masculine thing to do. Meanwhile, most girls preferred to work with poultry or cows.

To the surprise of the agricultural supervisor, Dorech, I chose to work with the sheep. I became a shepherd for several reasons. First, caring for them required rising early to lead them into the hills, a routine that came naturally to me after years of waking at dawn with my father. Second, I was drawn to their quiet nature; their rare cries matched my own need for peace, and the solitude suited me far more than being among the crowd. Third, the wide desert air gave me space to heal my spirit and begin to release the haunting memories of the Fountain. And finally, shepherding restored my strength and confidence. The responsibility of guarding the sheep's well-being gave me a sense of purpose and responsibilities.

Having grown up on biblical stories, I knew that many of its great figures had once been shepherds. My favorite, King Saul, had even preferred tending his flock to leading his tribes. Still, I was surprised to find how many of the children at the boarding school despised the work. To them, it was grueling. The early mornings demanded discipline, and the lingering smell of sheep made it hard to attract the attention of girls. The duties stretched far beyond grazing: daily milking, feeding, shearing, and even assisting with the spring mating season.

Most of the children were likely unaware that the school was surrounded by Bedouin nomads, who roamed freely in the desert with their flocks. I would watch them lead their herds from one hill to another, resting under dried oak trees as the sun beat down. Being alone with the sheep allowed me to guard my embarrassing past. Wandering the hills with the sheep—moving

CHAPTER SIXTEEN

from one pasture to another, free to roam for most of the day, and for the first time truly in charge—was more than I could have hoped for in my wildest dreams.

I reflected on my feelings during my interview with the headmaster and some teachers, who determined shortly after my arrival that my destiny would be as a shepherd. I accepted this challenge with open arms. When I shared my new assignment with other students in the large dining room, they responded with laughter and compassionate looks, acknowledging what I was about to experience. Their laughter wasn't mocking; it was empathetic, which I welcomed after having felt ignored for so long.

This positive atmosphere, the warmth of the staff, the acceptance from my peers, the absence of derision and the fact that no one unleashed anger on me by lashing out created a foundation for my healing process, a journey to rebuild my confidence, self-esteem and trust in others.

As if life had prepared me for this moment, my days began once again in the dark morning hours. At dawn, I needed to lead the sheep out to the open fields where they could graze while the desert temperature was still cool, encouraging them to feast on the wild weeds that grew in certain areas. Later in the day, when the temperature soared to one hundred degrees or more, the sheep would combat the heat by sticking their heads under each other's tails, forming a fantastic circle of wool before me. As the heat began to dissipate several hours before sunset, the flock was ready to return home for fresh water and grain. I would lead them back to the sheepfold, creating a cloud of sand that rose with every step.

Walking among the sheep always made me feel connected to them. I watched their humble eyes and dry mouths, longing for water and grain. They reminded me of us, struggling with life and hoping for better things to come.

An old donkey lived among the sheep. It is believed that having a donkey in the flock helps relax the sheep, which is essential for milk production.

Donkeys can also be fearsome guardians when needed. Reflecting on those days, I can't help but think about how the sheep and the donkey have become important symbols in Christianity and Judaism. Jesus is often depicted with sheep and lambs, symbolizing simplicity and humility. Despite our sins, we are no more than a flock of sheep in the eyes of the Creator. For religious Jews, the Messiah is prophesied to arrive on a white donkey, symbolizing humility and submission. And for my father, the Messiah did come.

After a long day of wandering in the desert, the flock entered to feed on grain served on long conveyor belts. Head-locking stalls allowed us to milk them while they fed, which we wanted to do correctly, or they would kick us with their tiny feet. I would sit on my wooden stool and fill buckets of milk, sheep after sheep.

In the spring, the mating season, the ingenious process of impregnating the females fascinated me. We used the opportunity to insert them as they fed on the grain, which was critical for artificially breeding them. This was a unique process for a thirteen-year-old boy to experience. First, we needed to identify the females in heat. Out in the field, a couple of the males would join the flock and, as sheep are very active, with red paint I would mark every female that would not resist the advances made by Samson or Goliath—yes, each male had a grand, biblical name. The following morning, the marked females would undergo insemination.

I would stand over each sheep as she ate, lifting her tail while another, more experienced shepherd administered the injection. This approach, while less natural, was necessary for seven rams to successfully impregnate over two hundred sheep. When the time came for the sheep to give birth, we assisted in pulling out the lamb to help reduce the high mortality rate associated with a sheep's natural delivery. We cleaned the newly born lamb, enabling the mother to feed on the placenta—another fascinating aspect of being a sheep caretaker.

My responsibilities also included shearing the sheep, carefully removing

CHAPTER SIXTEEN

each one's fleece using specialized shearing scissors. In those days, we didn't have electronic milking machines or electric shears; everything was done manually. I enjoyed pressing my head against the sheep's woolly hides and always felt it was a mutual experience, as the sheep seemed more secure releasing their milk into the bucket. The soothing sound of the milk filling the bucket was like calming music to both of us.

Shepherding was an immersive and demanding trade that earned my deep respect. My only day off was Shabbat. On Shabbat, both the sheep and I rested.

The only thing missing in my new life as a shepherd was a synagogue where I could conduct the Shabbat service. In retrospect, I realize that most of the staff at the agricultural school were survivors of the Holocaust. For them, God and religion were things of the past; they had left God behind in the concentration camps. I had left my God buried in the crawl space of the building at the Fountain.

Tending to the sheep taught me important lessons in responsibility and accountability. A shepherd is a humble leader who must address the immediate needs of the flock. It's essential to be attuned to the demands of the sheep because ignoring their needs denies us the milk and wool they provide. Over time, I learned to sense their pain and distinguish their health by observing their eyes, faces, and movements. This dedication to understanding how sheep function later contributed to my effectiveness as a coach.

My intense schedule tending to the sheep often prevented me from participating in the social activities that other kids enjoyed. Walking those quiet, dark, dusty roads to care for the sheep and then wandering through the few green pastures available required me to march several miles each day. Those days of wandering through the desert gave me the opportunity to reflect on my identity and consider what I wanted to do with my life. There were moments under the desert sun when I imagined myself as Moses, standing before the burning bush, hoping to hear the voice of God. I longed to receive a signal from above that would guide me with a clear vision of my purpose.

However, that calling never came. I ultimately concluded that any such calling must originate from within.

Amid those lonely days, I met Rina. I first saw her in the noisy dining room during dinner. Unlike the other loud kids, she sat quietly, shy and princess-like. Her braided black hair, blue eyes and soft features captivated my imagination. It was love at first sight.

I knew that other boys were better looking than me and certainly didn't have the unpleasant odor that came from working with sheep. For the first time, I became aware of the scent that lingered from my body. It is well known that working with sheep could affect a person's smell. The pungent aroma lingered no matter how many times one bathed or showered. I was certain that any attempt to attract Rina was a hollow dream—yet the idea of falling in love and allowing myself to dream was tantalizing.

Every dinner, I summoned the courage to glance at her. I wanted her to know how beautiful she was, and I was mesmerized by her presence. When she walked away, I left the dining room and followed her, escorting her to her dorm. She never looked back, but I knew she was aware of my presence just a few steps behind her. I imagined her stopping to ask for my name or at least offering a smile to encourage me to pursue her.

But it never happened.

One evening during dinner, I mustered the courage to leave a note next to her plate. I wrote that I would like to see her after dinner by the bench next to the dining room. I waited there for more than two hours, but she never showed up. Despite continued notes, she continued to ignore me.

I learned from others that she and her parents came from Morocco and, like my own family, struggled to make ends meet in this new land. Rina was quiet and graceful, and unlike the other girls, she rarely socialized or walked hand in hand with a boy. I discovered that her family lived near my father's

CHAPTER SIXTEEN

synagogue.

Despite her rejection, I carried thoughts of her with me. As I tended to my responsibilities, I imagined her in my arms, holding hands and roaming the wild desert hills together. I envisioned us like the Bedouins, who married off their children at a very young age. I even toyed with the idea of leaving the farming school to join the nomads with her by my side.

One of the greatest gifts in life is love, a gift I never thought I would get to explore. Rina's calm presence later drew me to quiet women who didn't need to show off to mask their insecurities. Her name means "the voice of happiness," and she truly had a soothing, harmonious voice that filled me with warmth—a boy burdened by emotional storms and an insatiable hunger for love and to be loved.

Rina and I never developed any form of intimate relationship. After all, a first love story rarely works out. Nonetheless, I refused to give up. My first courageous act was sneaking into the orchards at night, where I managed to pick some beautiful peaches and plums. I placed the stolen fruit in a basket I found in the dining room and left it on her bed while she was away. The next day, she waited for me outside the dining room and, with a shy smile, thanked me for the beautiful fruit. I was overjoyed; I felt I was making real progress in getting her to notice me.

From that point on, she came alive in my imagination. She was with me when I milked the sheep; she accompanied me in the vast, open spaces of the desert. I carried her with me wherever I went and in everything I did. In my heart, she was my first love, my guiding light, and a lasting hope amid isolation. She embodied my search for warmth and love that inspired me to push forward. Despite her rejection, I didn't give up.

On one of those Saturday mornings, when the weather was beautiful and most students relaxed outside their dorms, I decided to impress her. I enlisted the help of the donkey that lived among the sheep. I believed Rina would like me more when she saw me valiantly riding the white donkey in front of her dorm. Riding a donkey doesn't require a saddle, but these animals, like many others, are not easily fooled.

Recognizing that I was a novice, the clever donkey led me to believe he was collaborating with me. Tired of being around the sheep and doing nothing all day, the smart donkey allowed me to hop on its back without any resistance. I opened the gate, and there we were, the donkey and I riding together. I felt like a hero. I managed to steer the donkey towards the building that housed the girls. Most of them sat on the front porch, staring at me in amazement. I spotted Rina among the girls, unsure whether she was smiling or anticipating the miserable outcome that was about to happen.

The loud sounds of the mocking boys and the laughter of the girls scared the donkey off. Without warning, this clever donkey kicked its rear feet and took off quickly. I fell flat on the ground; my face covered in dust. Ashamed and embarrassed, I picked myself up, wishing I could disappear. I stumbled to my room, feeling lower than the ant crawling on my pillowcase.

But this was not the end of the story. The donkey was clever enough to gallop to the border crossing into Egyptian territory. This forced the border police on the Israeli side to negotiate with the Egyptian soldiers to return the stubborn animal. It became the talk of the entire community, and I was the laughingstock for several days. Eventually, the donkey was brought back to rejoin the sheep.

Upon the donkey's return, I was summoned to the headmaster's office. I sat there as he told me never to attempt something as foolish as I had. Despite my embarrassment, I felt proud to have done something no one else had done before. In fact, the whole episode impressed the girl I loved, and she decided to see me that evening after dinner.

This was one of those memories that never fades away. We walked for an hour as she shared stories about her early years in Casablanca and her parents' struggles in the new land. I simply listened; her words flowed like a beautiful stream of fresh water, refreshing my spirit. As we walked back to

CHAPTER SIXTEEN

her dorm, I extended my hand and held hers. The warmth radiating from her small palm warmed my heart, and in that moment, I felt like the tallest boy on the farm.

Chapter Seventeen

RISING FROM THE ASHES

As the months passed on the farm, I became fascinated by the lifestyle of the neighboring desert nomads. Whenever we crossed paths, our sheep never mixed; each flock remained loyal to its respective shepherd. I admired the Bedouins' free-roaming ways and how they cared for their families, flocks and the few possessions they owned. They didn't possess any property, yet they mastered the desert, learning to live with its unpredictable nature, including sudden shifts in heat, winds, floods and sandstorms.

The nomads exhibited a quiet resilience. Without complaint, they simply adapted to the desert's whims. They were constantly on the move, embracing change like no other people I had known. When the green grass vanished overnight, they would fold their tents and load their few belongings—dishes and sheepskins—onto donkeys or camels, moving on in search of greener pastures for their sheep and new landscapes to explore. They were known for their hospitality, kind demeanor and strong will to thrive as the eagles of the desert. In many ways, I felt envious of them.

One nomad even saved my life. On a scorching day in August, when temperatures soared to one hundred and ten degrees, every creature sought shade to escape the heat. My sheep were already huddled together, their heads tucked under each other's tails, as I leaned against an old oak tree, its leaves gone, having been eaten by camels. I fell asleep, only to be awakened by unusually loud bleating from my flock. Although I had some experience, I still needed to learn the various cries of the sheep and didn't understand their agitation. Ignoring their warning, I continued to rest. Unbeknownst to me, the sheep sensed a black scorpion crawling towards the trunk of the oak tree, desperately seeking shade from the blazing sun. When I spotted the large scorpion, it was right by my bare foot. Startled, I jerked away in fear, causing the scorpion to whip its tail and sting me, injecting enough venom to render me unconscious.

I remember feeling dizzy and then waking up in a hospital. I was later told that a nearby nomad had understood the sheep's cry of distress and had come to my rescue. He carried me to the highway and hitchhiked on a military vehicle that brought me to the hospital. I never saw my rescuer, but from that day on, my admiration for sheep and nomads deepened.

After several days in the hospital, an administrator picked me up and drove me back to the farming school. As the car pulled in, I felt a surge of emotion. I made a critical decision that would change my destiny: I was convinced it was time to leave the farm. Although I loved being a shepherd and had begun to heal from the misery of my past, I was ready to move on and explore opportunities I had never dreamed of. I was prepared for a new beginning.

On the Shabbat following my return from the hospital, I strolled along the path leading to the dining room when I saw a young couple holding hands. The young man's white uniform, pristine and crisp, caught my attention. The sight of the uniform against the dusty desert backdrop was striking, though I couldn't fully understand its impact on me at the time. It contrasted sharply with my own appearance: dusty, pale and covered in bug bites. The cadet, about seventeen years old, walked with pride, his body erect, head held high, and a pleasant smile on his face. He looked like a royal prince, exuding authority and presence. In addition to visiting his girlfriend from the poultry section of the farm, he had come to see his youngest

CHAPTER SEVENTEEN

brother, who was training as a cattle rancher.

I learned that the man in white was attending a naval school in the northern part of the country and was happily on track to become a naval officer. His brother shared more details about the academy, explaining how difficult it was to gain acceptance. From that moment on, I became mesmerized by the idea of the blue ocean, sailing the seas, and exploring the world.

I made up my mind: I would go there.

While I tended the sheep, my thoughts were consumed with dreams of leaving the farm. I pictured myself on the deck of a ship, dressed in the gray and white uniform of the Navy. As a child often mocked and pushed aside, I imagined the uniform as a shield, protecting me from ridicule. I saw myself walking down the main street of Ashkelon in crisp white attire, certain that the laughter, the whispers, and the taunts from those back home would finally be silenced.

One March day, as I wandered with the flock, I decided it was time to go. I devised a plan: I would return the sheep to the farm ahead of schedule. By moving the hands of my watch—a bar mitzvah gift from my mother—I thought I could persuade the head instructor that my early return was due to blurred vision. I knew he would be furious, that bringing the herd back too soon would earn me shouts, perhaps even a slap or punch. But I needed that reaction, a justification strong enough to make my departure acceptable. The truth was, the treatment I endured here was nothing compared to my earlier days in Ashkelon. Still, the mind of a fourteen-year-old is often both naive and daring.

I signaled to the sheep that it was time to head home. The confused animals stared at me with puzzled expressions; their biological clocks weren't ready for them to return just yet. However, despite their confusion, they followed me back to the farm. It was three hours before my scheduled return, and I felt scared, but there was no turning back now. I was prepared to face the consequences.

As we entered the gate, the supervisor noticed a cloud of dust rising from the hills, signaling my early arrival. This was not the first time he had dealt with young boys trying to pass off a malfunctioning watch as an excuse. He was far more prepared for me than I was for him. He ordered me to stop, got off his tractor, and approached with his hands on his hips, yelling furiously about my breach of schedule.

My voice shaking, I tried to explain that my watch was to blame. He snatched it from my wrist and threw it into a haystack behind him, then ordered me to return to the field and made it clear that I was to stay there until he came to tell me when I could return.

Torn between searching for my watch and obeying his order, I realized I had lied, and I had no choice but to comply. Angry, feeling sorry for myself, and regretting both my lost watch and my deceit, I remained resolute about leaving that night.

That evening, I searched through the haystack for the watch but never found it. I felt terrible about my loss, knowing how hard my mother had worked to buy it as a gift for my bar mitzvah, and how many coins she had to collect just to afford the down payment.

With nothing holding me back, I packed my few shirts and pants into a small duffle bag and tiptoed outside near midnight. I tossed my bag over the fence, crawled under it, and made my way toward the highway, leaving behind the school and my days as a farmer. It would be decades before I would return with my family to show my daughters and grandchildren the place that filled my lungs with fresh air and rebuilt my courage and stamina; the place where, for the first time, I looked to the future with confidence and the conviction that whatever came my way, I could face it, struggle with it and overcome it.

I spent two years at this farming school—two years of hard work, waking up before sunrise, tending to the needs of the sheep, wandering in the desert and meeting the humble and resilient Bedouins while learning

CHAPTER SEVENTEEN

their way of life. My time here was filled with invaluable lessons that shaped my character.

Though I couldn't fully understand the clarity of the road ahead of me, I knew I had to move forward with grit and courage. That night, as I walked the path from the dorm to the highway alone, I inhaled the cold air of the desert night and felt no fear. I knew that if anyone tried to chase or stop me, I would run fast along the highway. Unlike when I arrived at the agricultural school as a hunched and weak child, I was now tall and strong. Strength and endurance were born from wandering with the sheep for miles each day, milking them by hand, and an inner force that compelled me to do the impossible and to do what was right.

I needed to hitchhike several rides to reach the academy that long night. The cars that stopped to pick me up were military vehicles driven by young soldiers who looked surprised to see a teenager hitchhiking in the middle of the night in the desolate desert. They offered me biscuits and soda to quench my thirst and satisfy my hunger. I was straightforward with them, explaining that I was heading to the academy to apply for the Navy. Sitting next to the drivers in the dark cabin, I could sense their mixed emotions and doubts, but also their admiration for a young kid like me making his way to a prestigious school that only a few could get into without connections or an outstanding performance record.

When I arrived at the school, I stopped at a faucet near the entrance to wash my face. I used my fingers to comb through my long, unruly hair. Given the early hour, I was the only person around and it was tranquil. I searched for a sign indicating the direction to the superintendent's office. After finding it, I sat on one of the benches in the parking lot, shaded by a tree and soon fell asleep.

I woke up to the sound of a trumpet and saw the cadets gathering on the field not far from where I was sitting. They were in gray uniforms, marching on the orders of the officer in charge. As two cadets raised the flag, the group sang the national anthem. I was in awe.

When the office opened, I entered and found the receptionist already sitting at her old IBM typewriter. She looked at me as if I were from another planet. My wrinkled clothes, long, unkempt hair combed back, tired face and wide-eyed expression certainly contributed to that impression. I could tell the smell from my time working with the sheep made her uncomfortable, and she did not hide her feelings toward me. I managed to whisper a greeting in a shaky voice.

"What can I do for you?" she asked sternly.

"I came to apply," I told her.

"Where are your parents?"

"My mom works, and my father is almost blind," I responded, quickly realizing that I had encountered someone unkind.

"I'm very sorry, but you must bring your parents."

"Ma'am, I spent the whole night traveling to reach the academy, and I'm not going back," I insisted in a trembling voice. I explained to her that becoming a Navy man was my dream. I had met one of the senior cadets visiting my agricultural school, and I was amazed by his story about the academy and the future it offered. But to no avail. She refused to budge and repeated coldly that I must return with one of my parents. She stood up and walked toward the door, indicating that I needed to leave.

I tried again to explain that I couldn't go back, that I had run away from school and would most likely be expelled and sent home. Just then, as I approached the door, I heard a man's voice.

"Come here, young man."

I didn't realize it was the superintendent's voice, a tone I would never forget. To me, it was a voice from heaven. I didn't know he had been listening to our conversation from his office. He stood tall, handsome in his uniform, and commanding as I approached him. He was a Romanian Jew, a partisan who had escaped a concentration camp and joined the Russian partisans

CHAPTER SEVENTEEN

fighting against the Nazis.

Leading me into his office, he asked me to tell him who I was. So I did. I shared my whole story: I was the son of a rabbi, I knew how to read, I had memorized the Bible, and I had been taken out of regular school and placed in a "special education" school. My father had spoken to a friend who managed to transfer me to the farming school. One day, I saw a cadet visiting his girlfriend, and I was captivated by the thought of being at sea. I told him I was not going back to the sheep.

He listened, and I felt as though an angel had descended upon me, that my prayers had finally been heard. He stared at me for a while and then warmly asked about my knowledge of math, English and history. I answered negatively to all his questions but emphasized my in-depth knowledge of the Bible and my love of reading. He didn't seem impressed, and once again, I felt deflated.

"It'll be very tough to get in," he explained.

"I know," I replied.

I decided to be open and let him know everything about my past, including the bullies I had faced. I could see that my story touched him; at one point, he even closed the door. I felt safe in his office and sensed his empathy. I would never know what touched him the most. Perhaps it was my time as a shepherd, my days at the Fountain, my courage in arriving alone without my parents after a long night hitchhiking, or the fact that my escape reminded him of his own. Did my disheveled look and wrinkled clothes remind him of his days in the forests wearing the same clothes every day? Was I the son he never had?

He then proceeded to order breakfast for both of us. He explained that I needed to use the remaining months before the September start date of the new freshman class to catch up on math and English. His smile and openness warmed my heart, and I knew then that something about me had touched the core of his being. I was not one of those kids who arrived with parents who held honorable positions in public office or business enterprises. I was a poor teenager with an unyielding desire to make something of myself.

The superintendent offered me cash for my bus ride home and asked me to write to him weekly to keep him updated on my progress. As he walked me out of the office, I could sense the warmth of his heart and the generosity of his soul.

He placed his hand on my shoulder and said, "I will see you here in September, and don't worry, I will call the farming school and let them know that we will accept you for the coming academic year."

There are moments in our lives when all seems broken, and spirits are crushed. Something happens to us that leaves a mark on who we are. It requires conviction, a belief in oneself, and a refusal to surrender. This was a transformational morning for me, as I was coming from the desert to a lush, green land, from the darkness of the night into the light of a better day.

On the way back to the highway, I wondered if I should hitchhike home and give my bus fare to my mother, who would be shocked to see me back. In the end, I was too exhausted and opted to take the bus. As I boarded the bus to Ashkelon, I reflected on the superintendent's unbelievable words informing me that I was accepted into the naval academy. His words of acceptance felt as warm as the wool of sheep.

As I walked the mile from the school to the bus station on the main road to Ashkelon, memories of walking on the beach with my father came to mind. The encounter with the head of the school filled me with warm feelings of love and care. While there was no hug—only a handshake—I sensed his generous heart and commitment to my future. His acceptance of me as an incoming student at the age of sixteen convinced me that there are angels among us. They appear in difficult times to teach us the importance of generosity and to make a lasting impact on who we are and what we can become.

His tough exterior, tempered by a warm heart, inspired me to dedi-

CHAPTER SEVENTEEN

cate myself to helping others. Despite his experiences in the forests fighting the Germans and his journey to Israel, where he educated young cadets to become warriors, he never lost his humanity. There was no anger in him. I never heard him complain about his past—not even about the execution of his parents and siblings. He approached life with a stern look and deep compassion. He reminded me of Moses, leading his people in the desert and preparing the newly born to be pioneers who would revive the land, sailing naval vessels to protect and defend it, creating a generation that would not suffer the pain of exile. He was a giant in my eyes and certainly touched the core of my soul.

I smiled the whole way back to Ashkelon and felt worthwhile for the first time in a long time. I knew I was about to attend a great school that would allow me to showcase my ability, strong will, courage and conviction. I would be among the smartest, and I knew I had to invest every ounce of my energy to excel. I fell asleep, only to be awakened by the bus driver announcing our arrival in Ashkelon.

As I walked from the bus station to my parents' home, I remembered that I should stop by at the school where my mother worked as a janitor. I wanted to share the news of my acceptance with her. As I approached the two-story building, I was shocked to see my mother standing on a second-floor windowsill, cleaning a large window from the outside. I couldn't believe my eyes. My mother was balancing like an acrobat, with her feet on the base of the window and her body tilted to one side, trying to reach the far side of the glass. My first thought was that her surprise at seeing me might cause her to lose her balance and fall to her death in the schoolyard. I rushed into the building from another entrance and ran upstairs to the classroom. When she noticed me, there was a smile on her face, and she slowly maneuvered her way back inside.

I wanted so much to hug her, but she wasn't one for holding or being held. When I finally managed to catch my breath, I raised my voice to her.

"How could you engage in such a dangerous action?" I demanded to know.

She looked at me with her warm eyes and replied with a smile, "My son, when you do anything, you can't do it halfway. You must do it fully, or not at all."

We walked home together, and I shared the exciting news of my admission to the naval academy instead of the agricultural school. I sensed her pride and saw the sadness in her eyes, knowing all that I had been through to finally find the right school—a place that most parents dreamed of for their children, envisioning them becoming men of the sea.

Chapter Eighteen

THE JOURNEY TO CONFIDENCE

When we arrived home, I was exhausted from the sleepless night, the heartfelt interview, and the long journey.

I found my father sitting at his desk reading the Psalms. He stood up, extended his arms and held me tight. Feeling his warmth and his long prickly beard gave me comfort I had not known for so long. My mother had managed to share the news with my father. He smiled with a sign of approval, although I sensed a gesture of pain at the prospect of missing me as I used to walk him to the synagogue. Later I learned that my sister started to walk with him daily. I always felt that my father let me choose. He never forced me or tried to convince me to become a rabbi. I remember telling him that my admission to the new school would enable me to bring pride to the family and extra income down the road to help with the mounting expenses.

I had six months on hand, during which I needed to find work, learn English and math, and get ready to start school in September. I walked out of the house and climbed onto the mosque tower, escaping from the noisy street. The steep spiral staircase, with the scent of the old stones and the reflection from rays of light sneaking from the small openings in the wall, delighted me. From the mosque's top, I screamed with joy and thanked Heaven for being accepted to the new school.

I was overwhelmed by the moment, especially as I stared with a cold face and anguished heart at the Fountain glaring at me from a distance and stood alone in the mosque's tower. I reflected on life and the struggle accompanying us as we make our way in a complex and sometimes unkind world. From the tower, I scanned the landscape of the town below and beyond.

Things look so different from afar. They become less noisy and disruptive, enabling us to reassess and reset our minds and hearts. As I walked down the tower and came home, I shared my climb to the mosque's tower with my mother. She didn't seem concerned or critical, nor did my father, who was sitting at his desk with his eyes glued to the book he was reading. Sometimes, I felt my father was from another universe, merely visiting the planet while his brilliant mind was elsewhere.

For the next month, I worked on a farm picking cotton. With a sack slung over my shoulders, I pulled the soft white blossoms and dropped them into the bag, day after day. One afternoon, returning from the fields, I passed a small print shop owned by a Hungarian Jew—an expert printer who had survived the concentration camps by proving his skills. His name was Abraham Hirsh.

Hirsh was a kind man, one who had stared into the abyss and emerged with deep compassion for others. He was short, with sorrowful eyes, yet carried a remarkable sense of humor. I often wondered how someone who had endured such horrors could still laugh, let alone make others laugh. But Hirsh did just that. He had a rare gift for drawing people in, a gift I hadn't yet learned to cultivate.

The first time I passed his shop, he was sitting on a small stool outside, smoking his pipe and sipping a tiny cup of Turkish coffee. The coffee came courtesy of the two electric grinders in the neighboring shop, whose owner generously let townspeople use them to grind beans or grains.

Hirsh greeted me with a disarming smile, lifting his small cup of coffee in salute, and I smiled back. It wasn't unusual for children to sit with adults over coffee, so when he pulled up a stool and invited me to join him, I did.

CHAPTER EIGHTEEN

With warmth etched into his wrinkled face, he asked my name. His eyes lingered on the cotton fibers clinging to my clothes, and I explained that I was working in the fields to earn money for my mother. He seemed surprised that someone my age wasn't in school, so I told him I'd soon be attending naval school.

With a smirk, he asked if I might prefer working at the print shop, adding that at least there I'd be spared the scorching sun. I accepted without hesitation and arrived early the next morning. From that day, he and his kind wife took me under their wing, teaching me everything I needed to know about printing.

Within a week, I was printing wedding invitations, funeral announcements, and announcement posters for special events. I learned quickly and could take orders for special requests from customers coming into the store. Once a week, Abraham Hirsh went to Tel Aviv to purchase ink and paper supplies for the print shop. One morning, just as I entered the print shop, Mrs. Hirsh told me that the town's deputy mayor was on his way, requesting twenty-five large posters announcing the arrival of a government official to visit the town. He expressed his desire to lecture in the public park the same day at six in the evening. The deputy was anxious to post those posters on the town's wall, encouraging people to show up. As she explained the challenge ahead of us, the deputy, a chubby and nervous-looking man, entered the store.

We listened to the specific information he needed for the posters. I looked at him and said we would have the posters ready for him within two hours. I immediately drafted a poster design and approached the drawers with various sizes of letters made from lead. I arranged the letters, making sure that the name of the official visiting the town was in a large typeset. The large metal frame holding the poster's details was placed in the old printing machine. Mrs. Hirsch prepared a blue ink, which I rolled over the assembled letters. I then placed the first large white paper in the press machine and with my foot, I closed the pressing metals against each other. When I opened the pressing metals, I was amazed to see the beautiful poster shining with the dark blue printed letters announcing the name of the governmental official, the place, the time of the speech and that coffee and cookies would be served.

We printed twenty-five posters and hung them at various places in the shop to dry. The sight of the posters hanging all over the print shop, with the smell of fresh ink, filled me with pride. I couldn't wait to see the posters glued to the walls all over the city.

We rolled out the posters with Mrs. Hirsh, and by noon, they were ready for delivery. The deputy showed up, and when he saw the newly printed posters, he expressed his gratitude to Mrs. Hirsh. When he left with the posters, she gave me a memorable hug that, till today, I can still feel its warmth and admiration.

When Mr. Hirsh returned to the store, Mrs. Hirsh intentionally kept one of the posters she hung on the wall over his desk. She shared the entire event with him, speaking in Hungarian, her voice trembling and her eyes watering. I remember his beautiful gray eyes staring at me with respect and gratitude, then extending both hands and shaking mine with a smile and admiration.

Mr. and Mrs. Hirsh were both educated people. They spoke Hungarian, English, German and Hebrew. At the end of each day, Mrs. Hirsh spent two hours teaching me English and history. They also found me a tutor to help me understand the basic concepts of computation and algebra. The power of love and kindness, though, has no substitute. It completely transforms people.

I kept my promise to stay in touch with the superintendent of the naval school and had Mr. Hirsh write him a letter about my progress. When the letter formally informed me of my acceptance, I decided to have my mother join me for the trip to the new school. We sat together on the bus, and I

CHAPTER EIGHTEEN

enjoyed the warmth of her body pressing against me. When we got there and walked along the manicured lawns with beds of flowers, I could sense her pride and surprise that her son would be attending a good school.

We stopped in the main office, where the superintendent greeted my mother, who spoke little Hebrew. The superintendent handed me an envelope, which he asked me to open later. He thanked my mother and told me that the uniforms must be purchased from a tailor shop in Tel Aviv. One of the cadets gave us a tour of the school: the boats anchored in the small harbor, the neatly kept rooms of the dorms, the modern classrooms and the beautiful landscape.

On the way back, I sensed my mother's rising spirit. She whispered in my ear how proud she was to have her oldest son get into a reputable institution and how important education was for us. I asked her why it was so important. She responded that education is the only way out of poverty. She fell asleep while her head, covered with her colored scarf, was leaning on my left shoulder.

While she was asleep, I opened the envelope to find a check signed by the superintendent—made out to the tailor shop to purchase my uniform.

Chapter Nineteen

THE SEA WITHOUT HORIZONS

I awoke early in the last week of a hot August day. I took a cold shower that our neighbor had installed. Slowly and deliberately, I dressed in my gray naval uniform. My mother and siblings watched me as I stood in front of the mirror, my spine straight. There I was, barely sixteen years old, wearing my ironed shirt and straight pants, topped off with new shiny shoes, ready to leave home and my family behind to attend a prestigious boarding school and become a navy officer.

My father, sitting quietly in his office, called me over. He placed his aged hands over my head, which was topped with a new navy cap adorned with an anchor and an olive branch insignia. He blessed me, and I could sense his mixed emotions. There I stood, his son, stepping away from a rabbinical path toward the secular life of a navy man dedicated to defending our sea border against any enemies attempting to sneak into our new land.

My mother walked me to the bus station, where I boarded a bus to Tel Aviv and then connected to another bus that would take me to Haifa, stopping at the school known as Mevohot Yam, which means "the path to the sea." Sitting in the back during the long ride, I tried to keep my new uniform wrinkle-free as I watched the landscape pass by.

I was determined to work hard to prove to myself and my peers that I could compete. Knowing that most students accepted to the school came from well-off families that invested significant time and resources into their education and well-being made me anxious. I reminded myself that I came from a wonderful home, with a loving family and a long tradition of survival. I promised to excel and make my family proud, vowing to overcome any challenges that came my way.

I will never forget my first day at school. Each cadet arrived with their parents, but I came alone—my mother was busy working and caring for my siblings, and my father was too frail. When I reached my dorm room, I found my roommates included the son of a police chief from a major city, the son of a chief engineer in the Military Corps of Engineers, and the son of the owner of Tel Aviv's largest retail store. I watched with envy as the other cadets were welcomed with baskets of fruit and cookies, tokens of love from parents reluctant to let their children go. Their puzzled glances fell on me when they noticed I had no one by my side. Nervous and uneasy, I sat on my bed, pulled the new blue blanket over my lap, and opened the Book of Psalms my mother had given me.

When the parents finally departed, the dormitory supervisor gathered us together. He laid out the code of honor, the discipline required, the mandatory assignments, daily drills, swimming schedules, and the standard of professionalism expected of anyone who hoped to graduate. We were shown photographs of former cadets who had gone on to become leaders in the Navy and in other military branches, reminders of the path we were expected to follow.

The disciplinary instructor for our class, Yehuda Gill, was in his mid-thirties and appeared in his white uniform, looking stern and intimidating. He laid out the rules, which we were required to repeat loudly and clearly. He instructed us to prepare for the daily run and swim. While most of my peers struggled to keep up, I completed the run, the march, and the swim with ease. I enjoyed the classes, the drills, the hours of rowing and sailing and learning to navigate the unpredictable sea.

CHAPTER NINETEEN

Soon, I noticed the cultural gaps among the cadets. Although the strong code of conduct reduced the sting of prejudice between those of European backgrounds and their counterparts from Arab countries, it did not eliminate the invisible walls of prejudice and stereotyping.

I found myself among intelligent and well-educated cadets who came from middle class families. I felt the need to master all aspects of naval training to stay ahead. I was compelled to prove that we were just as intelligent and capable and that our heritage was rich and powerful. We, too, had carried the flame for two thousand years. We, too, paid the price. We, too, were people without land. We, too, were strangers in our host countries, awaiting the day we would return to our ancient homeland, where we could cultivate the soil and build a nation that contributes to humankind.

However, this sentiment was not widely shared among the young cadets who were away from home for the first time. They assigned me unpleasant nicknames and often tried to intimidate me by shouting slurs. My years at the Fountain and my time at the agricultural school had helped me endure both physical and mental pain. I never responded; I simply looked back at them with a dismissive gaze.

In my new training, I witnessed the impact of rules that treated every follower equally—practices where merit and performance mattered more than family name or country of origin. At the naval academy, it didn't matter if you came from a wealthy or poor family, or whether your parents were from the West or the East, Germany or Libya. I saw the power of equality and its effects on meritocracy. Competition was fierce and discipline was strict. Excuses did not sway the faculty, who adhered to the same code of conduct. All the teachers were exceptional; they had mastered their subjects and knew how to present them effectively. Without exception, they were firm and demanding, expecting our full participation, beginning with homework that had to be submitted at the start of each class.

The system operated on what was known as the "point system". Every cadet started with one hundred points, and any violation of the code of conduct would result in a deduction of points. A cadet would be expelled if they lost more than sixty points. Each infraction carried a specific point deduction based on its severity. For example, smoking would result in a deduction of twenty-five points, incomplete homework would cost ten points, and a physical fight would lead to a loss of thirty points. Disobeying or showing disrespect to any staff member would result in a reduction of fifteen points. The rules were clear: compliance was the only option.

We had to balance physical activities such as swimming and sailing with rigorous academic studies and enhancing our expertise in ship building and navigation. That taught me the importance of structure and protocol, which I later applied when leading a naval school. It became my life's purpose to ensure that a diverse group of individuals from various cultures understood and applied the rules without favoritism. While the idea that rules are made to be broken may be thought-provoking, it only applies in certain cases.

One night, early in the school year, I reflected on all the changes I had experienced. My new life revitalized my weary soul. I embraced the sudden order and structure of the naval academy, with its set schedules for each day and the precise execution of those plans. I understood the importance of punctuality, the necessity of making my bed, the requirement to walk with proper posture, and the expectation to conduct myself with professionalism and mutual respect. I enjoyed every minute of it. I appreciated the transition from feeling lost to having a clear sense of direction, from never feeling on solid ground to hearing my steps echo in those heavy military shoes. For the first time in my life, I found myself in a place where command and control represented something more than merely submitting to tyranny.

At the Fountain, I was told what to do and lived under strict, arbitrary and at times cruel supervision, which made me feel anxious and frightened.

Conversely, at the farming school, most rules existed to protect us and our livestock. There, I mostly moved about with too little supervision. Each

CHAPTER NINETEEN

day, I woke up at three in the morning and walked the dark path to the sheep alone.

There were moments when I struggled with the darkness as I spent time alone with the sheep. I often missed home, my father's synagogue and studying the Bible. Life as a shepherd unfolded without any real order, except for the routine established by others. The lack of a library, the absence of books and limited classes heightened my thirst for learning about history, philosophy and other subjects typically covered in more academically oriented high schools. The agricultural school's mission was to train farmers, not academics.

However, in my new school, I found comfort in the rules and the structure they provided. The appealing rooms, comfortable beds, private desks, table lamps, uniforms, manicured lawns and academically demanding subjects—engineering, navigation, shipbuilding, history and the sounds of the waves—were all new, refreshing and somewhat intimidating.

There were moments when I considered staying in Ashkelon to become a plumber or a carpenter, believing it to be a clear and safe choice. Yet I was driven to prove to others that the power of the mind and the strength of one's will make life worthwhile, enabling us to lead lives that are more than mere existence. The willingness to confront challenges rather than retreating from them became my guiding principle. Through my work with others—encompassing teaching, lectures and workshops—I emphasize the necessity of changing ourselves first. Otherwise, it is all too easy to succumb to the dark voices that may arise in our minds.

I wondered if I had the stamina, courage and intellect to thrive in this new and challenging environment. I thought about my father, too old to walk to his synagogue; my mother, who was still working hard; and my younger siblings, who were without their eldest brother. I missed opening my father's volumes of sacred texts, a collection representing thousands of years of Jewish philosophy and wisdom. Although I missed my home, I knew I had chosen a different path—one that my ancestors, including my grandfather, the baker, and my father, the rabbi, could never have imagined. That night, as I lay in bed reflecting on what lay ahead, I felt ready. I was prepared to face whatever challenges came my way. Regardless of how frightening the changes might be, I was determined to learn, understand, adapt and fight.

And my determination to stand up for myself was tested that very night. Just after midnight, cadets from the senior class shook us awake and ordered us to get dressed and line up for a long walk. Later, I learned that it was a tradition for the senior class to "discipline" the incoming freshmen. They ordered us to run for three miles. Then, each freshman had to lower his head into a barrel of water filled with dead fish while they hit our backs with sticks. I remember grabbing hold of the long stick from the guy about to hit me. I dragged him toward me as I stared at him with loathing eyes. He punched me right on my nose. Outnumbered and woozy, I acquiesced to the absurd command. By the time we were released back to our dorms, it was almost four o'clock in the morning. We were dirty with mud, reeking of dead fish, my nose bleeding, and we were exhausted from the ordeal.

No one spoke a word. Later, I resolved to put an end to the tradition. During my junior year, after being elected president of the student association, my team and I met with the council and school administrators to argue for its termination. We insisted that such a practice had no place in an institution devoted to shaping great military officers and strong leaders. Instead, we proposed a new system: each senior cadet would mentor a first-year student, guiding them in understanding the school's mission and values.

The administration accepted our recommendation. They ruled that any attempt to harass a freshman would result in a severe penalty of twenty-five points—a punishment heavy enough to deter even the strongest supporters of the tradition. And so, the long-standing practice was finally abolished. After the meeting, I received rare words of praise from the superinten-

CHAPTER NINETEEN

dent, the very man who had championed my admission. As we walked out together, he told me how proud he was to see me engaged in student leadership and advocating for policies that mattered.

At the academy, however, the relentless pressure and competition proved unbearable for some. One cadet, in particular, struggled under the weight of constant ridicule from his peers. Soft-spoken and unable to withstand the turbulent environment, he faltered under the unyielding demands to perform. His lack of confidence, compounded by loneliness, wore him down. I remember his curly black hair, his faraway eyes, and the way he drifted through his days, most often alone.

It was lunchtime on a beautiful sunny day when he managed to get to the locked room where the rifles and guns we used for our training were stored. He pulled out a rifle and loaded it with bullets. He made his way to the end of the pier where he held the gun under his chin. It was a surrealistic sight carved in my memory. Within several minutes the cadets and the faculty gathered all around the pier watching this young boy holding the gun and warning everyone not to get close to him.

We watched as the chief disciplinary officer, Yehuda Gill, tried to get close to him and softly told him to put the rifle down. To our dismay, he pulled the trigger. He was thrown several feet away, his head nearly severed from his body, and blood pouring on the rocks. He lay there on those rocks before he was picked up by the crew who carried his body to the ambulance. The trauma left many of us numb, silent and confused. I was selected as one of the students to attend his funeral in his village near the city of Ashdod.

His mother refused to let the burial crew lower him into his grave. She clung to his body, pleading to be buried with him. As his body was being lowered, his mother yelled at us for not having the courage to stop him. I wanted to hold her in my arms but as a uniformed cadet I was forbidden from displaying my emotions. I stood there frozen.

On the way back, I sat in silence, reflecting on the fragility of life and the consequences of a lack of love. Later, when I became the head of the maritime academy, I insisted on holding weekly meetings with the cadets. I encouraged the staff to get to know the cadets, understand their stories, fears and needs.

We implemented a policy to assign a married couple, specializing in child psychology, as guardians for each dormitory. We were convinced that having two adults living alongside the cadets could provide better supervision with care and empathy. In many ways, these two supervising adults became like surrogate parents, and the relationships with the cadets lasted for many years after graduation.

As our daily routine settled in, I noticed that the heads of the dormitories displayed different leadership styles. The dormitory next to ours, which housed the sophomore class, had a strict, firm and straightforward leader. He held his cadets accountable and never allowed one to overpower another, either physically or mentally. His strong presence deterred any conflicts, and he motivated his charges toward outstanding performance and mutual respect. As a result, the sophomore class always seemed mature and professional.

In contrast, my dormitory supervisor, Shimon Teshuva, had a more laid-back approach. He was less visible and less involved, believing that we needed to learn to get along independently. Instead of strictly enforcing rules and correcting misbehavior, he chose to view conflicts as topics for discussion during our weekly meetings. Shimon was sensitive and held a strong belief that one shouldn't simply tell people what to do; rather, he aimed to help others find their own way.

Unfortunately, this hands-off approach led to disastrous results. A tradition known as "fair fight" thrived, in which conflicts were settled through fistfights. Because physical fighting incurred penalty points, these bouts took place in secret. After the lights went out and everyone was supposed to be in bed, the opponents would sneak out of their rooms with their friends and

CHAPTER NINETEEN

make their way to the beach. There, amidst the muffled sounds of the waves and cloaked in darkness, they would face each other like fierce roosters, throwing punches, kicks and applying chokeholds until one person either gave up or passed out. Once a winner emerged, he and his friends would quietly celebrate the victory as they walked back to the dorm, while the loser would be silently carried back by his friends.

Once again, for reasons I could not understand, I found myself facing hostility. I became a target for what were called "fair fights." Was it jealousy of my academic achievements? Was it my still unimpressive physique? Did they see the defiance in my eyes? I would never know.

On several occasions, without warning, a cadet would approach me, often with witnesses present, and challenge me to a fair fight. The informal code of conduct among cadets was straightforward: first, you could never decline a challenge; if you did, you would be labeled a coward for the rest of your days at the academy. Second, no member of the staff or faculty could be informed about these fights. Third, regardless of the outcome—no matter how wounded or bruised you were—there could be no snitches and no reporting.

The term "duel," which comes from ancient times and is now referred to as a "fair fight," originates from European traditions. This concept was foreign to the Arab-Jewish culture, which never encouraged physical fighting. The idea of scheduling a time to stand before another cadet and attempt to knock him out with my fists was strange to me. Each time I was challenged to a duel for seemingly no reason, I would walk to the beach alone. Those fights were short-lived; I was typically knocked out within a minute or two. I stood in front of my opponent, feeling helpless and bewildered. I had never learned how to fight or defend myself, nor had I ever thought self-defense would be necessary until that moment.

When the discipline officer, Yehuda Gill, offered weekly training in wrestling and aikido, I immediately signed up. Our group consisted of about two dozen cadets learning how to wrestle and defend ourselves. While my confidence grew and my skills improved, so did those of my opponents. After losing five fair fights, I began searching for a quicker and more effective way to combat an opponent.

During a weekend trip back home, I learned about a relative named Rachmanino, who worked as a lifeguard on the beach. He was a man of impressive strength, known for his ability to lift a camel on his shoulders. Rachmanino was from Tripoli, and I heard that some local gangs had tried to persuade him to serve as a bodyguard, but he refused. Despite his strength, he was a simple man with a great passion for his job, often referred to as the king of the beach as he watched over the waters from his lifeguard tower.

When I visited his home, his mother welcomed me with a delicious Libyan dish, shakshuka, made with eggs cooked in a flavorful tomato base and hot sauce.

Although Rachmanino had tall stature, broad shoulders and a tough physique, he was reserved and non-imposing. He loved the sea and supported his family by watching over the beachgoers.

I confided in him about my struggles. He advised me to learn how to use my forehead to quickly knock out anyone who tried to attack me. Following his guidance, I practiced breaking light branches with my forehead, solid wood and even simulated defenses against attackers. Over time, I developed a noticeable bump on the top of my forehead, almost like an invisible horn that could cause real damage to anyone who tried to provoke me.

As I honed this technique, I began winning fair fights. By my senior year at the academy, I had become the protector of anyone who felt threatened. Those who were bullied quickly learned they could call on me for help. I would take on their enemies as well as my own.

I had become a fighter, transitioning from the boy I once was, who would take abuse without any reaction. But this change required effort. I focused on building my skills, strength and intelligence to fight effectively

CHAPTER NINETEEN

and quickly. My time practicing grappling ended abruptly when my instructor grabbed me by the collar one day while I was dominating my opponent in class.

"Saada, this is a sport!" he yelled at me.

"To you, it is a sport. To me, it is survival," I replied.

That was the last time I attended the class. I realized that using my wits was my best option. I honed my skills by practicing on various tree branches, as it provided the quickest and most effective way to end fights. I never enjoyed the matches; if anyone wanted a fair fight, I aimed to finish it quickly. Chokeholds and swinging fists seemed like a waste of time. They only gave others the opportunity to invade my personal space, which I had come to see as sacred.

I didn't want anyone near my body. Instead, I would grab their heads and use mine against their foreheads, right between their eyes. Fights would conclude in seconds. This approach had nothing to do with cruelty; to me, fighting was about survival.

The challenges I faced began to wane, allowing me more time to enjoy life's deeper pleasures. On Israel's Independence Day, we had the day off and permission to go to Netanya, a vibrant city near our school. A friend and I made our way there to savor good food and a change of scenery. Dressed in our white uniforms and walking among the crowd, we spotted two girls at a vending booth selling aromatic fried dough.

The taller girl caught my attention. She had beautiful blue eyes that sparkled like the sea. Her brown hair cascaded over her shoulders, and her figure resembled waves rolling toward the shore. Her face radiated warmth and liveliness. We exchanged glances, both captivated. With a smile, I mustered the courage to approach and introduce myself. The four of us strolled along the busy street, munching on sunflower seeds and sipping soft drinks, filled with the youthful energy around us.

She was one year older than me, a top senior at her public school, already poised for a career in intelligence with the army. I was just a junior at the academy. I learned she lived in a nearby village with her Romanian parents, who had managed to escape Europe just in time to avoid persecution. Her father held a high position in the Israeli government.

After walking and talking for a mile, she signaled to her friend to leave with my classmate, and I found myself alone with her. Suddenly, I felt nervous and stumbled over my words. We reached the sandy beach, took off our shoes and walked barefoot on the hot sand. My mind raced with images of running into the water with her and swimming as far as we could. I entertained thoughts of holding her hand and walking along the shore, even imagining kissing her like in the movies. However, I also knew I had to keep my thoughts in check, fearing she might leave and take my dreams with her.

In just two hours together as total strangers, we shared things that we wouldn't dare discuss with family. I told her about myself, including my dreams of mastering navigation to one day command ships. With caution, I also opened up about my past struggles.

I could see from the corner of my eye that she was listening, sensing her empathy for my experiences. I shared my time at naval school and what I learned in self-defense. To my surprise, she took my hand in hers. My palm was sweaty, but I felt an undeniable connection that would remain with me for a long time. It taught me about the power of love and the importance of authentic bonds; without them, we roam aimlessly in the universe.

After that beautiful Independence Day, we agreed to continue seeing each other. Back then, we wrote letters to one another, and she was always on my mind. Once a month, usually on Saturday evenings, with permission from my dormitory supervisor, I would get five-hour leave. I would hitchhike to her village, which was fifteen miles away. She would come out of her home, and we would stroll in the dark among the orchard trees. We talked about her school, and how she was the only child in her family to escape the Holocaust.

CHAPTER NINETEEN

I did most of the listening during those evenings. Holding her hand filled me with joy, especially when she was willing to share an evening full of charm, her brown hair flowing down her petite shoulders. In her beautiful village, I forgot everything else—my family, my school, my past. I felt as if I melted in her arms. When we lay down on the warm soil, heated by the sun from earlier in the day, I would place my head on her chest. My heart raced faster than it did during my morning runs. Those evenings of walking together and knowing how much she desired me made my days worthwhile.

We often entered the football field, where we held each other tightly, kissing and touching each other as if it were the last time. Those were moments of pure happiness, and life suddenly seemed meaningful.

During vacations, I would take her to my home, where she met my family. I could see the shock in her eyes as she compared her beautiful house in the rolling hills, surrounded by orchards of orange and peach trees, to our old, worn home. In our house, she had to use a toilet in the corner, which was just a hole in the ground with no toilet paper—only a pitcher of water to wash herself. She never complained or looked down on me. Instead, she always wore a wonderful smile and remained kind to everyone. Unlike my own temperament, her amiable nature may explain why we managed to maintain a delicate relationship for over two years.

I was amazed at how well she got along with my mother; I recognized the same shy yet strong and mature character in her. She enjoyed watching my mother cook. She would hug us when we arrived and kiss us goodbye upon parting.

Despite this closeness, however, I felt ashamed of our differences. One day, as we walked out of the house toward the beach—where only the sound of the waves echoed in my ears—I felt the urge to end the relationship. Here there was someone from the elite class, accepting me as I was, a product of the underclass. I felt inadequate, and that feeling haunted me. In my heart, I understood then that nothing would come of this.

I decided to focus on my academic work and aimed to become a leading cadet to make my family proud. Instead of becoming a rabbi, I wanted to be a ship captain. I envisioned myself standing on the bridge of a ship, sensing its every move as well as the condition of the sea. I wanted to learn astronomy and how to determine the ship's position using the stars and the sextant, a navigational instrument invented in ancient China. From the command room of the vessel, I would maneuver these great ships over open water as if by magic. I also imagined commanding a racing boat with twelve cadets rowing in unison, learning how to harness the wind to sail our boats as far as Cyprus.

The sea became my playground, my secret lover. At night, I slipped into its darkness, immersing myself in its waters and discovering courage. I loved its shifting moods. Some mornings it lay still as glass, and days later it raged like a tiger, tearing through everything in its way. I often saw my own restless temperament mirrored in it. I believed it was God's invisible hand stirring the waves.

I loved its colors—the calm turquoise of quiet days, the gray and muddied tones of crashing surf. Its fury fascinated me even more than its peace. At night, the waves thundered like timpani in a grand crescendo, their rhythm calling me. On those nights, when I slipped from bed at midnight for a secret swim, it felt like meeting a lover, surrendering to a powerful and beautiful presence. In those moments, I felt wrapped in God's embrace. I wept, my tears disappearing into the ancient, tumultuous sea.

I graduated with the highest honor. Commencement was a day of reflection rather than celebration. Naval officers, commandos and skippers of war vessels filled the graduation field. Flags waved everywhere. I walked by the sea in my newly tailored naval uniform. Parents and grandparents arrived with bouquets of roses, and girls wore beautiful dresses, filling the yard with joy. I went to the field to meet my mother, who had arrived by bus with my sister. Although she seemed uncomfortable with the crowd, I could sense

CHAPTER NINETEEN

her pride in her uniformed son standing tall with a rare smile. After showing them to their seats, I left them to enjoy the parade and joined my fellow cadets to march into the field, loud drums echoing in the background and proud parents celebrating us.

I felt humbled when I was called to the stage to receive my diploma. I approached the superintendent—the man who had guided me to this moment, the one who saw potential in me that I couldn't see in myself. He was my angel. As I saluted him, I wanted to hug him to express my gratitude, but the protocol wouldn't allow it. Instead, with tears in my eyes, I said thank you, and he returned my salute. He resembled an old soldier saying one last farewell.

Holding my diploma and looking toward my mother and sister, I couldn't help but reflect on how changeable life could be. Standing before the crowd, I was only steps away from a painful, unforgettable past. I looked up at the sky and thought of my father praying back home and my mother, with her colorful scarf over her head, looking up to heaven and blessing me, as she always did until her last breath.

Chapter Twenty

STIRRING THE MELTING POT

One month after graduation, I was drafted into a bootcamp in southern Israel.

The first three months proved to be physically and mentally demanding. We woke up at four in the morning for a ten-kilometer run while carrying over forty pounds of gear. After the drill, we had only a few minutes to wash up before heading to the training field to learn how to shoot and accurately throw hand grenades.

Following the firearm training, we tackled an obstacle course that required stamina, critical thinking and, most importantly, teamwork. We were all drafted together, a solid class of cadets in boot camp. We faced the most unyielding officer. His tough demeanor pushed us to our limits. We ran every morning for miles, crossed obstacle fields filled with muddy water, learned to shoot, tossed hand grenades and found our way back to base alone in the isolated desert.

For the first time in my life, I witnessed the power of the IDF (Israel Defense Forces) to remove cultural barriers, ethnic differences, and various forms of prejudice. After years of doubt, I began to see this institution as a unique institution driven by merit and performance rather than ethnicity or skin color. Individuals were measured by their ability to withstand pressure and collaborate with others; penalties for racist remarks or conflicts resulted in severe punishment, followed by coaching sessions. I fell in love with the military's informal nature.

Unlike most other military forces worldwide, the IDF promotes an informal and direct communication style between commanders and soldiers. It is not unusual to see a general sharing a snack or coffee break with a group of soldiers or lower-ranking officers. The IDF is known as the "Army of the People," characterized by its casual atmosphere. Today, both men and women visibly carry their firearms in the streets or along highways, often hitchhiking to get rides home or back to base. This informality has significantly contributed to the IDF's successes in various wars since the establishment of the state. The easy flow of communication and minimal bureaucracy has made the organization a subject of study for scholars attempting to understand its accomplishments, both on the frontlines and as a genuine melting pot of Israel's diverse population.

From the age of eighteen, we trained, fought, socialized, and learned the fundamental aspects of teamwork. We worked as a cohesive unit, regardless of ethnicity, skin color or accent. An enlisted member from a European country whose parents survived the Holocaust had to rely on and trust members of his unit from Middle Eastern or North African countries and vice versa. Inclusivity extended to the Druze, a tribe in northern Israel, who have been staunch supporters of the country even before its establishment. Druze soldiers, known for their fierce fighting spirit, have also risen to high-ranking positions in the military.

In its early years, Israel grappled with the concept of integration. Nevertheless, the IDF was the only institution actively stirring the pot through its policies and practices. Once drafted, any recruit in the IDF could express a desire to learn and demonstrate the courage to take initiative. The IDF encouraged high school dropouts, primarily Sephardic Jews, to complete their basic education before being commissioned as officers. The doors were wide open for training and development. IDF became a pathway out of

CHAPTER TWENTY

obscurity, where potential talent could be nurtured and cultivated. The IDF was, and still is, one of the fiercest military forces that relies heavily on cooperation and collaboration among its units and recruits.

Here, I found myself. Once a shepherd in the desert, I now served as a full-fledged member of the Israeli Defense Forces. Contrary to what some political analysts believed, I was first assigned to the crew of the Navy's torpedo boats. Our role involved patrolling the coastline for invading terrorists. These torpedo boats, remnants of World War II, were made of wood and powered by robust Packard engines. Standing on the deck and watching the coastline from the sea was one of the most beautiful sights imaginable. Maintaining a naval ship is no small task. The work included consistently oiling the guns, inspecting the torpedoes and repainting the vessel regularly.

During my time in the Navy, I experienced a sense of freedom within the military structure for the first time while things outside remained unchanged. Discrimination and racism persisted. I was still dating the woman I had met during my years at the Naval Academy. She had also joined the military, serving as an intelligence officer. Her quick mind, composed demeanor, and charm were essential to her new role. Unfortunately, our schedules made it difficult for us to see each other as often as we wanted. One Friday night, when we were both available, she mustered the courage to invite me to her parents' home for Shabbat dinner.

I arrived at her home in a beautiful settlement near Netanya, a city known for its significant population of Libyan Jews. As I parked my motorcycle and walked to the house, I noticed her father standing at the entrance. She came out to greet me, but her expression was stern. Her father signaled for her to return inside with a sharp hand gesture. She obeyed, leaving the door open as she watched her father approach me. We shook hands, and he commented on the beauty of the approaching Shabbat evening, inviting me to join him for a cup of coffee at a nearby café. Shocked and bewildered, I agreed and rode with him to the coffee shop, where I ordered a Turkish coffee while he requested tea. This was early afternoon.

Without a preamble, he told me that she was his only child, and he was concerned about her relationship with me after two years. I responded by praising her intelligence and wonderful qualities, but my words had little impact on him. He was focused on expressing his desire for me to end my romantic involvement with his daughter, citing our cultural differences as his primary concern. He asked if I would be willing to stop seeing her. I remained silent for a long moment.

When I asked what he meant by our cultural differences, he replied, "You come from an Arab country where women are not treated the same way as in European countries." Internally I was fuming as I was reflecting on how my father treated my mother with the utmost respect and love. Instead, I looked at him and responded that I was only three years old when I arrived in Israel, that I was the son of a well-known rabbi, that I was serving in the Israeli Defense Forces, and that my love and respect for his daughter were genuine. I mentioned that she had visited my parents' home numerous times over the years and enjoyed being with us. I added that she loved my mother and felt more comfortable with us than with her own community.

None of my words seemed to sway him. He had come with a clear mandate: He wanted me out of his daughter's life and out of his mind. I could only stare at him, my blood boiling within me. I wondered if I should feel angry at his prejudice or respond with patience and tolerance.

I suppressed my emotions and asked him if he had ever visited a military cemetery. He replied that he had attended several funerals of fallen soldiers from his village. I expressed my hope that he would never have to bury any members of his family. I then invited him to join me at the nearest military cemetery, reminding him that the gates would soon close for Shabbat.

We drove there silently, and I sensed his discomfort with my request. I wondered if he understood my intention. Upon arrival, the cemetery was quiet, as Jews do not visit cemeteries on the eve of Shabbat until Sunday

CHAPTER TWENTY

morning. We walked into the serene space, filled with simple gravestones that all looked alike. In a trembling voice but with a commanding tone, I said to him, "Let's walk through the gravestones and try to determine if the names carved on these stones are from European, Australia, Canada, America, Middle Eastern or North African countries."

His face changed color. At that time, many immigrants had yet to modernize their names. However, names like Rosenberg, Rothman and Eisenberg were unmistakably European Jewish. On the other hand, names like Hakim, Saadia, Haddad, Buzaglo, Azran, Hassan and Vaknin originated from countries like Yemen, Morocco, Libya and Egypt. Holding my anger deep in my throat, I pointed out that there were just as many young men from Arab-speaking countries as from European nations. If we are equal in death, having paid the ultimate price, why should we be treated differently while building a new nation?

"Here in this eternal place," I said, "these young boys from the four corners of the world paid the ultimate price to build one nation, one union and one Israel for all. Here we are all equal."

Back in the car, he seemed more comfortable with me. He told me that my empathy touched him deeply. Finally, he shared that it had been his wife's wish for him to have this conversation with me. I felt saddened by the unfair and unacceptable prejudice exercised by the very victims of the terrible Holocaust. It became clear to me that the struggle of Sephardic Jews would continue for many years to come. I realized that it might take two or three generations for the differences to fade and for people to forget where each other's grandparents came from. I have always believed that over time the differences will melt away and mixed marriages will eventually erase cultural boundaries creating one nation, one state, all equal in this old new land.

Before we parted ways, I looked at him—both annoyed and empathetic—and told him I would honor his request and would explain to his daughter his request. We shook hands, and instead of going into her home with him, I walked back to my motorcycle and drove away. That evening, I wrote her a lengthy letter explaining the factors and the reasons for us to separate.

Later, I learned from one of the crew members on the torpedo boat, who lived in her village, that she took my departure with great sadness and despair. Three months later, she surprised me at a bus station as I headed home for the New Year celebration. She opened her arms, hugged me, kissed me with a smile I would never forget, and whispered a final goodbye in my ear.

Her departure left a void in my heart, and I sank into a sea of melancholy. I stopped talking to my peers and spent most of my time alone. Out of nowhere, I became preoccupied with my acne, constantly trying to scratch the pimples off my face. I was surprised that these annoying pimples became such a concern. Later, I learned that trivial preoccupations often accompany depression and melancholy.

As a seaman, I knew that seawater and salt could cause constant oxidation that would quickly wear away a ship's foundation if it wasn't properly maintained. We would use anti-rust acid to make scraping off the rust easier. The acid would sizzle and bubble as we worked. I don't know what got into my head, but watching the sizzling paint melt upon contact with the acid gave me an insane idea.

I used to squeeze my pimples, which only led to more marks and additional breakouts. My mother would advise me to wash my face and be patient, explaining that it was just a matter of time until I grew out of it. However, for a young man in uniform dealing with severe acne, it felt like a monumental issue. Frustrated with my situation, I decided to take matters into my own hands.

One day, I visited a paint store, locked the heavy metal door behind me, dipped a cotton ball into anti-rust acid, closed my eyes, and applied it to my face. I could hear the acid sizzle on my skin, reminiscent of its reaction

CHAPTER TWENTY

with rust. I screamed, though no one was there to hear me. The experiment lasted about half an hour, but my face remained raw for several days afterward. To my surprise, I began receiving compliments about my skin two weeks later. When people asked about my secret, I replied, "Anti-rust." Admitting it to my unconventional remedy didn't seem wise, as I wouldn't recommend it; it could have resulted in severe burns. However, in a way, the burning sensation, the rawness of my skin and the pain felt like a therapeutic baptism, cleansing me of memories of my failed romance. Despite the physical discomfort and the psychological wounds, my acne never returned.

In the military, it wasn't uncommon for enlisted soldiers to question or challenge their commanders. Mine was a fair man and a true role model in my eyes. He had experienced suffering first-hand, having escaped the Nazis in Germany and joined the partisans to fight for the Jewish cause. During a mission to enter enemy territory, I noticed that his chosen strategy involved what I considered unnecessary risk. I suggested a less risky alternative, and to my surprise, he listened and changed his approach. We returned to base successfully, accomplishing the mission without casualties.

One of the Navy's key requirements for being on deck was to have a perfect vision without correction. Although I passed all the tests, I ultimately failed the eye exam, which revealed that my vision was defective. This discovery marked the end of my career on naval vessels; however, I was presented with several options and the one that appealed to me most was becoming a faculty member at the newly established Maritime School south of Ashdod.

Following the Six-Day War, Israel urgently needed to strengthen its naval presence in both the Mediterranean and the Red Sea, necessitating the training of a new cadre of naval architects. Israel needed additional academies to prepare young men and women to become agile sea warriors. Before the war, France had been a major supplier of Mirage fighter planes and specially designed missile boats crafted by Israeli engineers and built in French shipyards. After the Six-Day War victory, Arab nations-imposed restrictions on oil exports to any country supporting Israel, and many countries, including France, followed suit by imposing an arms embargo against Israel. Although Israel had financed the construction of six missile boats from France, the sudden embargo prevented us from acquiring these crucial vessels. In a secret operation, Israel managed to send six naval crews to France with the mission of sailing those boats back to Israel. This daring endeavor involved breaking into the French naval base at La Havre at night and maneuvering the boats out. Later, it became known that the French Navy had collaborated with the Israeli government to enable us to complete the operation.

One of the most lasting lessons from the navy was the notion that sailing a line from point A to point B is never a straight line. Facing strong headwinds, high waves and dangerous tides, we learned to zig zag toward point B. Life is very much like sailing the ocean. We need to learn how to face the storm and navigate our journey despite all obstacles.

Faced with threats from the north, south, and east, the Israeli Defense Forces (IDF) recognized the sea as Israel's only open frontier. These open waters provided significant opportunities for building a strong and effective naval force. Visionary leaders understood the necessity of expanding the Navy, which at the time was smaller than the world's most renowned air force, commando units, or elite paratroopers.

With only two naval academies in the country, naval leaders determined that expanding our maritime capabilities needed to begin with the design and establishment of additional maritime schools. These schools would aim to attract and prepare a new generation of Israeli naval officers to enhance Israel's naval capabilities.

They assembled a team to establish a naval branch in a flourishing youth village south of Ashdod. When the opportunity arose for me to join this team, I was excited to take on this new chapter, which would lay the foundation for my future as an educator.

Chapter Twenty-One

FORCING THE WINDS ON THE SAIL

My mission, along with that of other officers and administrators, was driven by the vision of building a new maritime school from the ground up to prepare engineers and deck officers for both the Navy and the Merchant Marine. After all, the sea has always represented the only open horizon to the rest of the world.

The village of Nitzanim, occupying a prime location near the sea, was located near the newly and rapidly growing city of Ashdod destined to become the largest seaport in Israel. The village of Nitzanim became an excellent location for the new school. There, the government constructed dormitory buildings to house the first class of fifty cadets. Each room contained four beds, a desk and a closet for each cadet. We collaborated with a landscaping crew to recreate the grounds of my previous academy, planting trees, shrubs and grass to create a welcoming and natural atmosphere. Naval units donated sailboats for training, and the government financed the cadets' expenses. There was a palpable sense of excitement in the entire team.

Many young and talented recruits preferred to join the larger, more prestigious military units. The dream of becoming a pilot or wearing the Red Berets drew the best of Israel's youth. Since our program was still new, we had to go out and actively recruit boys and girls for the first class of 1970. We visited development towns where unemployment was high and school dropouts were common. We also connected with the Jewish Agency, which was bringing in young people from countries such as Morocco, Argentina, and Romania.

On opening day, when the recruits arrived, we greeted them with biscuits and lemonade. Their faces carried a mixture of hope and unease, the excitement of stepping into the unknown tempered by the weight of uncertainty. As I looked at them, I recognized pieces of myself in each one of those young cadets. I committed then to transforming them into proud individuals devoted to public service.

At first, they appeared unsure of themselves. Their movements were hesitant, their posture unsteady. The separation from their families weighed heavily on them, and I understood how difficult it was to leave home behind. My task was clear: to help them grow stronger by instilling in them the values of discipline, structure, vision, and self-worth.

We divided each dormitory into separate sides for girls and boys. Each dormitory building included an attached apartment for the supervisor, whose role was to ensure that the cadets' well-being adhered to established protocols and policies. I chose to live in the apartment next to one of the dorms. By being close to the cadets, I was able to merge my supervisory role with their need for nurturing and care. Right there, I recognized the importance of authentic leadership. When leaders are focused on the mission while demonstrating genuine compassion, their team will follow them with conviction and commitment.

The first step in addressing the newcomers was to unite them as a cohesive team, not by instilling fear and anxiety, but by appealing to their hearts and helping them see the strength of one team driven by a shared dream.

On the first night of their arrival, I woke them up just after midnight with the sound of a bell we had transferred from an old ship. I told the

CHAPTER TWENTY-ONE

confused recruits to get dressed for a long run. Despite their shock, every cadet was ready outside the dormitory just a few minutes later. In the darkness, under a half-moon, I spoke to them about the importance of being physically fit and mentally healthy. My tone was firm and demanding as I explained that this exercise would become a daily habit. Here, I learned that leaders are apart from their teams but an integral part of the people they lead. It is not about talking to them but walking the talk as a clear demonstration of caring and compassion. As the famous Chinese Sun Tzu , the author of the Art of the War wrote that when there is harmony between the leaders and their followers, they will be willing to sacrifice everything they have.

As we started with a fast walk that gradually increased at pace, they all complied. One of the cadets began singing a marching song, and soon, everyone followed suit. That night run helped to forge connections among these young people from all over the world, encouraging them to think and act as one team dedicated to fulfilling the dream envisioned by their ancestors. As we ran the long course along the sea, I could hear their huffing and puffing, blending with the sound of the breaking waves, and I saw my father's face before me, bearing a rare smile of blessing and approval.

"One for all and all for one," I assured them, borrowing a phrase I had learned from my commanding officer. As we ran along the hills and the beach, the surrounding darkness, their shared task and the novelty of the experience created a sense of excitement. I noticed one cadet struggling to keep up with the group, so I ordered everyone to stop and sit in a circle on the sand to rest. This moment of vulnerability was an opportunity, and I seized it. Sitting by the sea, I encouraged them to share their stories, fears and aspirations. Still breathing heavily, they listened attentively to each other's narratives. I witnessed the beginning of their transformation into a team composed of individuals who genuinely cared for one another. On the way back, we walked in silence, reflecting on the personal stories they had shared with a group of strangers who would ultimately become lifelong friends. For many of them, it was likely the first time they felt a sense of purpose and belonging.

The days at the new school were structured and disciplined. Each morning began with making beds, followed by washing up, running three kilometers, conducting drills and raising the flag. After breakfast, we headed to the sea, where they learned to swim, rescue others and row harmoniously. They needed to feel comfortable in the water and develop a love for the sea, adapting to its changing moods. They also learned to repair various pieces of naval equipment and navigate a boat in stormy conditions. After lunch, they had a break to wash up and dress for their afternoon classes in literature, mathematics, English, navigation and world history.

I would occasionally visit classes unannounced to ensure that the cadets were learning, taking notes, completing their assignments and behaving like future officers. I shared with them our vision: to graduate each of them without a single dropout or discharge. Together with the instructional team, we created an environment where the entire class was responsible for everyone's performance. If one cadet misbehaved, the whole class faced consequences, such as canceling a movie night or losing a free evening in town. I was pleased to see how they came together as a team. These challenging experiences fostered a sense of cohesiveness and unity that lasted throughout their military service and beyond.

Within three months, most cadets became disciplined and committed to their education and the sea. By the end of their first year, we managed to take the entire class sailing on one of the Israeli naval vessels to Marseille, France. The long voyage enhanced their skills in engine maintenance, painting, scraping rust, cleaning and serving as lookouts on the bridge. The warm reception from the crew, representatives of the French Navy, and the Jewish community made the cadets feel proud and important as they took part in various ceremonies and enjoyed wonderful food. Watching them interact with members of the Jewish community and other officials in their white

CHAPTER TWENTY-ONE

uniforms reinforced my belief that what I was doing was worthwhile, and I cherished every moment. Seeing those cadets, marching in their white uniforms with a great deal of pride convinced me of the power of education in transforming individuals and organizations.

On the return journey from Marseille, we took several opportunities to reflect on the experience, with each cadet committing the vision of becoming an officer and a public servant. I remember the excitement on their faces as they shared their moments of walking in their white uniforms, representing the new state of Israel.

Upon returning to Haifa, we expanded our program from two classes of thirty-five cadets each to three classes. We needed to increase our outreach. One of our best recruiters was a teacher named Yehoshua Geta. He was six feet tall, handsome and engaging. He was known for riding his motorcycle to school every day. Legend had it that he had made his way to Jerusalem on horseback, donkeys and camels, crossing the borders of Libya and Egypt. He traveled along the coastline, passing through Alexandria and El Arish on his long journey to Israel. Yehoshua had served as the bodyguard to David Ben-Gurion, Israel's first prime minister. Educated in France, he was well-versed in philosophy and the classics. Yehoshua spoke eloquent French and could cite poems in Arabic. He was tough yet respected and loved by the cadets, who enjoyed listening to his stories of his journey from Tunisia to Israel.

We became close friends. Sometimes, we would venture into the neighboring towns for a scrumptious meal or to recruit a juvenile delinquent or a school dropout. My mother loved him and always had a Libyan dish ready for him. Despite having left behind his parents and home country of Tunisia, he always smiled, even when he complained about discrimination against the Sephardic Jews. One day, he didn't show up for class. I quickly sensed that something was wrong. He had diabetes, but he had never taken any medication or adjusted his diet to renounce sweet pastries like baklava and fried dough coated with sugar and honey.

I drove to his home in Ashkelon. His motorcycle was parked by his tidy garden. When no one answered the door, I broke in, only to be confronted with the awful smell of a decomposing body and the sight of my friend lying on the sofa with the book he had been reading before his heart stopped.

The loss weighed heavily on me. Like many others, I admired this extraordinary man who had been passionate about teaching and doing good. People from around the country came to his funeral, including military officers, friends and students. I had my cadets prepare a military procession for him. With their white uniform and rifles on their shoulders, they marched him to his final resting place in Ashkelon's cemetery.

The Chief Rabbi of Ashkelon delivered a deeply touching sermon. He said, "We never know the true height of the tree until it is cut down; only then, when the tree is laid down, do we truly know how tall it was." Yes, he was a tall man of significant impact. I learned then how fragile life can be. My thesis advisor at Harvard, Professor Badi Foster, used to say, "Life is an unguaranteed loan and can be called back by the Maker anytime without any warning or early announcement."

After that, I worked relentlessly to convince authority figures in the Ministry of Education that the naval school should operate as a four-year institution instead of three. In those days in Israel, high schools fell into two categories. The first and most prestigious academic route consisted of four-year schools. Students took the matriculation exam in their senior year to be accepted into universities. The least desired way was the three-year option, better known as the vocational high school, after which graduating students received a diploma disregarded mainly by the universities. Most Sephardic students attended the vocational three-year high school, while the Ashkenazic children filled the four-year schools that assured their university admission. More than 80 percent of the student body in primary schools came from a Sephardic background. By twelfth grade, 90 percent of the

CHAPTER TWENTY-ONE

graduates were of Ashkenazic origin. As a result, through the sixties, seventies and eighties, all universities accepted almost exclusively students whose parents came from Europe or North America.

At school, most of us viewed this educational cycle as unfair and unethical. The new nation was heading toward an infrastructure built on three levels: the Europeans, whose social status assured them the power; the Sephardic Jews as the second-class group to occupy all blue-collar positions; and the Israeli Arabs, who had the least opportunities to merge into the new society.

In meetings with representatives from the Ministry of Education, I faced criticism for my disruptive views on what I regarded as discrimination and mistreatment. The struggle was intense and, at times, demoralizing. Despite my efforts to extend the new naval school to a four-year program, I was unsuccessful. I believed that cadets should complete a fourth year to qualify for matriculation, which would open the doors to universities. However, the Ministry of Education had a different perspective.

My battle ended after an emotional meeting with the Inspector General of the Ministry of Education, who made it clear that without a college degree, I had very little credibility when discussing education. Following that meeting, I realized it was time for me to pursue my education after three years at the new school. Although it was painful to leave everything behind, I decided to resign myself to pursue my college education. I recognized then that education is the most powerful vehicle to get a meaningful break from poverty and prejudice.

The realization that I was leaving the very school I had helped create filled me with feelings of remorse and sadness. However, I recognized that it was essential for me to obtain my college education and avoid the trap of becoming stagnant in my career. In retrospect, I refused to live a vertical life. I made up my mind that getting education and using it to empower others was my calling and aspiration. In many ways it was the process of shifting from being a rabbi to becoming a teacher.

I returned to my apartment to pack my belongings and gathered the cadets during lunchtime to inform them of my decision to continue my education. They lined up to wish me well, expressing how much I had impacted on their lives and futures. I then departed from the school, leaving behind the cadets and the beautiful sea, and headed back to my mother's home to share my decision with her.

Chapter Twenty-Two

RECOVERING IN DENMARK

It was difficult to leave my life behind—yet my desire to explore, to learn, and continue investing in my development couldn't be denied. I learned then that when one's vision is clear, the inner power of finding ways to reach the target becomes not only clear but also feasible.

I decided to study naval architecture, becoming a designer of new and revolutionary naval vessels. I considered schools in cities like Stockholm, Glasgow and Copenhagen, all known for their reputable naval architecture programs. Ultimately, I chose Denmark.

Denmark is renowned for having protected its entire Jewish community from the Nazis. It has a history of tolerance, exemplified in the legend of its king, who wore the Jewish star during the Nazi invasion, as well as tales of heroic individuals who helped Jews escape to neutral Sweden aboard fishing boats, saving them from the invaders. The Jewish community holds immense admiration for the Danes who risked their lives to save the Jews of Denmark.

I applied to Elsinore Shipbuilding Technical School, and once accepted, I left Israel in August 1968 for Copenhagen. At the airport, I was greeted by one of the engineers, who drove me to the beautiful city of Elsinore, known for Hamlet's Castle. Nestled by the sea and only a few miles from Malmö, Sweden, it offered tranquility and beauty. The locals were generally calm and content, in stark contrast to the louder, angrier people back in Ashkelon.

Instead of a dorm, I was offered a place in one of the most beautiful homes in Elsinore, owned by a famous Danish national photographer named Mrs. Louis Larsen. She was highly admired in town and gained national recognition when her exquisite photograph of Hamlet's Castle was selected as the best image of the castle and printed on the five-kroner bill. Having lost her husband several years earlier, she found herself alone in her beautiful home and decided to call the school to offer her place to an international student. During the sixties, there was hardly any demand for international students in Denmark, and I was the only one accepted; thus, the admissions staff felt it would be best for me to take her up on the offer. It felt like a gift from heaven.

Entering Mrs. Larsen's estate remains one of the most memorable moments of my life. A cobbled path led to the Victorian house, surrounded by a rose garden with flowers hanging from several lattices and fragrant apple trees. A riot of colorful flowers covered the manicured lawn, creating a paradise-like image. In contrast, I reflected on the dismal appearance of my city, Ashkelon, which had filthy streets, open sewer lines infested with rodents, and dogs and cats covered in ticks everywhere. I thought I must be dreaming.

Mrs. Larsen welcomed me with a glass of lemonade, a warm smile and Danish cookies as I entered the house. I stood in that beautiful living room, with its Steinway piano, impressive paintings and an air of tranquility. Here I was, a young man surrounded by everything I desired but could not have. Mrs. Larsen was an elegant older woman filled with pride, grace and trust in someone she had never met before.

She led me to the second floor, where she had prepared a bedroom. It featured an old-fashioned bed, a personal bathroom, a desk with an empty bookshelf and a large vase of flowers from her garden. I was in awe.

Her voice broke the silence when she said in beautiful, clear English, "My young and handsome man, you must be tired. Rest, and at six, we will

CHAPTER TWENTY-TWO

have dinner together."

From upstairs, I gazed out at the tranquil garden and thought about how much we had lost back home. I imagined how wonderful life could have been if my family had experienced even a fraction of the beauty I was witnessing there. Everything seemed so far away, and I felt reborn. I closed my eyes and fell asleep on the sofa.

I woke up to the beautiful sound of piano music playing downstairs. After washing up, I went to the living room, where Mrs. Larsen played the piano and the housemaid set the dinner table. Both women spoke perfect English, and I was comfortable enough with the language to communicate with them. Whenever the housemaid switched to Danish, Mrs. Larsen kindly reminded her to speak English. This became my home and refuge for the entire year to come. Every day after school or at the shipyard, Mrs. Larsen would play the piano, and during our delicious dinners, she taught me to speak Danish. It was the highlight of almost every day in Elsinore. The time spent with Mrs. Larsen taught me the physical boundaries and geographical borders melt down when it comes to the power of love and compassion.

I took an intensive Danish course while working at a large shipyard near Hamlet's Castle. My technical training consisted of two months in the shipyard and one month at school. My time at the shipyard included working in the drafting room, where I learned conventional and unique methods, such as helium welding. I shadowed engineers and architects during their meetings with suppliers, clients and union representatives.

One day, after welding all day and feeling frustrated with my eye protection shield, I returned home with dry, painful eyes. Blinking became difficult due to the dryness. I lay in my room, trying to avoid making any sounds of discomfort. I remember Mrs. Larsen calling an ambulance to take me to the hospital to flush my eyes. We were there for more than four hours, and she stood by me the entire time, holding my hand with a smile I will never forget. Her presence made the entire staff very attuned to my situation.

Being the only foreigner at the shipyard subjected me to much curiosity from the Danish workers. I got to know them, joined them for dinners at their homes with their families, and attended special services at their beautiful old churches. Sitting in the classroom with other Danish students was a treat of friendliness and acceptance. I fell in love with the design of ships and other commercial vessels. We used traditional drafting methods then, including a tall draft table, high stool, large paper scroll, ruler, pencil and eraser.

My project at the shipyard was to design a commercial ship from scratch. I spent more than six weeks, including weekends, working on it. I had to post several blueprints on the walls for a committee of three engineers to inspect. The weekend before the Monday morning presentation was intense, filled with many sleepless nights as I reviewed and redesigned the blueprints. Mrs. Larsen stayed with me all night, serving coffee and pastries while playing music in the background. Despite being over seventy years old, she provided me with an incredible love that was given without expectations or conditions.

I learned then that true love knows no boundaries and no age. The heart can be sparked at any time by an act of kindness and grace.

On Monday, I was thrilled when the three engineers approached my blueprints hanging on the wall. They looked at them silently for a moment before bursting into wild laughter. I didn't know how to respond until they explained that I was a descendant of the Vikings in both English and Danish. I took them seriously and shared that my roots were in Spain and North Africa, which only made them laugh even more.

I realized that I had designed a full-fledged ship without bathrooms or toilets, much like the Vikings who used to relieve themselves over the ship's side. Although my design was passed with a minor change, I walked home feeling both satisfied and disappointed for overlooking such an essential

CHAPTER TWENTY-TWO

detail. Upon my arrival, Mrs. Larsen was waiting for me at the gate with a rose and a cold bottle of champagne.

After dinner, we lay next to each other on the sofa, her head resting on my shoulder as we listened to music. For the first time in a long time, I felt safe and secure and wondered if we were in love. That night, I learned an important lesson that guided me throughout my life: wealth and fame do not guarantee satisfaction. Finding a purpose in life and being in a psychologically safe environment can uplift one's spirit, reminding us that life is precious and often beautiful when all is said and done.

Living in Denmark made me contemplate the nature of its people, whose courage was unmatched by any other European nation. They managed to smuggle their entire Jewish population onto fishing boats, taking them to Sweden under the cover of darkness. Where did such courage come from? Why didn't other nations follow their example? What was it about the Danes that gave them the bravery to defy the Nazis' orders to turn over the Jews?

During the weekends, I traveled throughout the country in a small Fiat I had purchased from a local dealership. I spent much time in Copenhagen and ventured into Sweden, visiting Stockholm and Malmo. I took a ferry to Oslo, enjoying every trip and every visit. These experiences allowed me to see and understand the character of the Scandinavian people and their aspiration to live peacefully with others. The tranquil landscape was so unlike the place I had left. Whereas life in Scandinavia was serene, I had come from a place filled with external and internal enemies.

During one of my trips to Odense, I met an incredible woman named Ruth Rasmussen. Ruth was a Holocaust survivor. At the outset of the war, when she was fourteen, her parents put her on a train leaving Berlin for Copenhagen. She was protected by a family friend who lived in the old town of Odense.

Ruth later married a Danish entrepreneur who built one of the most sophisticated radiators. They had two beautiful children and a retreat home by the ocean. Despite her painful background and limited knowledge of Judaism, I became a good family friend to them. Her non-Jewish husband offered her all the love she had been deprived of after losing her parents in one of the concentration camps. She grew to love her heritage and made several trips to Israel. I enjoyed relaxing times with her family, spending time doing enjoyable activities with their children and two dogs.

During our hikes with her kids, Ruth shared the horrible experiences she endured after being separated from her parents. Like many other survivors, she had resorted to silence about her past. She told me she never discussed her experiences as a young girl in Berlin during the war. Her new life in Denmark, filled with her loving husband and children, helped her avoid dwelling on those painful memories. However, as I shared my narrative with her, she opened up. Tears streamed down her face as she recalled the traumatic nights and days she had to endure to survive. Her entire family was sent to Auschwitz, their home in Berlin was ransacked, and the precious artwork her parents had accumulated over the years was stolen, never to be found again. In that moment, I reflected on the stark contrast between her nightmares and Denmark's serene, beautiful landscape.

My year in Denmark taught me much about art, architecture and the importance of maintaining a harmonious relationship with nature. I learned to trust again and connect with others. For the first time, I didn't have to worry about anything—neither my siblings, nor the Minister of Education nor my cadets. It was an incredibly healing time for me. I began to understand the power of recovery; it's a time to set everything else aside, including those we love the most. Taking a break from the burdens of life is essential for healing.

Although I missed my cadets and family dearly, being away from the intensity and pressures of life in a stress-ridden country felt like a blessing. Denmark, with its beautiful landscapes, caring people, peaceful relations with every nation and relaxed way of life was like a breath of fresh air in a

CHAPTER TWENTY-TWO

suffocating basement. Among the Danish people, it felt warm and inviting.

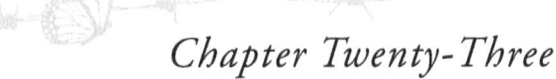

Chapter Twenty-Three

EVENTS BEYOND OUR CONTROL

By the end of the academic year at Elsinore, I was missing my family and my cadets. I decided to return home and spend the summer in Israel.

On the plane from Copenhagen to Tel Aviv, I sat next to a vivacious woman from Los Angeles who was making her first trip to Israel. Her name was Gail Weiner, and she was the daughter of a Jewish businessman from Philadelphia. She chose to visit Israel for her summer vacation, feeling that exploring the land of her ancestors might provide her with some respite from her restlessness.

At 25, Gail was a hematologist working in one of the hospitals in Los Angeles. She felt increasingly dissatisfied with her life there, and her friends suggested that a trip to Israel might alleviate her stress. We immediately liked each other. Gail was open about her life in America, expressing her yearning for a place with purpose and meaning. She had read extensively about Judaism and Israel and was aware of the socio-economic differences among various factions within Israeli society. Despite her vulnerability, she possessed a strong inner resilience. I, too, shared my life experiences and struggles with her. Our conversation flowed easily, and I found myself drawn to her natural happiness and unburdened spirit.

The six-hour journey felt like the fastest I had ever experienced. It's fascinating how two strangers can discuss topics they might never broach with family or friends. Gail's sense of humor and bubbly personality were refreshing, and I felt emotions I had never encountered before.

Without hesitation, as we landed and made our way to collect our luggage, I invited her to stay with my family in Ashkelon. She accepted my invitation eagerly and asked me to cancel her hotel reservation in Tel Aviv. After renting a car, we continued our conversation on the drive to Ashkelon. When we arrived home, my mother and siblings were taken by surprise.

Gail brought her smile, her warmth and her curiosity; I brought the story of how we had just met. My mother and family seemed pleased to have a new visitor. During her stay, Gail developed a love for Libyan cuisine and helped my mother during the long hours of cooking. We traveled throughout the country, from the Golan Heights down to the Dead Sea. We visited the agricultural school and the sheep herd I had worked with for over two years. My mother took a liking to Gail and whispered in a mix of half-Italian, Arabic and some English that we should get married. The thought of marrying someone I had known for only three weeks felt strange to me. Yet, many aspects of her personality left a strong impression on me.

Gail had a zest for life and a deep curiosity for learning. She made my mother laugh, playfully teased me about my intensity, engaged with strangers and demonstrated compassion for those in need—qualities that drew me to her. What impressed me the most was how comfortable she felt in our old home. Despite the thick walls, the presence of mice, the hole in the ground that served as a toilet, the lack of hot water, and the absence of air conditioning—all amenities she was used to in Los Angeles—Gail adapted remarkably well to the changes in her lifestyle.

As her departure for Los Angeles approached, I felt anxious about not seeing her again. What were the odds that I would ever meet her again? At the same time, I thought that marrying a loving, compassionate woman who

CHAPTER TWENTY-THREE

paid me undivided attention could help my restless soul find some stability. Seeing how my siblings were motivated by her care and witnessing my mother's laughter for the first time made the idea appealing. After all, my mother had once reminded me that she fell in love with my father at first sight. So, proposing after three weeks didn't seem out of the question.

I proposed on a hot summer day during the last week of August 1969, before Gail returned to Los Angeles. It was by the Wailing Wall in Jerusalem. As we exited this sacred place, I asked her to marry me, and Gail accepted with tearful eyes. However, on the way home from the airport, I started to question my decision after saying goodbye to her. Did I do the right thing? Was I ready for married life? What would I do about my studies in Denmark?

The new marriage excited me and instilled a sense of promising stability. Coming from a different cultural background, Gail accepted and enjoyed mine. The Libyan dishes, the loud voices, the visibly expressed emotions, and the commotion during disagreements—behaviors often stereotyped in Israeli society—became a source of joy for her.

While Gail was in Los Angeles preparing to leave everything behind and join me in Israel, I had my hands full with a long list of activities. I spoke with Rabbi Chaim Sharvit, a good friend of my father's, who agreed to officiate the ceremony and give blessings. I arranged for our wedding to take place in the newly erected synagogue at the naval academy, with two rows of my former cadets in their white uniforms. I also called the school in Denmark to inform them that I would skip the Fall semester and return in January with my newly wedded wife.

I rented a beautiful house in the countryside, near Ashkelon, to celebrate our new life together. Using my savings, I purchased an old BMW to explore the country's beauty together. And in smooth Danish, I called Mrs. Larsen and explained that I had met a wonderful woman, and we were getting married.

After a long silence, I could sense her sadness. I promised her that I would return with Gail to continue my studies by Christmas. However, two months later, the engineer who introduced me to her wrote to inform me that she had passed away.

On the day Gail landed from Los Angeles via New York, I was beside myself with excitement. She walked toward me with her beautiful smile and open arms, and we embraced for a long moment. As we drove home, I updated her on everything that had happened while she was away. The following day, we headed back to the airport to pick up her parents, who had flown in from Philadelphia to join us for the wedding and our honeymoon at the Dead Sea. Her father looked frail, suffering from severe hardening of the arteries. During the wedding, Gail whispered to me that this might be the last time she saw him on his feet.

Our wedding was beautiful. Many members of my extended family, friends from my Navy days and cadets attended the lovely event. Gail looked magnificent, and everyone remarked about how she resembled Elizabeth Taylor. She was warm and brought so much happiness to my family. After the honeymoon, her parents returned to the States, and we began our new life together.

Gail quickly bonded with my family and adapted to the Libyan cuisine, much to the delight of my siblings. They genuinely loved her and often teased her about her American accent and her obsession with cleanliness. She happily scrubbed the floors with my sisters, washed dishes and planted flowers in the small patch of land in our courtyard. Gail brought life to a house that had rarely experienced such joy.

We traveled around the country together, spending time working in a kibbutz, picking oranges, milking cows and collecting eggs. She loved every moment of it.

Two months into our marriage, Gail told me she was pregnant. I was overwhelmed with joy and excitement at the thought of becoming a father. However, our wonderful months in Israel ended abruptly when her mother

CHAPTER TWENTY-THREE

called us at midnight to inform Gail that her father had passed away.

Gail's journey to Philadelphia for her father's funeral marked a turning point in my life. Being the only daughter in her family, and very close to her mother, I understood through our long-distance calls that leaving her mother alone in the suburbs of Philadelphia was not an option. Moreover, her mother's age and fragility meant she couldn't travel. Gail's absence cast a shadow over my family; my siblings were silent, and my mother was somber. I missed her terribly. My mother and siblings realized that I would once again leave them behind to join Gail in Philadelphia.

Unlike the journey to Denmark, when I felt guilty about leaving everything behind, this time it felt different. Everyone agreed it was the right thing to do. My mother blessed me, telling me that I needed to be with Gail as a husband and soon-to-be father. My siblings and friends felt the same way. It was clear that I had to leave everything behind, and despite my tradition of honoring my parents first, I decided to be with Gail and let destiny take its course. All I wanted during those difficult hours was to be next to Gail, the source of my happiness, to hold her in my arms and be there for her.

Chapter Twenty-Four

THE POWER OF EDUCATION

Moving from one country to another is never easy or trivial. The Talmud states, "He who changes location changes fortune." Whether the change is for the better or worse is up for interpretation.

The night before I went to my father's synagogue. Alone there, I opened the Holy Ark, placed both hands on the scripture, and asked for blessings. In my heart, I felt that I was withdrawing from Israel. I was tired of my struggle for identity and found it hard to let go of my past. My stolen childhood haunted me; nightmares never ceased. I had a nagging feeling that Gail's love and commitment to her mother would make it nearly impossible for her to return to Israel or any other place.

Everything I heard about America was positive: it was described as the land of endless opportunities, advanced education, authentic democracy and a place where dreams could be realized. While I knew my trip to Philadelphia was to be with Gail, I also felt it was a journey of destiny—a journey to a land of choices and endless possibilities. As I stood before the Holy Ark, I realized that my heart was not at peace with the idea of becoming a naval architect. Instead, I felt I was destined, like my father, to be there for people and help them transform their lives. I enjoyed the process of listening, probing and guiding others toward the truth without telling them what to do. I could not imagine spending my life confined to an office, designing naval vessels. Instead, I felt my calling was to be a modern version of a rabbi—not to lead, but to facilitate; not to direct, but to mentor.

As I continued to touch the scripture, my heart trembled, my eyes filled with tears and for the first time, I felt the presence of God communicating with me through my father. I sensed his words of encouragement urging me to venture forth and deepen my education to make a difference in the lives of others.

Adapting to a new country and culture requires more than simply going with the flow. It demands the agility and courage to let go of the past. Immigrants are called to complain less, blame less and focus less on their former lives. The only way forward is to look ahead, invest time and energy, take responsibility and, as a result, grow and develop. This is the essence of life in America: arriving in this great country not as a burden, but as someone who dreams and works hard, just like many immigrants from difficult backgrounds who have contributed to the endless landscape of opportunities.

Coming to America is a battle for every new immigrant. It is a struggle between the past and the future, between anxiety and hope, between guilt and freedom, and between randomness and intention. Upon my arrival in Philadelphia, Gail and I moved into her mother's home, a simple townhouse located on the outskirts of the city in a small town called Havertown. While we were happy to be close to each other, it was a challenging time. We had to care for her mother, who could no longer manage the house on her own. We also needed to erect a gravestone for Gail's father, who was buried in the local Jewish cemetery. Above all, I had to look after Gail, who was expecting our child to be born in a few months.

As someone who is naturally active, I found that my responsibilities didn't fully occupy my time, so I began searching for work to help with expenses, including sending money to my mother, who continued working as a janitor at a local school in Ashkelon. I managed to secure a teaching position at a nearby Hebrew school. During the interview, both the Rabbi and

CHAPTER TWENTY-FOUR

the school principal were excited to learn about my religious background. They wanted me to teach young children about Jewish history and prepare them for reading from the scripture on their Bar Mitzvah Day. As Rabbi Berkowitz got to know me better and witnessed my positive impact on the children, he became my first mentor, providing guidance and support, and eventually encouraging me to apply as a freshman to the University of Pennsylvania.

I made a case to the admissions office, arguing that my experiences in Israel would add value to the university community, particularly since very few international students attended at that time. Despite being relatively older than the typical freshman and having a late start, the university made an exception and admitted me to begin my undergraduate studies. My daughter was born on a hot August day, two weeks before the fall semester began.

Becoming a father while starting my undergraduate work was no small challenge. The arrival of my daughter changed many aspects of my life, and I now realize that I wasn't fully prepared for fatherhood. The intensity of my classes at the university was overwhelming. I struggled with my English as I took courses in economics, statistics, psychology and philosophy. I aimed to excel academically and be the best student I could be, and in retrospect, I regret that my role as a father became secondary to my studies. Gail's mother was thrilled to have a grandchild, and with Gail's family nearby, I felt I could step back from my responsibilities as a father and fully invest my energy in my academic pursuits.

To create a suitable environment for studying, I converted the old, unfinished basement into an office. After giving it a fresh coat of bright white paint and adding some lights and bookshelves, I created a quiet space to read, write and learn. Balancing my academic work with my teaching responsibilities while being a husband and a young father made me intense and moody.

OUT OF THE CUCKOO'S NEST

Life is rarely a straightforward journey. It consists of ups and downs, with periods filled with light and happiness followed by days of darkness and despair. My college peers were much younger than I was, and as a twenty-five-year-old man, I found that they preferred to socialize and party with their contemporaries. Most focused on demonstrations against the Vietnam War, marching with posters and loud voices along Walnut and Chestnut Streets. Meanwhile, I observed the similarities between these protests over the policies of their government and the demonstrations in Israel by Sephardic youth who protested unjust policies and demanded opportunities.

Attending large, impersonal classes was not my vision of a university education. I sensed the lack of personal connection between the professors and the students. Many students seemed more focused on their grades than on mastering the material and applying it to real life. Everyone was busy taking notes and memorizing facts, overlooking the joy of learning, questioning and exploring the underlying causes of issues. There was less interest in subjects like history and philosophy, with a stronger emphasis on courses that would help them gain admission to medical or law schools. I felt lost and puzzled by the education system, especially at the University of Pennsylvania, a leading institution known for producing great scientists and renowned scholars.

One cloudy October day, I made an appointment with my advisor, Professor Janet Pack, who would later become a great friend. I shared my frustrations and feelings of being disconnected from the true learning experience. I confided in her about feeling adrift after my efforts to improve the quality of education back in Israel. As a Jewish professor who had visited Israel multiple times, she was aware of the struggles faced by Sephardic Jews and showed great empathy.

She looked at me and said, "You don't belong here. You need to be in a place where learning is highly valued and where the faculty is more engaged with the students' well-being." She informed me that such a school was not

CHAPTER TWENTY-FOUR

far away, only fifteen miles from Philadelphia. "It is not easy to get admitted to Swarthmore College, but you should try."

The morning after our conversation, I decided to visit Swarthmore. The small college, nestled in beautiful rolling hills, radiated a sense of tranquility. As I walked from the train station toward the main campus, I was mesmerized by its serene presence. I observed students discussing their impressions from lectures, captivated by their mature expressions despite their youth.

Upon entering the main hall, I realized that this was a place founded by those who opposed any form of war or aggression. The Quaker philosophy was alien to my own experience; I had come from a country torn by wars and internal struggles, and now I found myself in a place built by pacifists. I was in awe in that hallway. In that moment, I felt that destiny was guiding me to the right place—a place where learning is genuinely valued and embraced.

An elderly woman named Margaret Webb approached me and asked if I needed help. Even after all these years, I can still picture her long white hair cascading over her shoulders and her blue eyes focused intently on me as she led me to the Admissions Office. In that moment, I decided that Swarthmore was where I wanted to lay down my arms and immerse myself in the world of the classics—reading the works of great thinkers and asking the questions I had always been reluctant to voice.

As I listened to the admission officer, Lynn Mifflin, describe the academic demands and high expectations for incoming students, I felt a surge of excitement. Though her words seemed intended to deter me, I didn't waver. She sensed my aspirations and determination.

Choosing to be completely open, I shared my story with her—the years I spent in the wrong school, my escape, my parents' struggles in a new and unwelcoming land, the wars and my battle against injustice. We spoke for three hours. By the time I finished, she was fully invested in my narrative. I could hear the tremor in her voice as she helped me navigate the admission forms. She requested that I send my SAT scores, my TOEFL score and letters of recommendation from two professors at the University of Pennsylvania.

Several weeks later, just after the Thanksgiving holiday, I received an acceptance letter. What touched me the most was that Swarthmore College had accepted an incoming student for mid-year admission for the first time. This meant I could begin my college studies in January of 1971. Furthermore, the college offered me a scholarship and a stipend of $200 a month.

Holding that letter in my trembling hands felt like the gates of heaven had opened before me. I promised myself that I would master the English language and embark on a journey of learning, exploring the beauty of knowledge and wisdom.

Swarthmore should serve as a model for other colleges and universities. Its halls of learning are dedicated to helping young women and men delve into the classics, arts, sciences, painting, music and, most importantly, cultivate friendships and relationships that last a lifetime. Unlike larger institutions, where many students often feel lost and intimidated by certain faculty members, Swarthmore offers a different experience. The close relationships between professors and students stand out, and the small classes taught by famous yet humble faculty members, who serve as mentors, are truly remarkable.

Teachers at Swarthmore encouraged active participation and questioning, creating an atmosphere reminiscent of ancient Greek schools where Plato and Socrates fostered learning. The emphasis was on inquiry and exploration, helping us seek a deeper understanding of the universe, natural forces and human experiences. We examined the role of culture and rituals in navigating diverse societies while grappling with the search for meaning in a seemingly purposeless existence.

One particularly fascinating aspect of the curriculum was its emphasis on public service. Many Swarthmore students spent their summer vacations volunteering in underprivileged neighborhoods in cities such as Chicago, Philadelphia and Detroit. Others traveled as far as Africa and Asia to serve

CHAPTER TWENTY-FOUR

as teachers and provide healthcare in clinics for the sick and needy. In this environment, I engaged with some of the brightest and most humble young men and women, all deeply committed to learning. They prioritized understanding over grades, focusing on how politics and social science shape societies and cultures.

The goal of each faculty member was to enhance our understanding through engagement and thoughtful questioning rather than by providing definitive answers. This was a place where critical thinking flourished, encouraging us to delve into root causes and comprehend the human condition. Throughout my time there, I often felt the presence of my father. I remembered his unique ability to guide people toward their own truths by listening closely and helping them reach their own conclusions, rather than adhering strictly to textbooks or rigid rules. Swarthmore became an extension of my father's philosophy of learning and personal growth.

Instead of focusing solely on traditional texts, I explored a wide range of materials, from Thomas Aquinas to Machiavelli, examining the role of leadership in shaping societies. I immersed myself in poetry, spent hours fencing and engaged in sculpting. Horticulture was a vital part of Swarthmore education and wandering among the trees and shrubs allowed me to appreciate nature's beauty and reflect on my thoughts. I cherished every moment, finding solace in this experience.

The overall philosophy of the college revolved around the concept of "doing well by doing good." As English was my third language, I dedicated more time to my studies than many other students. I read every page twice, took detailed notes and rehearsed them to deepen my understanding. Many evenings, I found myself in the library, sometimes even hiding in the restroom until closing so I could continue reading. I often carried a blanket in my bag to cover myself when I got tired from studying so much.

I cherished the moments when faculty members invited us to their homes for dinner and discussion. In those informal settings, fueled by home-cooked meals and the warmth of a fireplace, conversations flowed freely and honestly. Surrounded by such brilliant minds, my soul soared to heights I had never experienced before. I felt as though I was reborn and reshaped. At Swarthmore College, I was rediscovering myself and learning to trust again, witnessing firsthand the transformative power of education on personal growth and development.

I studied psychology under the world-renowned Professor Hans Wallace, who escaped from Germany with the assistance of the Quakers, saving him from the gas chambers. I delved into economics under the guidance of Professor Howard Pack, who became a lifelong friend and advisor. I spent hours in the lab working with the famous Professor Barry Schwartz, author of the best-selling book *The Tyranny of Choice*. The beautiful campus, the intellectual prowess of its students, the small class sizes, the group discussions and the collaboration between faculty and students felt like heaven on earth.

The study of human behavior—particularly the root causes of madness, brutality, compassion and sadism—fascinated me. I was especially interested in economics, as human behavior often drives economic forces. During my sophomore year, I faced the challenge of selecting a major. Torn between psychology and economics, I ultimately chose to double-major in both and graduated with honors.

My upbringing in Israel sparked my curiosity about human behavior and helped me understand the causes of maladaptive behaviors. I volunteered as a teaching intern at Chester High School, a school predominantly attended by Black and low-income students. This experience provided me with invaluable insight into the struggles faced by many in the Black community in the United States. I witnessed their resilience and came to understand their anger, anguish and resentment towards their challenges. I observed the strength of their convictions and their commitment to their faith. Throughout the year, I assisted teachers in calming down angry students who were

CHAPTER TWENTY-FOUR

often searching for attention and identity. Those young people embraced me as one of their own, greeting me with wide smiles and hugs each time I walked in.

During summer vacations, I secured an internship at the Philadelphia Psychiatric Center, where I worked with patients who were business leaders and public servants. These individuals had become dangerous to themselves and others and were therefore confined within the institution. I assisted physicians and nurses in administering electroconvulsive therapy (ECT). Although the treatment is often viewed as cruel, it effectively alleviated some of the patients' symptoms. My senior thesis focused on various theories explaining why ECT worked despite public objections, culminating in a discussion of the movie *One Flew Over the Cuckoo's Nest*. I discovered an intriguing fact: this treatment had been used three thousand years ago by the ancient Egyptians, who submerged the heads of mentally ill individuals in tanks swarming with electric eels.

At college, I formed lasting friendships with various students and faculty members. One of my closest friends was David Baskin, a classmate who became like a brother to me. His brilliant mind and exceptional talent for crafting essays were invaluable during challenging times, particularly when I struggled with lengthy research papers and sought to improve my mastery of English. Our bond grew so strong that I had the privilege of meeting his parents, who treated me as if I were one of their own, especially during the stressful periods leading up to final exams, when I doubted my abilities to graduate from Swarthmore College. David pursued a career in medicine and has since become one of the top neurosurgeons in the world. Our friendship and mutual support have served as a pillar of love and care throughout our lives.

Additionally, Mrs. Lynn Mifflin and Dr. Howard Pack became dear friends during my time at Swarthmore, and we maintained that friendship for many years after graduation. I also became actively involved in clubs, such as the Afro-American Club, and formed friendships with students from Algiers, Morocco and Lebanon. My years at Swarthmore were transformative, teaching me how to think critically, write effectively, and, most importantly, maintain my passion for learning throughout my life.

Swarthmore's tradition of emphasizing the importance of liberal arts education and public service has had a lasting impact on who I am today. Swarthmore graduates continue to lead, teach, heal and serve the public. Upon graduation, I received attractive offers from prestigious institutions such as Princeton, Stanford, and Harvard to pursue my doctorate. Ultimately, I chose to attend Harvard University.

Chapter Twenty-Five

THE THICK WALLS OF ACADEMIA

My move from Swarthmore to Cambridge, Massachusetts in the summer of 1974 was filled with both excitement and sadness.

While Gail and I continued to love each other, my deep commitment to my academic work took a heavy toll on our marriage. Gradually, we began to grow apart. Gail seemed increasingly dedicated to her mother and our daughter. In hindsight, she understood me better than I understood myself. She recognized my hunger for knowledge and my desire to break away from my past. Although she wanted me to succeed, it came at the cost of our time together.

I knew it was difficult for Gail to leave her mother alone in Philadelphia. Additionally, my mother-in-law developed a close bond with our daughter, which made the separation even harder for her. I suggested that she join us, but she was uncomfortable leaving her home. In retrospect, I believe she wanted us to be independent to see if our marriage could withstand the challenge. She was right to let us have that space, but my obsession with being accepted to Harvard significantly impacted on our relationship.

Never in my wildest dreams did I think the timid, shy and wounded boy from Ashkelon would even consider Harvard, let alone be accepted to pursue a doctoral degree there. I reflected on my father's teaching that in every blessing, there is a curse, and this encapsulated my situation: attending Harvard would come at a considerable cost.

Pursuing my master's and doctoral degrees at Harvard University was challenging, but I found it less difficult than my time at Swarthmore College. After spending several years as a graduate student, fellow and teacher, I concluded that, despite its greatness and global reputation, Harvard fell short of the quality of education offered at Swarthmore. Harvard primarily focused on preparing students for specific careers, while Swarthmore served as a vibrant laboratory for ideas and public service. In comparison, Harvard felt isolated from its surroundings.

Harvard excelled at training its graduate students to become competent lawyers, sophisticated consultants, capable physicians, and accomplished academic researchers. Most of my peers were focused on achieving outstanding grades as a way to advance their careers. I found, however, that many faculty members were self-centered, highly competitive, and often reluctant to share their research.

Being a doctoral student at Harvard was not easy. I frequently walked around campus deliberately avoiding the Admissions Office, haunted by the fear that they might discover a mistake had been made in admitting me. That sense of insecurity stayed with me throughout my years there. Still, I was determined to make the most of the opportunity. To prepare for the future, I immersed myself fully in the study of educational psychology, public policy, and organizational behavior.

Gail and I settled into university housing for married students on Kirkland Street, next to a well-known Jewish grocery store. Gail was thrilled to be with me. Being apart from her mother provided a unique opportunity to rekindle our fragile marriage. She found a wonderful job as a hematologist at Mass General Hospital, and our daughter began kindergarten at a local school in Cambridge.

CHAPTER TWENTY-FIVE

One of my most cherished memories is biking with my daughter every morning on our way to kindergarten, with her sitting in front of me on the bike. I would rest my chin on her hair while my arms protected her, feeling both proud and joyful. It reminded me of my walks with my father on the beach at Benghazi. My life had changed completely from those times. And after several twists and turns—some cruel and some revitalizing—I was here leading a more normal life, being a protector to my little daughter, just how my father was to me. I was determined to make these rides meaningful to her. Since Gail had to leave early for work, I took on the responsibility of getting our daughter dressed and ready for school. I managed to balance my academic work while being a caring father and loving husband.

As my routine in Cambridge became more established, I began to enjoy my time there. I decided to engage with the local community and got involved with an organization called ABCD (Action for Boston Community Development). Founded by prominent community activist Robert Coard, ABCD aimed to provide "human renewal" and became Boston's leading anti-poverty agency. The organization was launched with a $2 million grant from the Ford Foundation. It assisted unemployed youth, offered support programs for low-income, inner-city single-parent women, and helped poor tenants keep their homes heated during Boston's harsh winters. ABCD dedicated itself to uplifting the city's impoverished populations, which primarily included Black and Hispanic residents. Given that the city was predominantly run by Irish politicians, the relationship between City Hall and the Black community was often tense. In this context, ABCD emerged as the voice and defender of the poor in Boston.

Robert Coard proved to be a shrewd leader with strong connections in Washington and the White House, enabling him to secure funding for essential employment and education programs. Through him, I had the privilege of meeting an incredible woman named Margaret Goodwin, the Director of The Women's Inner-City Educational Resource Center, known as WINNER. The organization's mission was to help unemployed women in areas like Roxbury, Dorchester, Mattapan and Jamaica Plain find meaningful work to support their families and transition off the social welfare system. Most of these women were single parents with one or two children, struggling financially and often isolated from mainstream American life.

Margaret and I connected immediately, and I committed to leveraging my Harvard connections to secure funding for WINNER. Together, we established skill-building workshops and implemented mentoring programs by recruiting graduate students to serve as counselors. We connected these women with college volunteers who could help them pursue education and seek employment. They reminded me of my own mother, who spent most of her life as a single parent providing for her children.

I also had the opportunity to meet Mayor Kevin White and his team, advocating for support from Harvard and the University of Massachusetts to prepare a funding request for the Department of Labor. ABCD greatly benefited from a stream of federal funding and private foundation grants. My role involved monitoring various programs to ensure compliance. I interacted with community organizations, engaged with politicians and fought to ensure that the recipients received most of the funding—a constant battle. Through these experiences, I learned a great deal about influence and constructive negotiation. My driving force was seeking win-win outcomes: politicians wanted visibility, city employees sought job security, ABCD members fought for resources and the inner-city women and unemployed youth were eager for mental support and encouragement.

The often polarized and conflicting environment taught me the importance of listening and allowing others to express their voices. While I had to navigate challenging and ego-driven individuals, my real passion lay with the remarkable women I met. Their dedication to learning, determination to provide for their children and resilience in protecting their kids from threats in their neighborhoods left a profound impact on me. I came to believe that,

CHAPTER TWENTY-FIVE

ultimately, women are often the stronger gender in many societies.

In one of my classes on Statistics and Social Science, I was fortunate to be taught by an impressive professor named Dr. Marcia Guttentag. An accomplished academic, she received funding for most of her research proposals from federal agencies and private foundations. As the Principal Investigator on more than half a dozen research projects, she generated millions of dollars for Harvard each year. However, while she excelled in research, Dr. Guttentag struggled with managing her team of researchers.

I was surprised when she invited me to her office and asked if I would be willing to manage various projects and oversee the work of more than ten graduate students. I accepted the challenge and took on all the tasks necessary to run the research projects. This included traveling to Washington, D.C., to meet with funding agencies and report on our progress. We arranged a strategic retreat for the entire research team, resulting in a clear vision and roadmap that outlined responsibilities and milestones. Dr. Guttentag became my doctoral thesis advisor, and we developed a positive and constructive working relationship. Together, we authored a handbook on Evaluation Research, published by Sage, which became a required textbook for individuals interested in assessing the outcomes and impacts of programs funded by foundations and governmental agencies.

Then, in January 1978, during a conference in Washington, Dr. Guttentag was found dead in her hotel room. She had died of a massive heart attack. The news of her sudden and untimely death shattered me. Afterwards, I met with a dear friend, Father Robert Drinan, a Jesuit priest, human rights activist and Democratic U.S. Representative from Massachusetts; we were introduced by Benjamin Netanyahu, who was then a graduate student at MIT. Father Drinan, a staunch supporter of Israel, invited me to join him at a monastery outside Portland, Maine. He was like an angel to me. I shared with him everything that was hurting me—my mistakes and my blindness—and he listened like a father. He offered no specific solutions, but suggested that I complete my dissertation and work on rebuilding my broken family.

When I returned to Boston, I resigned from my position running research projects at Harvard and focused on completing my doctoral thesis to advance my professional career and mend the pieces of my fractured marriage.

While my academic work at Harvard and my involvement in the community were going well, my personal life was in turmoil. One morning, just as I was about to attend an early class, my mother called. She sounded anxious and expressed her concerns about two of my brothers. She felt they were getting lost amid the chaos in the poor city of Ashkelon. The rise of gangs in the area had placed my siblings in a very vulnerable position. Large families were losing daughters to prostitution and sons to gangs that were breaking into homes, stealing and vandalizing public property. Synagogues began to lose their influence over the younger generations, and parents struggled to discipline their children. The widening gap between the wealthy and the poor fueled growing anger and discontent.

My mother, who had never asked for anything, was adamant that I had to do whatever I could to bring my brothers to Boston. The Libyan Jewish community was disintegrating, and my mother was starting to lose her stability. Burdened by her work and saddened by my absence, she was losing her focus and determination. The loss of my father, along with the fact that I was thousands of miles away, weighed heavily on her, leading to her depression.

My middle brother had quit school and started coming home later and later at night. He was a big guy and an excellent target for gangs looking to recruit members with cash and guns. My youngest brother, the most intelligent of us all, was serving in the military. He was closest to our mother, but he became restless and wanted to leave.

I went to the Office of Immigration and Naturalization and success-

CHAPTER TWENTY-FIVE

fully obtained immigrant visas for both of my brothers, bringing them to Boston. I helped my middle brother open a restaurant in Brookline, while my youngest brother found work as a construction worker for a small but successful contractor. I also applied for one of my sisters to move to Boston. Upon her arrival, she met a man from Israel who had been born in Iran. They married and had three beautiful children, who grew up in Boston and became successful professionals.

My fourth sister met an American Jew who worked as a banker, and together they had five magnificent daughters who grew up in Boston and Miami. Like my other nephews and nieces, these five daughters became physicians and successful lawyers.

The only siblings left in Ashkelon were my two oldest sisters, both of whom were married. One had three children, and the other had four—All committed to learning and servicing others.

Having five of my siblings in Boston significantly increased my responsibilities. I found myself under increasing pressure to excel at Harvard while looking after my siblings and dealing with my own family, which was falling apart.

Despite being busy with my academic work at Harvard and assisting my siblings, my relationship with Gail was deteriorating. I often took my immediate family for granted, hardly spending any time with Gail or our daughter, Edee. Instead, I poured all my energy into my studies and the well-being of my siblings in Boston, neglecting my own priorities.

Gail dedicated her entire salary to our family's needs, while I was blinded by the allure of Harvard and the pressure to support my siblings. The strain on Gail, along with her perception of me as a husband, became too much to bear. One night, while waiting for me to return home from the library at midnight, she sat at the dining room table and asked me to sit down and listen. She presented me with a heartfelt request.

"You need to decide: Are you married to me, or are you married to your work and your siblings? I will not accept being the last item on your list of priorities. You need to make a choice."

I made a choice that I later regretted. I told her that in my culture, siblings and parents are part of the family; when one gets married, the wife must support her husband and his family. Looking back, I realized how foolish and unreasonable my words were, and I failed to express gratitude for all the sacrifices she had voluntarily made. But at that time, I was young, wild and stubborn.

"That is not the American culture," she responded. "Once you get married, your new family—your wife and child—are the most important people in your life."

It was late, and I was exhausted. Although I knew she was right, I reacted impulsively and said, "My siblings come first, then my work, and then my family."

It was foolish of me to say that, but by then, my fate was sealed. While I was asleep, she spent the night packing. The next morning, her belongings, along with Edee's clothing and toys, were loaded into her car. I stood in a daze as I watched her drive away with my daughter, who waved goodbye. Gail moved back to Philadelphia to be with her mother.

Every other Friday night, I drove to Philadelphia to visit Edee, then returned home—a thousand-mile journey that took more than fifteen hours. The long ride was exhausting, and I began to accept that perhaps I had to move on without them being an integral part of my life.

One night, as I walked back to my car, I felt a heavy weight on my heart. I wished more than anything for Gail to come outside and say, "I am coming home with you." But how could she say that, when I couldn't bring myself to declare, "Yes, you are right; you must come first"?

Those words never came. I longed to express how much she meant to me, but I felt dishonest doing so. I was blind to my true priorities and paid a steep price for my obsession with my education. I neglected my roles as

CHAPTER TWENTY-FIVE

a husband and a father, becoming like many faculty members who place a heavy emphasis on their academic careers while overlooking their most valuable asset—their families.

Reflecting on my journey to the top of academia, it became clear that completing my education at Harvard was my primary objective. I believed that all personal costs were justified. I desperately wanted to earn my degree at Harvard; obtaining diplomas bearing the university's name, along with the titles of Master's and Doctorate, became my singular focus. I wanted to be recognized not as a second or third-class citizen back in Israel, but as an accomplished scholar—an accomplished man who, despite all odds, had made it. Deep down, I thought that after graduation, I could return to Gail and my daughter, and they would welcome me back as if nothing had happened.

I was wrong.

Unlike my cheerful graduation ceremony from Swarthmore, my graduation from Harvard was subdued. Gail and my daughter didn't attend. A week before, Gail had forwarded divorce papers for me to sign.

I knew that Gail's love for me was deep, and she longed for me to be beside her. I never came through. To some extent, our different values clashed. But deep in my heart, I know it was not the culture that broke us; it was my obsession with Harvard. I walked around feeling like Judas. I had betrayed the most sacred thing; I sacrificed my wife and daughter for the glory of a doctoral degree from Harvard.

When my daughter grew up, she went on to Brown University, and Gail struggled in Philadelphia. She eventually moved to Manhattan to work as a social worker. She was not able to find herself. Her bipolar personality took the best of her, resulting in terrible mood swings. Ten years later, on a cold and snowy night in Philadelphia, she committed suicide by driving her car into the Schuylkill River. All attempts to pull her out of the water and bring her back to life were in vain.

There is a statement in the Catholic scriptures that whatever a man soweth, that also shall be reap. Our sins eventually catch up with us in time. They chase us in our dreams and twist us during our waking hours, causing us to act out of character—almost like self-flagellating, but without blood gushing out, only the spirit broken down into small pieces.

Gail was gone, and a part of me died with her.

Chapter Twenty-Six

REVISITING THE PAINFUL PAST

Life is a mosaic of memories. For some, these memories are mostly pleasant, filled with joyful images of a happy childhood, providing comfort and serenity even in adulthood. For others, however, these memories are marked by pain and sorrow.

Making peace with my past was difficult. Often, it felt impossible. Still, I learned to turn my memories into fuel, pushing myself forward, though often at the expense of my own well-being. I devoted my life to helping others, yet I struggled to help myself. In many ways, I lacked self-compassion. I set out on a hard journey that left no room for self-pity or complaint. With intensity and determination, I pressed on, driven by a relentless need to prove to others that I was both capable and willing.

Nightmares and mood swings haunted me constantly. I found it nearly impossible to build deep, lasting relationships. When people drew too close, I withdrew. On visits to see my mother in Israel, I carefully avoided the area around the Fountain. At times, I wished for that old wooden structure to be torn down by the largest bulldozer imaginable. Other times, I prayed for desert winds to topple it. And in darker moments, I longed for God Himself to strike it with lightning, to set it ablaze and burn it to the ground—erasing every trace of its existence.

One evening during a visit to Israel, after my mother had fallen asleep,

I ventured out to walk around the Fountain. The entire facility was shut down, surrounded by a commercial fence. It was a full moon night, and I mustered the courage to jump the fence and explore the buildings. The night was quiet, but I could hear the echoes of the past—the crying, the screaming—and I could smell the stench of urine and see the place where I had been lashed with a belt.

I sat there for several hours, weeping as intense memories flooded my mind. I found myself lost in the past, the past I refused to revisit, and feelings of anger and sadness overwhelmed me. There was no way to reclaim what I had lost. The very place that had shaped my ambitions for the future also contributed to my melancholic state.

As I walked away, I picked up stones and tossed them behind me, a ritual that Jews practice when burying family members. Flashbacks of those dark days crashed over me like a series of endless waves lashing my soul. I continued throwing stones behind my back and then turned around to throw one at a window. The shattering glass produced a loud noise that brought me a sense of relief. Quietly, I made my way back to my room, ensuring that my mother's sleep was not disturbed.

Eventually, the city hall demolished the entire facility to make space for new housing for another wave of immigrants arriving from Russia and Argentina. The new school was relocated to a more upscale neighborhood and continued to offer mental health services to less fortunate children in the town. For a while, I believed that the collapse of those buildings would erase my experiences there once and for all. But, as in most cases, this was merely an illusion. Such memories linger like a fallen tree with roots still alive underground. It takes a long time for the roots to decompose and disappear. Sometimes, they sprout a twig or two, rising again and bringing back old memories that refuse to fade away.

There were three occasions when I returned to Israel, believing I could reintegrate into mainstream Israeli society. However, all attempts were insuf-

CHAPTER TWENTY-SIX

ficient to pull me out of the American landscape where I felt most secure.

The first attempt occurred during my doctoral studies at Harvard. The plight of the development towns stirred considerable concern in Israel and among leaders of the American Jewish Federation. Many Jewish donors felt that the funds allocated for these towns were not being utilized as intended. There was widespread belief that the funds had been diverted to other projects in Israel. At the time, the President of the Jewish Federation was the well-known philanthropist Max Fisher, of Fisher Body. Max Fisher was a giant, loved and respected by all Americans. He dedicated his life and wealth to helping Israeli institutions as well as various charitable organizations in the United States and abroad. To address the donors' concerns, he reached out to several leading Jewish professors from Harvard University to form a fact-finding task force. The mission of this task force was to visit these towns, review the budget process, and determine whether the funds were appropriately invested or diverted to other initiatives.

The task force included academics from Harvard Business School. During one of my courses there, I was invited to join the task force by Professor Joseph Bower, who was familiar with my background. He knew that I was a Sephardic Jew who had grown up in a similar town and spoke Arabic fluently. I embraced the project enthusiastically, teaming up with other faculty members, including Professor Richard Hammermash and the late Dr. Richard Rosenbloom, as well as two Israeli students studying at Harvard. Together, we formed a dedicated group determined to uncover the truth and propose meaningful recommendations for future initiatives in underdeveloped towns.

Ofakim was one of the towns selected for this project. My role involved immersing myself in the community and interviewing local officials. I had a list of projects funded by the agency, and my task was to evaluate the extent to which these initiatives had materialized.

I was provided accommodation with a local family originally from Rabat,

Morocco. Despite their financial struggles, they welcomed me warmly. The husband, who had previously worked for a bank in Rabat, faced challenges securing a job in any local bank despite his extensive experience in finance. Eventually, he found employment as a janitor in one of the elementary schools.

I interviewed many residents of the town, most of whom hailed from Morocco and Algeria. They primarily relied on support from social welfare agencies. Those fortunate enough to find work were typically seasonal employees at nearby *kibbutzim*, picking fruits and gathering tomatoes and cucumbers. The town lacked factories or an industrial base, resulting in high unemployment rates. This situation contributed to increasing rates of school dropouts and juvenile delinquency, which overwhelmed the few probation officers available through local government.

The residents expressed their frustration to me, feeling misled by the government. They had been relocated to these towns near the border without any job or educational opportunities. I became their sounding board. Living close to the Gaza border and far from any major city deprived them of opportunities for growth, and their anger resonated deeply with me. I had to work hard to remain objective and conceal my emotions.

We met with government officials in Jerusalem to investigate how financial resources were being allocated. The findings were shocking and disheartening: a significant percentage of the funds from American Jews did not contribute to the development of these towns. Instead, the government allocated these funds to other projects, such as the military and the importation of resources like oil and steel. I summarized my observations in a case study titled "Ofakim: A Case Study of Undeveloped Towns."

This case study, along with other reports written by the Harvard team, was presented to the American Jewish Federation. The positive outcome was that this lengthy report eventually changed how the Jewish Agency in Israel allocated the funds collected from American Jews. The new policy

CHAPTER TWENTY-SIX

allowed donors to designate specific projects from a list generated by the Israeli government.

However, in retrospect, this change had little meaningful impact. It was merely a diplomatic gesture to appease the donors, while a policy of neglect continued. These development towns remain impoverished and are often visited during election seasons when aspiring politicians promise to elevate them to the same standards as the rest of the country. Despite some progress, towns like Kiryat Malachi, Kiryat Shmona, Sderot, Ofakim, and others still face high rates of school dropouts, drug addiction, and unemployment.

At the core of our findings was a troubling perception held by the founders: that Jews from Arab countries were collectively "not up to par" compared to Jews from Europe. This notion included judgments about their lifestyles, arguing styles, religious practices, family dynamics, and levels of ignorance regarding Western culture, as well as their feelings of silent resentment. For the immigrants in these development towns, there was a blend of love for the country and deep resentment for the lack of opportunities and inadequate social infrastructure to support a suffering generation. One of my friends summarized the situation well, noting that while Israel made considerable efforts to bring Jewish immigrants from all over the world, it fell short in meeting their needs and assisting them during their challenging transition.

My second opportunity to return to Israel arose in the winter of 2016 when I took on the role of strategic advisor to Moshe Kahlon, an Israeli with Libyan Jewish roots who had climbed the political ladder within the Likud party. I met him in Boston while teaching at MIT; he had been accepted into the prestigious Executive Program at Harvard Business School. During dinner, he shared his struggles growing up in Givat Olga, a small town south of Haifa overlooking the beautiful Mediterranean Sea. His father worked as a bricklayer for a large construction company, and his story touched my heart, prompting me to leave academia despite my director's objections.

Kahlon's plan was to establish a new political party called Kulanu, which means "all of us." The party aimed to improve the dire conditions faced by Israeli families living in poverty. My role was to formulate a clear campaign strategy focused on promoting greater equality and inclusion of all ethnic groups in Israel. We were committed to having representatives from all walks of life, including a representative for the growing number of neglected elderly individuals in Israel. We aimed to increase the number of women representing all age groups and sought accomplished individuals, including Michael Oren, the former Israeli Ambassador to the United States; Yoav Galant, a former military general; and Eli Cohen, the CEO of a large Israeli enterprise. I had the honor of interviewing more than thirty candidates.

We spent four months traveling the country, scouting every corner and campaigning tirelessly in the lead-up to Election Day. We met with hundreds of families in towns along the border, assuring them that Moshe Kahlon would bring policies to strengthen economic growth in development towns, build new housing for young couples, and attract industry to areas long burdened by neglect. Mr. Kahlon's advisors nominated candidates, and my role was to interview them and evaluate how closely they aligned with the party's vision and values. We recruited representatives from Kiryat Shmona in the north, Arad in the south, and Be'er Sheva in the Negev. Strategic meetings were held with these future representatives to forge a unified front—one that would transform the way resources were allocated and finally bring relief to Israel's neglected regions.

It was equally important to ensure that women held strong representation on our candidate list, reflecting the diverse sectors and ethnic groups of Israeli society. We placed representatives from the Russian immigrant community, the elderly population, and the Arab community in prominent positions. With determination and energy, we secured a significant victory on Election Day, winning twelve out of 120 seats in the Knesset and establishing the Kulanu party as a key player in forming the coalition.

CHAPTER TWENTY-SIX

However, to my dismay, Moshe Kahlon ultimately disappointed his voters. After the election, his accomplishments fell short of his promises, and his shifting priorities contributed to his downfall. I returned to MIT feeling defeated and disappointed/. I failed in my assessment of Moshe Kahlon as a leader and for falling into a political trap without the knowledge or skills to navigate it effectively. I was blinded by our shared background and made the grave mistake of judging him based on his ethnicity rather than other attributes.

In the subsequent election, his party failed to reach the required minimum threshold. Blinded by the allure of the political arena and his self-centeredness, Kahlon collapsed the Kulanu party and merged it with Likud. He then disappeared from the political landscape to accept a senior position with a credit card company, which was ironic, given that his campaign had focused on fighting credit card companies that exploited low-income individuals in Israel.

From my office in Cambridge, I watched the party's demise unfold with shame. It was disheartening to see Kahlon rise to the top only to roll downhill like a snowball. This regret lingered with me for a long time, creating disdain for all forms of political life. To my dismay, I discovered that the Israeli public has lost trust in its elected leaders. Since then I declined any calls or invitations to join political parties, recognizing that I was not cut out to be a politician. I knew I was more effective as a teacher and a coach. I lacked the stomach for secret meetings held behind closed doors—and I had learned painfully that personal agendas, the drive for power, and political payoffs distract many politicians from delivering on their promises.

On the positive side, I met many wonderful people in those towns, including Israeli Arabs in the North, Israeli Druze near Syria, and a diverse group of individuals from all corners of the world. Listening to their pain and hopes and feeling embraced by them made the journey meaningful, strengthening my conviction that true leadership is all about removing fears, instilling hope, and doing the hard and right as opposed to the easy and wrong.

My third and most memorable visit to Israel occurred when one of my graduate students at Harvard, a film producer from Israel, arrived to study organizational behavior and public management. He was one of ten public officials selected each year to attend the Harvard Kennedy School, where he pursued a master's degree in public administration, an initiative supported and financed by the Wexler Foundation. This remarkable individual chose to take my elective course, titled "Know Thyself," which focused on conflict resolution, building high-performance teams, motivating oneself and others, and leading organizational change. The course was quite popular, as it was hands-on rather than purely academic. The objective was to equip graduate students with practical tools that many academic institutions often overlook. I cherished every moment of teaching and mentoring my students, who came from diverse backgrounds around the world.

Just before his graduation, he approached me and shared that he represented Channel Ten, a popular TV station in Israel. He wanted to produce a documentary about my life in Israel. Having researched my background, he believed that the film would significantly impact Israeli society, particularly young people. He titled the twenty-minute documentary *From Cuckoo's Nest to Harvard University*.

I flew to Israel for the filming and was impressed by how much the crew knew about my background. Along with the filming team, we visited several significant places: the agricultural school, my father's synagogue, the demolished house in Ashkelon, the naval academy, and the Fountain in its new location. Each place we visited brought back a mix of painful and pleasant memories. I tried to maintain my composure, but there were moments when the memories and sights overwhelmed me, leading the camera to capture tears streaming down my face—a torrent of locked emotions flowing like a hidden river.

CHAPTER TWENTY-SIX

When we entered the Fountain, I was taken aback by the joyful sounds of children in the classrooms. The teachers, mostly women, were smiling and appeared supportive and nurturing. The tense atmosphere of the past, characterized by indifference, had dissipated. The classrooms were clean, adorned with children's drawings on the walls, and vases filled with fresh flowers decorated the teachers' desks. The children showed no fear in their eyes; they seemed secure and well cared for. Although the unpleasantness of the past was behind us, the memories still overwhelmed me. The building, constructed from beautiful Jerusalem stones, was attractive and inviting.

As I struggled with my emotions and tried to hold back my tears, I caught sight of an older man with a long white beard. His head was covered with an old Libyan Talmudic kippah as he walked toward me. I was overwhelmed when I realized this was Mr. Nissim G'ean, the man who had helped me escape from the Fountain and directed me to the agricultural school in the Negev.

He approached me slowly, with a cane in one hand and his wife holding onto his other arm. He looked like an angel descending from the heavens. I embraced him tightly, tears in my eyes. Despite his frail appearance, his warm and kind eyes had never lost their brightness.

I recalled the day he entered my old classroom, determined to help me leave that place behind. After so many years, I finally had the chance to express my gratitude for his courage in opening new doors and providing me with the opportunity for a different life. This man had rescued me from a stench-filled, miserable environment, leading me to the open expanse of the desert. He was my prime mover, instilling in me the power to resist, the determination to move forward, and a compassion that knows no bounds. Because of him, I uprooted myself from a hostile environment and worked my way up to become a compassionate professor. He was a messenger who ignited a fire within my soul, empowering me to swim against the tide and move forward without fear or hesitation. He truly was my angel; without his divine intervention, I cannot imagine where I would be today. The documentary concluded with me giving a lecture at Harvard, emphasizing the importance of change and transformation.

I believe there is a shining light at the end of most dark journeys. Amidst the cruelty, indifference, and ignorance we often face, a small ray of light can guide us during our darkest hours, leading us to higher ground and better places.

Unlike the miracles depicted in the Bible, real miracles do not come marked by thunder, but in much more subtle ways, quietly announcing their presence. There is something powerful about prayer, even for those who may not consider themselves believers. Miracles require faith, inner spirituality, and the conviction that, despite all the pain and humiliation, something good will emerge like lotus flowers blooming from the depths of murky waters.

When the documentary aired nationwide, I received hundreds of calls and emails from people across the spectrum, including school administrators and old friends. One of the most impressive calls came from Sherry Arison, the Chair of Bank Hapoalim. We met, and she encouraged me to teach at an innovative university known as Ben Hatchumie in Herzliya. I also received messages from people who knew my father, urging me to consider becoming a rabbi or taking a seat in the Israeli Parliament. All these responses truly touched me.

Another intriguing trip to Israel happened when the Bertelsmann Foundation asked me to facilitate a weeklong session in Jerusalem and another weeklong session in Berlin for fifteen young Israelis working in the media, all descendants of Holocaust survivors. They were joined by another group of fifteen young German professionals engaged in the German media, most likely descendants of those who served in the German military or held positions in the government during WWII. The mission was to foster communication and explore the impact of the war on their identities. It was an

CHAPTER TWENTY-SIX

amazing gathering, revealing that all participants had little to no information from their parents or grandparents about their family histories. There was a deafening silence from the older generations; Holocaust survivors and those involved with the Nazi regime chose not to discuss those dark days. The program had an incredible impact on the participants, who formed friendships that lasted for many years after completing the program.

During university breaks, I made several trips to Israel, delivering speeches to students and public organizations. Reflecting on these experiences reminds me of a movie that profoundly impacted me: *Cinema Paradiso*. In the film, young Toto discovers an escape from his war-torn Sicilian village at the *Cinema Paradiso* movie house, where the projectionist, Alfredo, instills in him a love for films. When Toto grows up and becomes the projectionist, Alfredo encourages him to leave his small town and pursue his passion for filmmaking. Toto follows Alfredo's advice and moves to Milan, ultimately becoming one of Italy's greatest movie producers. I felt a similar sense of leaving my roots behind, moving forward but never truly returning to my childhood town.

The thought of returning to Israel has never left me. I always thought that I could make a meaningful contribution there more than any other place in the world. However, the pain endured during my early childhood left a mark that can't be erased. Several factors contribute to my reluctance.

First, being rejected by Israeli universities while being accepted by leading academic institutions in America instilled in me a deep sense of gratitude toward a country that opened its gates and welcomed me to its academic institutions. From Swarthmore to Harvard, MIT, and other institutions of higher learning, as well as governmental agencies, I was accepted for my knowledge and ability to contribute valuable insight. To my surprise, I never encountered any form of discrimination based on my ethnicity, religion, or skin color. The United States, despite its shortcomings, remains a land of opportunities. Here, I have never felt like a second-class citizen. At both

Swarthmore and Harvard, I was among the wealthy and influential, yet I was treated for who I am. My thoughts and ideas were welcomed, and my advice was judged based on its merit. This kind of acceptance is truly a rare gift.

Second, despite my achievements, the years of being labeled as mentally underdeveloped have left their mark on me. Fear and insecurity have created deep scars. The constant pressure to prove that I am not inferior and that I possess the aptitude and desire to grow and contribute has significantly affected my self-image. Although I may appear confident on the outside, I grew up believing I was dumb and worthless. Those feelings still haunt me, making it difficult to revisit my past. When I am there I still have the urge to hide my insecurities. For me this is the last unconquered frontier: going back to the place that shaped me and truly being myself—free of old and rusty shackles, liberated from deep wounds of past prejudice, and yes, free at last.

Today, I recognize that the country has changed significantly. Mixed marriages between East and West, greater mutual respect for all cultures, technological advances, rising socio-economic conditions among the Sephardic population, and improved education have transformed the landscape. While I hold dual citizenship, my loyalty lies not with a country or a flag but rather in serving others, listening to silent voices, and encouraging people to venture out, take risks, explore, and make life more meaningful. This has been my guiding principle, my purpose, and my true North.

Chapter Twenty-Seven

SPREADING MY WINGS AND FLYING HIGH

Graduation day with my doctoral degree in organizational behavior and education at Harvard was filled with mixed emotions—joy from my achievements, and sadness at my personal failures.

As I walked onto the stage to receive my doctorate in education and organizational behavior, I felt a deep sense of emptiness. After the ceremony, I returned to my apartment, a place I had shared with Gail for less than two years, and realized I needed to escape Cambridge to find a fresh start in a new place, free from memories. With my daughter starting her first year at Brown University and my siblings settling in Boston, I made the decision to leave Harvard and embark on my own journey.

My colleague from Harvard, Walter McCann, who was the Associate Dean of the Graduate School of Education at Harvard, had accepted a new position as the Dean of Business Administration at the University of Hartford in Connecticut. He invited me to join him as the Chairman of the Department of Public Administration and to oversee Executive Education. The ambience at Hartford was markedly different from Harvard's elitist atmosphere, which often seemed indifferent to the needs of the city of Cambridge. By contrast, the University of Hartford engaged actively with city officials, placing the university at the heart of its community. I relished the chance to strengthen that bond.

Where Harvard's culture emphasized personal fame focusing on research and publication, the University of Hartford faculty focused on the development and growth of its students. The faculty was unpretentious and eager to collaborate. I sensed the possibility for programs and initiatives that Harvard's competitive environment and culture of silos might have stifled. My commitment was clear; to use education as a catalyst for transformation, enabling organizations to harness human potential. From leading a boarding school in Israel to my personal experience, I became convinced in the power of education to shape the future of societies in general and the underserved in particular.

As the new chairman, my role was quite demanding. When I arrived, the faculty members were functioning individually rather than as a cohesive team. I took the time to meet with each of them individually to share my vision for what we could achieve together. I was surprised to learn that their concerns focused less on compensation and more on visibility, spacious offices, research assistants and opportunities to connect with local and national organizations to share their work.

Together, we crafted a compelling vision for the department, along with a set of activities needed to enhance our competitiveness. After extensive negotiations, we successfully relocated the entire department from the cramped basement to a more appealing space, where each faculty member was provided with a private office with new furniture.

We established several task forces aimed at improving students' experiences on campus and reached out to corporations and public agencies to recruit our graduates. We hired a team of five staff members and six full-time instructors. Additionally, we transformed several traditional classrooms with designs that encouraged student interaction.

We launched some of the most innovative executive education programs

CHAPTER TWENTY-SEVEN

for members of the legislature, senior managers in state and federal agencies and executives from the largest insurance companies based in Hartford, Connecticut. We also designed programs for Chiefs of Police from cities and towns across Connecticut. Furthermore, we created a weekend program to help working individuals attain their master's degrees in public management and health administration.

One morning, a young man named Dr. Alex Parnia from Iran walked into my office seeking a job. He had completed his doctoral studies at Claremont University under the supervision of the renowned management guru, Peter Drucker. Despite his accomplishments, he was struggling to find work, especially during the Iranian Hostage Crisis, a time that severely impacted the Carter administration.

From the moment he entered my office, I sensed his potential. He had a spark that reminded me of myself, of my own struggles to find my place in a new home and gain acceptance in a foreign land.

When I approached my dean and president with the request to hire him, I faced resistance. Both were concerned about the implications of hiring an Iranian during such a tumultuous time. This response was particularly frustrating, given that my dean had Irish roots—his grandparents had escaped Ireland—and the president was a descendant of Russian Jews who immigrated to New York in the early twentieth century.

I confronted them, offering to take a one-third pay cut to bring Dr. Parnia on board. I assured them that he would be instrumental in developing our executive education programs. We had several discussions. I refused to give up due to their unfair prejudice, and ultimately, we decided to hire him.

Dr. Parnia made an extraordinary impact on the faculty and staff. He displayed a calm yet firm demeanor, had an exceptional ability to listen and tirelessly worked on creating brochures and meetings with city officials and business executives. His efforts began to yield remarkable results. Together,

Dr. Parnia and our team developed and implemented several executive education programs. Within two years, we generated over $5 million in revenue, attracting hundreds of executives from across the state to our programs. We also created a specialized program for newly elected state representatives, assisting them with courses in economics, finance and negotiation.

We focused intently on the needs of our adult students. Whenever a student missed a class or confided to a staff member that they were thinking of leaving the program, I was notified immediately. I reached out to those students, offering the support they needed to stay the course and finish their studies. Because most of our programs were held over the weekend, we invited the spouses of our students to join us once a month. These gatherings included special seminars and workshops designed to spark curiosity while also giving couples time to enjoy one another's company. On Saturday evenings, after classes ended, we hosted receptions and dinners. Sometimes a band from the School of Music performed—classical music to accompany dinner, followed by rock 'n' roll that filled the room with dancing and laughter. The festivities ended by ten, leaving participants and their spouses time to return to their hotels, rest, and prepare for Sunday's classes. By noon on Sunday, courses wrapped up, giving students enough time to head home and ready themselves for the busy week ahead.

Dr. Parnia went on to become a provost and eventually a college president in California. Despite the years, our friendship endured. That chapter of my life deepened my belief in trusting others to help shape a better future, just as the naval school superintendent had once trusted in me.

The experience I gained during those early years of executive education eventually allowed me to travel across the country, giving lectures on the power of student-centered learning and the role universities can play in transforming adult education. I also came to fully appreciate the vital role immigrants play in strengthening a nation's capacity in science and technology. I have always believed that new immigrants, eager to achieve

CHAPTER TWENTY-SEVEN

the American dream, work tirelessly to provide their children with better opportunities and a higher quality of life. This has held true for every wave of immigrants who have arrived on these shores. So when I read the current policies of making it almost impossible to come to this country, I wonder if we as a great nation will continue to benefit from the flow of new ideas and breakthroughs. I remain convinced that managing waves of legal immigration infuses a country with fresh energy and innovative ideas, opening doors for renewal and development.

While executive education was in its infancy, we embraced it enthusiastically. At that time, many corporations were disappointed with the quality of graduates coming from high schools and universities. Consequently, there was an increase in private companies offering adult education to meet the demand for employees who were creative and possessed strong learning agility. This became my calling, and I worked tirelessly to connect our programs with corporate partners.

Throughout my entire career, I have never had a team like the one at the University of Hartford. I was fortunate to work with the best people: a balanced mix of men and women, as well as team members from various countries, including Vietnam, Iran, Kenya and Puerto Rico. We were very supportive of one another. Our weekends were often hectic because most degree and non-degree programs were conducted during that time. It became a tradition for the entire team to meet at least once a month at a local restaurant for informal interactions. We felt like family.

These were unforgettable days, when I saw firsthand the immense power of education to transform both individuals and institutions, fueled by the strength of effective teamwork. We built a psychologically safe environment where faculty, staff, and students alike felt free to share their feelings and ideas for improvement. Our focus was always on continuous progress; stagnation was never an option.

In a relatively short time, our efforts began to ripple outward, making an impact across the entire state and throughout the New England region. Chiefs of police, state administrators, legislators, and business executives eagerly lined up to take part in our programs and classes. Recognition soon followed, with numerous awards from both business and government agencies. I saw with my own eyes how education could dismantle barriers, breathe life into dormant organizations, and clear away the blockages of cumbersome structures.

Our efforts extended beyond the borders of Connecticut. Collaborating with Dr. Michael Hargrove from Harvard University, we moved forward. We partnered closely with Aetna Insurance Corporation to design executive education programs for its senior managers from around the world. We worked diligently to enhance the skills of its underwriters and claims professionals by establishing a targeted curriculum designed to refine their capabilities. Additionally, we brought in professors from leading universities to facilitate discussions aimed at improving customer service and fostering an engaging corporate culture. Since Aetna relied on independent agents to sell its products, we created customized training programs for leading agents who came to Hartford for development at the Aetna Center for Executive Education, focusing on skill enhancement and nurturing a true sense of partnership with the company.

My work with Dr. Michael Hargrove extended beyond the borders of the United States. We collaborated with global corporations such as Marriott Hotels, where we engaged with managers to address the challenges of leadership in working with hotel staff. We dedicated time to supervisors at British Airways, discovering that addressing employees' professional and personal issues significantly enhances customer service and retention.

We initiated a global program for LVMH, training general managers to empower store managers to prioritize the needs of both existing and potential customers. Our efforts took us to Germany, where we worked with the senior leadership team at REWE, a supermarket chain operating throughout

CHAPTER TWENTY-SEVEN

Europe. Additionally, we collaborated with Bertelsmann, the largest media company in Europe, and we coached supervisors at Boston Scientific to actively listen to their employees and facilitate difficult conversations.

Our engagements continued with companies like Berkshire Heathway, Marriot, Heineken, Bacardi, and Deutsche Bahn, where we coached managers to foster an engaging culture that encouraged employee contributions and expression. We trained over eighty Bacardi managers from around the world to build high-performance teams. Furthermore, we worked for three years with Bacardi women to prepare them for leadership roles in their global expansion through the Women in Leadership Development Series (WILDS). We also delivered lectures on leadership for companies like DAVITA, Alibaba, Baidu, and Johnson & Johnson.

For General Re, an insurance company owned by Warren Buffett, we assisted managers worldwide in exploring strategies to merge two distinct cultures: the American culture of the acquirer and that of Cologne Re, the oldest German reinsurance firm. Our work with Champion International, a paper company now owned by International Paper, involved training union representatives to become facilitators of change. By guiding them, they became change agents who helped their members identify ways to reduce waste and enhance product quality. We influenced them to value a common vision and meaningful core values, leading them to establish a belief system focused on maximizing people's potential.

Over the years, we created a robust platform that encouraged companies to empower their managers to unlock the full potential of their employees. Our motto emphasizes that culture and leadership are the most sustainable competitive advantages, advocating for organizations to invest in employee development. These investments consistently led to increased loyalty, talent retention, improved efficiency and better customer service.

On a personal level, I learned that sharing knowledge, investing time in others, uplifting their spirits during times of change, instilling the courage to act and building the skills needed to move forward provided the greatest satisfaction and sense of achievement. I often advised my students to follow their passion and to focus on doing the right things rather than just on financial gain. I believe that when one concentrates on these principles, fame and financial success will naturally follow.

Chapter Twenty-Eight

FALLING IN LOVE WITH THE DRAGON

Years ago, just weeks before my father passed away, I spent a Shabbat evening with him. Despite the growing tension at the time between Egypt and Syria, including the potential for war involving Israel and its neighbors, I managed to secure permission from my commander to visit my family for Shabbat dinner.

After dinner, my father and I were the only ones left at the table. The flickering lights from the Shabbat candles, the white tablecloth, the leftover challah that my mother had baked the day before, and the sound of my mother rinsing the dishes are still vivid in my memory.

My father seemed eager to share his thoughts with me. He reminded me that he was growing old and fragile. Then, unexpectedly, he asked if I knew anything about China. His question surprised me, and I admitted that I knew nothing about the country. Despite being almost completely blind, he fixed me with a piercing gaze and said, "You know, my son, we Jews are indebted to the Chinese people."

Before I could ask why, he reminded me how during the war he was in a state of shock; indeed, he had to bury his family in a mass grave. But he never lost his faith in God. I remember him looking at me with his blind yet burning eyes and saying, "When the world closed its gates to Jewish refugees, there was only one country that opened its arms and hearts to us. That country was China."

His knowledge of world history stunned me, especially since we had never studied that topic in school. My father raised both his arms and placed them on my head, saying, "My son, I know you have to look after your mother and your six siblings, but when the opportunity arises for you to visit China, please express our gratitude to them for saving the lives of our people."

As the years passed, I completely forgot about the moments when my father spoke of the war in general and China in particular. Caught up in my own challenges and caring for my mother and siblings, his request regarding China faded into the recesses of my mind.

Years later, while lecturing at Harvard, a representative from Shanghai Jiao Tong University attended my class. He waited until everyone had left the auditorium before asking if I would mind having lunch with him. As we dined at a Szechuan Chinese restaurant on Harvard Square, he inquired whether I would be interested in coming to China to give lectures. Intrigued by the invitation, I accepted. A few weeks later, I was invited to spend the summer of 2002 in Shanghai, teaching graduate students about the meaning of leadership in challenging times.

My hosts took me to the Jewish Quarter in Shanghai, where the old synagogue had been converted into a museum. I walked the streets where many Jewish refugees lived. While most Jews left China after the 1950s for Israel and Australia, the photographs on the museum walls depicted a lively and vibrant Jewish life. Later, during the Shanghai World Expo 2010, I was honored to visit the Israeli Pavilion next to the Chinese Pavilion. At the entrance, a large piece of Jerusalem stone was inscribed with: "We, the Jewish people, are forever indebted to the Chinese people for opening their doors to our people." There is a significant admiration for Jews in China,

CHAPTER TWENTY-EIGHT

primarily due to their contributions to science and medicine. Throughout my visits and time spent in China, the image of my father, along with his gratitude for the Chinese people, remained with me.

My summer in Shanghai led to many more visits, and eventually, I spent the entire academic year of 2011 teaching full-time at the China Europe International Business School, better known as CEIBS. This year became one of the most engaging experiences of my life, allowing me to learn a great deal about the Chinese people, their history, their sufferings, their revolution and their aspirations. I began to see commonalities between the Jewish and Chinese peoples. I often started my lectures by reminding my students that Jews and Chinese share a common background. Both groups have endured humiliation, discrimination and centuries of suffering. Our unique and shared characteristics explain the root causes of our survival. Dedication to family, investment in education for children, industriousness, entrepreneurial spirit and a positive mindset are the commonalities that have served as pillars of resilience for both our peoples.

My deep connection to China is rooted in my father's profound admiration for the Chinese people. Furthermore, I have a deep respect for their achievements in the last five decades. It is a testimony for two people rising from the ashes. In 2022, with the help of my dear friend Ming Yue, we published a book of poetry dedicated to the Chinese people, expressing my heartfelt gratitude for their history, for saving my people, and for embracing me as a friend. Here is the opening poem titled *Embrace Them, My Son*, which conveys my gratitude on my father's behalf:

Embrace Them, My Son

His eyes were burning with fire and life,
His fragile body just about to say goodbye.
He stood up and asked for his oldest son.

OUT OF THE CUCKOO'S NEST

He whispered words not to be forgotten.

You, my good son, let the world know,
As Jews we suffered and cried enough.
Our people paid the ultimate price,
Chosen by God was their crime.

Look after your mother and the tribe.
Most of all promise me to spread the word:
While all nations shut down their doors,
China opened its heart and arms.

This ancient nation saved innocent lives,
An influx of Jews crawled in without a cry,
No visa or passport to come by China with
Smiles and warmth gave them solid ground.

We Jews have been brothers to those guys,
Five thousand years have passed by.
We will continue to bless life and multiply.
Take the time, son, to embrace them on my behalf.

For the past twenty years, China has felt like my second home. I have taught at some of its most prestigious, engaging and progressive universities, traveled throughout the country, and immersed myself in its warm and hospitable culture. I have coached hundreds of Chinese executives and government officials, assisting organizations such as Baidu, Alibaba and various State-Owned Enterprises. These individuals have been open-minded and eager learners, absorbing and internalizing lessons with remarkable agility. This capacity for learning is a significant factor behind their rapid

CHAPTER TWENTY-EIGHT

growth. Many of them have become close friends, affectionately nicknaming me "Gege," or older brother, while they refer to themselves as my "Didi," or younger brothers.

There is a common misconception that China's economic success is solely due to cheap labor, but that is far from the truth. The hard work, dedication, loyalty and pride of the Chinese people have driven their economic and social achievements. As Napoleon Bonaparte once said, "China is a sleeping dragon; when she wakes, she will shake the world." Like any country, China has its imperfections, but its accomplishments over the past forty years serve as a valuable case study for others. Success is rarely accidental; it arises from a compelling vision, resilience and positive thinking.

After a tragic marriage, broken romances, and years of profound loneliness, I met an incredible woman in Shanghai who transformed my life—Ping He, the daughter of a judge in the city. Ping worked for over twenty-five years as a global executive at Maritz, one of the largest event management companies in the world designing and delivering meetings and tradeshows for governments, corporations and associations globally. As the global general manager responsible for the Asia-Pacific region, she became one of the most recognized names in the industry on the global stage.

One early morning, I walked into a restaurant at one of the Shangri-La hotels. As I approached my usual table, I heard a loud voice exclaim, "Leadership does matter!"

Intrigued, I followed the sound and saw an elegant and confident woman sitting at the head of the table, lecturing to six senior executives from the Shangri-La hotels. I paused, approached her table, and said, "Yes, she is right; leadership does matter."

She instantly sprang from her chair and asked if she could give me a hug. For the first time after so many years of desolation and loneliness, I felt connected. I felt the rare tingling of my soul when we know we are falling in love. I felt that somewhere in the far away past, and a long time ago we were together. Rumi was right when he said: "Lovers don't finally meet somewhere. They're in each other all along". Since that moment, our relationship has flourished. A good friend of mine once said that Ping and I had found our other halves in one another. For many years, I doubted I could ever love again. My nightmares, demons, insecurities and constant restlessness had made it difficult for any relationship to endure.

As the old saying goes, the ultimate love is to love and be loved. Perhaps I had never found my true soulmate—someone wise enough to understand me and secure enough to love me for who I am. But then I met Ping. Her brilliant mind, boundless energy, and constant support have helped me feel comfortable in my own skin, trust again and find happiness. She taught me the power of love as a transformative force that can shape people for the better.

Through her unwavering love and loyalty, I have slowly emerged from the dark hole I once inhabited and embraced life's endless beauty. She is my True North, gifted with beauty, grace, courage, compassion and loyalty. Through our love, I am becoming aware of the importance of learning from the lessons of the past but not living in the past. True love is the wind in the sails that help us forge ahead and make peace with ourselves. True love is the fuel that propels us to laugh again, and let the wounds of childhood be healed without the lingering scars.

Chapter Twenty-Nine

FLYING AWAY FROM THE CUCKOO NEST

As I reflect on my life and its challenges, I have come to recognize the importance of what the ancient Romans called *memento mori*. The phrase exhorts us to remember our death and to remember the importance of our lives. As mortal beings, we must actualize ourselves by becoming more empathetic towards others. Empathy and humility are paths to true happiness. By giving more and taking less, we bring purpose and meaning to our lives.

Both of my parents exemplified this principle. Their lives cannot be measured by their modest means, but by how they enabled others to express their voices and inspired empathy in those around them, making the best of what little they had. In every action, they prioritized the well-being of others. My father, despite the loss of his first wife and children, continued his journey of helping those in need. Being a rabbi was more than just a title for him; it was a lifelong commitment. Other people's pain became his pain, their struggles, his daily concern and their despair, his calling for hope and inspiration.

My father managed to lead a generation of people who left everything behind. He did so with compassion and humility. His ability to probe with a deep understanding of the human condition enabled him to inspire others and instill in them the power of hope and positive thinking. While he was respected for his knowledge, he was loved for his generosity, the generosity of serving others.

My mother, who was forty years younger than my father, stood by his side, ensuring his health and well-being. Recognizing the challenges of providing for seven children, she persevered with courage, working as a janitor and house cleaner. Despite her tough life, she reached out to other women who struggled to make ends meet. She spent hours listening to those who felt neglected by their husbands and burdened by their challenges in a new land.

She invited these women into our small home, serving them coffee and pastries. With her warm eyes and engaging personality, she encouraged them to express their emotions. "Edvi mhaya ya-azi," she would say, meaning "Talk with me, my dear," to those reluctant to open up. I remember her tearing up alongside them, and those women would kiss her hands as they left our home, just as men would kiss my father's hands in respect and gratitude. By simply listening to their pain, my mother brought them relief and hope.

My mother had the strength to do what many find difficult: she gave people the greatest gift, the gift of time and undivided attention. Both of my parents dedicated their lives to serving others, and in doing so, they found happiness and fulfillment. In their heart of hearts they believed in what the sages called *Tikkun Olam*—the need for any living Jew to make the world a better place. Their value became my guiding principle.

We all find ourselves, in one way or another, trapped in a virtual cuckoo's nest. This can manifest in various forms: a broken marriage, toxic bosses, an abusive childhood, unbearable betrayal or simply feeling stuck. The challenge is not to accept these unfortunate circumstances, but to muster the courage to take charge of our lives.

We must recognize that we are not alone. As social beings, we are interdependent and connected; this unique connectivity is essential to finding

CHAPTER TWENTY-NINE

our way out. The path forward is not through anger or resentment, but through extending a helping hand. In many ways, we are all searching for that hand to reach out to us.

This was my life story. As a timid and shy boy, I had to wake up as early as four in the morning to walk my father to the synagogue. By the time I arrived at school, I was exhausted and appeared unusual to teachers who were unaware of autism and other forms of maladaptive behavior. Later in life, I could have channeled my anger and experiences of abuse into lashing out at a society that looked down on us and was indifferent to our needs. Instead, I was guided by angels who helped me chart a more constructive path—a life of giving and serving. However, we must take the first step; we must be willing to take risks. I managed to escape from my difficulties, and in doing so, I opened horizons I never thought I could see.

I have learned that complaining rarely leads to answers, and anger over life's misfortunes offers no real solutions. To isolate ourselves from the journey of self-discovery is to undermine our very existence and well-being. The more we engage with the lives of others, the more we realize we are not alone, and it is through this engagement that personal growth becomes possible. We begin to see that the suffering of others often reflects our own struggles.

I often find solace in listening to people share their experiences. In learning about their fears, anxieties, and hardships, I come to a deeper understanding of my own. This process demands a great deal of vulnerability. Without the courage to be vulnerable, I believe change cannot occur; instead, we risk spending our lives merely tending to our wounds without ever healing them.

Despite all the challenges I have faced, my love for Israel, its people, and its achievements has never wavered. Though I have experienced pain, those experiences have shaped my character. Having lived in the United States for many years, America has become my home. Here, I have reclaimed my identity and rediscovered my capacity to reach out and contribute. I feel free to express my thoughts and emotions and enjoy the liberty of being my true self. I am evaluated based on what I can offer and the value I bring, rather than by my past. In this environment, I am judged by my character and my desire to inspire change in others.

This transformation has been made possible by this unique place called America. Here, I have been embraced and granted the opportunity to pursue my education, which I couldn't find elsewhere. The years I spent learning at Swarthmore College, the experiences I gained at Harvard University, the opportunities to teach at leading academic institutions, and the invaluable sessions of coaching and mentoring executives have all contributed to bringing me closer to who I am today—a man who has overcome obstacles and reclaimed his identity.

As I reflect on my early years in Libya and my upbringing in Israel, I feel saddened by the on-going conflict and the widening gap between Israelis and Palestinians. It is painful to witness the ongoing bloodshed and the loss of innocent lives on both sides. I believe that one day will come and Palestinians will understand that the Jews will not be pushed into the sea, and the Israelites will recognize the fact that the Palestinians are to stay. I often walk the old alleys of Jerusalem and stare at its ancient stones, stones that witnessed blood, smoke and fire for more than two thousand years, I know in my heart of hearts that one day will come and the old loop soaked in blood will be transformed into a beacon of light where Jews and Arabs will live in harmony. The prophet Isaiah once said, "They will beat their swords into plowshares and their spears into pruning hooks."

Like my father, I have spent most of my life listening to others. From my early years, I observed my father listening intently to those around him. He listened with his eyes, ears and heart. His unique ability allowed him to influence others and achieve the seemingly impossible. Following in his footsteps, I have listened to hundreds of personal narratives from people of all backgrounds.

I have heard from successful executives who felt unhappy with their

CHAPTER TWENTY-NINE

lives, I spent time among the poor who feared becoming homeless, and listened to patients confined to their beds, regretting their life choices. I have witnessed the elderly in several countries who felt ignored by their children, and the workers abused by their toxic managers. As I absorbed these stories, I realized that my experience is not unique. I came to understand that their struggles often felt deeper than my own, and my challenges seemed trivial in comparison to their journeys.

Each personal story is unique. But while our narratives are intimate, the pain we endure is universal. Life is not a straight line; it is a crooked path that stretches along peaks and valleys. We must gather the courage to navigate our journeys, take risks with limited knowledge of the outcomes and trust ourselves.

There are times, like in my story, when we face failure, encounter unfortunate circumstances, feel ashamed of who we are and become angry with everything and everyone around us. These moments are the true tests of our character. They are when we need to free ourselves from limitations to inspire and uplift ourselves. By doing so, we can rise from the ashes and transform ourselves into better versions. To me, this is the true process of *becoming*.

Our world is filled with heroes who, despite their pain, manage to transform their darkest hours into positive paths of redemption. With a positive mindset, they harness newfound strength and energy to confront their trauma constructively. The road is rarely easy; it demands inner strength and resilience. It requires surrendering oneself to a leap of faith and, above all, believing in the immense power of love. Once we allow ourselves to love and be loved, remarkable things happen. A genuine expression of love and care for others sparks the realization of life's primary purpose: I have come to believe that only by serving others and committing ourselves to empathy and generosity, we come close to the fulfilments of our purpose. Only then can we truly experience the true meaning of happiness.

No matter what valleys we traverse, life remains a beautiful gift. Embrace it. Enjoy the heights and walk through the valleys with courage, conviction and resilience. Character is shaped not by the peaks, but by how we navigate the valleys.

As my father once told me, "Out of destruction comes construction." He was always right.

We all possess a latent gift; it is inherent within us—the power to rise from the ashes and rebuild. Therefore, our purpose in life is to create a new and better world, a world without locked gates or high fences.

With that courage, with that strength of our conviction, we may find a way to fly out of the cuckoo's nest into a clear and boundless sky.

Acknowledgments

Memories tend to fade over time, and writing a personal memoir is an arduous journey. It involves retrieving experiences that are deeply buried in our subconscious and revisiting the wounds that shape our existence. Nonetheless, the desire to bring these memories to light has been brewing for a long time. While memories define us, they should not serve as strict guidelines for our lives. This book is the result of five years spent interviewing, collecting, recalling, writing, and revising.

I owe a great deal of gratitude to Jonathan Subar, who took a genuine interest in reading the first draft of this book and helped me organize my thoughts. I am also thankful to Robert O'Donnell for advising me on the storyline and encouraging me to structure the chapters thoughtfully. My appreciation extends to Meghan McCracken for her incredible skill in transforming the manuscript into a polished book, and to Eliza Graham for her enthusiasm and ability to connect ideas with people. The wonderful editorial work for the final version was done with the help of Neelima Mahajan, whose extraordinary literary insight and editorial expertise were paramount in refining the manuscript.

Finally, I want to express my deepest gratitude to my beloved Ping He, whose unwavering belief in me and constant encouragement served as a beacon of light during difficult moments, helping me to recall wounds from the past. Her positive mindset, contagious energy, and brilliant mind helped transform my narratives into a book that captures both the burden of pain and the power of love. It is this power of love that transcends despair into hope, ultimately lifting us from the abyss to solid ground, where we can breathe life again.

About the Author

Dr. Shalom Saada Saar is a globally recognized thought leader in organizational development and education, with over 30 years of experience transforming leaders and organizations. A Harvard-educated scholar, he has taught at top institutions including Harvard, MIT, SMU, and Shanghai Jiao Tong University, and has worked with global organizations like Adidas, General Re, LV, JLL, DB, Marriott, Dassault Systems, DaVita, Baidu, and Johnson & Johnson. His expertise spans organization diagnosis, strategic innovation , leadership agility, critical thinking, change management and executive coaching. A trusted advisor to global organizations and governmental agencies, he facilitates acclaimed programs that foster collaboration and individual transformation. Dr. Saar currently teaches at the University of Miami's Miller School of Medicine and delivers keynote speeches on culture and leadership worldwide.

www.ingramcontent.com/pod-product-compliance
Lightning Source LLC
Chambersburg PA
CBHW030248010526
44107CB00031B/1361/J